T0135044

Model-Driven Dependability Assessment
of Software Systems

Simona Bernardi • José Merseguer
Dorina Corina Petriu

Model-Driven Dependability Assessment of Software Systems

 Springer

Simona Bernardi
Centro Universitario de la Defensa
Academia General Militar
Zaragoza, Spain

José Merseguer
Departamento de Informática
Universidad de Zaragoza
Zaragoza, Spain

Dorina Corina Petriu
Department of Systems and Computer
 Engineering
Carleton University
Ottawa
Ontario, Canada

ISBN 978-3-662-50942-5   ISBN 978-3-642-39512-3 (eBook)
DOI 10.1007/978-3-642-39512-3
Springer Heidelberg New York Dordrecht London

Printed on acid-free paper

Springer is part of Springer Science+Business Media (www.springer.com)

Preface

Goal of the Book

During the last two decades, a major challenge for the researchers working on modeling and evaluation of computer-based systems has been the assessment of system Non-functional Properties (NFP), such as performance, schedulability, dependability, or security. We can say that this is still an open research challenge today, although considerable progress has been made and different approaches have been developed, which are of interest not only to researchers but also to practitioners in the field.

A class of successful approaches found in the literature relies on building traditional formal models for NFP analysis (such as fault trees, Markov chains, Petri nets, or Bayesian networks) from system descriptions based on the Unified Modeling Language (UML). UML is a widely used modeling language, adopted by both industry and academia, which has become the "lingua franca" for software modeling. Model transformations from UML to formal models are addressed either by providing informal guidelines (implemented, e.g., using Java) or by defining rigorous model transformations (e.g., using QVT 2011; Jouault and Kurtev 2006). The former is included under the umbrella of *model-based development (MBD)* and the second of *model-driven development (MDD)*.

MDD is a software development paradigm characterized by the fact that the primary focus and products of the development are models rather than computer programs. A key premise behind MDD is that the programs are automatically generated from the models. The advantage of MDD is that models are expressed using concepts that are much closer to the problem domain than to the underlying implementation technology, making the models easier to specify, understand, and maintain (Selic 2003).

On the other hand, in model-based development (MBD) the software models do not play the same key role of driving the development process as in MDD, although they still play an important role. For instance, models may be used to guide the writing of program code by programmers, rather than being used for automatic code generation as in MDD.

Validation of the models is another important aspect, which is addressed using assertions or constraints in MDD, while in MBD validation is usually carried out by hard coded parsers.

Most of the existing approaches for NFP modeling and assessment that are using UML as software modeling language do propose UML extensions for specifying NFPs, which in turn lead to the definition of ad hoc UML profiles for NFP specification and assessment. Such ad hoc profiles usually cover a limited subset of concepts from the NFP domain they are addressing, without any coordination with other similar profiles with respect to the coverage of the NFP domain, terminology consistency, or profile structure.

The situation is better in the performance and schedulability analysis domain, which is supported by two Object Management Group (OMG) standards, "The UML Profile for Schedulability, Performance and Time" (SPT) defined for UML 1.X and "The UML Profile for MARTE: Modeling and Analysis of Real-Time and Embedded Systems", defined for UML 2.X. Many researchers have used SPT or MARTE to add performance and/or schedulability annotations to UML models and then to define model transformations for deriving a variety of performance and/or schedulability models to be used for analysis. Unfortunately, there is no similar standard profile for dependability analysis of UML-based models.

Another OMG standard specifying UML extensions for a variety of non-functional properties, the Profile for Modeling Quality of Service and Fault Tolerance Characteristics and Mechanisms (QoS&FT), provides a flexible but heavyweight mechanism to define properties such as performance, security, or reliability by means of specific QoS catalogs. The annotation mechanism is supported by a two-step process, which implies catalog binding and either the creation of extra objects just for annotation purposes or the specification of long Object Constraint Language (OCL) expressions. However, this two-step process requires too much effort from the users and may produce models that are hard to understand.

In this context, our book describes the state of the art in modeling and assessment of dependability requirements throughout the software life cycle. Dependability is a term that encompasses several non-functional properties of systems: *availability* (readiness for correct service), *reliability* (continuity of correct service), *safety* (absence of catastrophic consequences for the users and the environment), *integrity* (absence of improper system alterations), and *maintainability* (ability to undergo modification and repairs).

In this book we are using three kinds of models:

(a) *software models* used for software/architecture development and represented in software modeling languages, for instance, UML or AADL;
(b) *software models with dependability annotations* obtained from (a) by adding information related to dependability properties;

- in modeling language allowing for standard extension mechanisms, such as UML, the extra dependability information is given by defining appropriate extensions (i.e., defining a UML profile for dependability);
- in other modeling languages that are not provided with standard extension mechanisms, the language definition must be extended with built-in features for dependability information (such as AADL).

(c) *formal models* such as fault trees, Markov chains, Petri nets, or Bayesian networks, used for analysis; such models are too abstract for software development, but have the advantage of being supported by existing analytic or simulation analysis methods.

The following three research challenges are related to bridging the gap between these three kinds of models. The first challenge, related to dependability modeling, handles the transition from model (a) to (b). In the case of extensible languages (such as UML) this amounts to defining a suitable dependability profile and then applying the profile to model (a) in order to obtain the corresponding model (b). The second challenge, related to dependability analysis, addresses the model transformation from (b) to (c); the actual analysis of model (c) is performed with existing solvers for the formal model used in each case. The last challenge, related to feedback from analysis results to advise for developers on how to improve model (b), relies on bridging the gap between models (c) and (b). The book addresses the first two challenges; in regard to the third one, there are still open research issues that will be discussed in the conclusion.

Emphasis of the Book

In this book, we consider cutting-edge model-driven techniques for modeling and analysis of software dependability, proposed in the last two decades. Most of them are based on the use of UML as software specification language. From the software system specification point of view, such techniques exploit the standard extension mechanisms of UML (i.e., UML profiling). UML profiles enable the software engineers to add dependability non-functional properties to the software model, besides the functional ones.

The book presents the state of the art on UML profile proposals for dependability specification and rigorously describes the trade-off they accomplish. The focus is mainly on the RAMS (reliability, availability, maintainability, and safety) properties. Among the existing profiles, we emphasize the DAM (Dependability Analysis and Modeling) profile, which attempts to unify, under a common umbrella, the previous UML profiles from literature providing capabilities for dependability specification and analysis. DAM is defined as an extension of the MARTE profile and reuses some of its definitions.

Another concern addressed in the book is the assessment of system dependability, which has been traditionally carried out using standard modeling techniques, some based on the use of formal models (e.g., fault frees for reliability analysis, stochastic Petri Nets for both reliability and availability analysis). We particularly address the construction of such formal analysis models by model-to-model transformation techniques that, given a UML software model enriched with dependability annotations, produce either automatically or systematically proper dependability analysis models. These models can be analyzed with known solution techniques specific to the formalism used by the respective models and supported by existing software tools. The book describes two prominent model-to-model transformation techniques, proposed in the literature, that support the generation of the analysis model and allow for further assessment of different RAMS properties. Case studies from different domains will also be presented, in order to provide examples for practitioners about how to apply the aforementioned techniques.

Target Audience

The book is research oriented and it is mainly addressed to students taking Master and PhD courses in software engineering. They will learn the basic dependability concepts and how to model them, using the current de facto standard UML modeling language and its extension by the profiling approach. In particular, the students will be able to apply the UML extensions defined by the DAM profile and the standard MARTE profile, on which DAM is based. They will also gain insight into dependability analysis techniques, through the use of appropriate modeling formalisms, as well as of model-to-model transformation techniques for deriving dependability analysis models from UML specifications. The book provides proper references for further readings on these topics and a discussion on open issues in this research area.

Moreover, software practitioners interested in dependability analysis are also a target audience for this book. They will find a unified framework for the specification of dependability requirements and properties with UML that can be used throughout the entire software life cycle. They will also learn, with the help of the proposed case studies, rigorous techniques for deriving different dependability analysis models, such as fault trees to Petri nets, from UML software models with dependability annotations.

Road Map of the Book

Chapter 1

Establishes the scope, objectives, and point of view of the book with respect to model-driven software dependability specification and assessment.

Chapter 2

Presents the main dependability concepts used throughout the book. The chapter is mainly addressed to beginners in the dependability field, since it provides useful references for creating a background in dependability. Readers already familiar with dependability could skip the chapter.

Chapter 3

Model-driven software dependability assessment, the topic of the book, is necessarily carried out using models, in particular software models. Therefore, readers need to know what languages features support software modeling for dependability specification and assessment. This chapter is devoted to both general purpose modeling language, such as UML, and Domain-Specific Modeling Languages (DSMLs) used in literature for dependability assessment. It describes first the use of UML diagrams for software modeling, with emphasis on diagrams used for dependability modeling and assessment, even though concrete proposals are not described yet. An important characteristic of UML is discussed next: its profiling mechanism as a technique to define DSMLs as lightweight extensions of UML. Although the focus of the book is on UML, the chapter briefly presents another DSML, concretely AADL, so that the reader can see an approach to dependability modeling and analysis that is different from those based on UML.

Chapter 4

Irrespective of the approach taken for defining a DSML, the domain model is usually the first step toward the DSML definition. A domain model, described as a UML class diagram, specifies a set of core concepts related to a specific problem or field. This chapter introduces a domain model for dependability characteristics, aimed at both dependability modeling and analysis. The dependability concepts, given in Chap. 2, constitute the basis for this domain model, which unifies the terminology used in previous dependability profiles proposed in the literature and provides a consistent vocabulary for software dependability modeling and analysis.

Chapter 5

Based on the domain model presented in Chap. 4, this chapter develops a UML profile for dependability modeling and analysis of software systems. The profile, called DAM, relies on the standard OMG MARTE (described in Appendix A). DAM consists of a set of UML extensions (i.e., stereotypes, tag values, and constraints) to annotate a UML model with dependability properties, requirements, and measures for dependability analysis purposes. To exemplify the use of DAM, the chapter applies the profile to two case studies. The first one is in the field of secure distributed systems and the second in the avionics field. Later, in Chap. 8, these case studies will be used for the illustration of dependability analysis.

Chapter 6

Dependability modeling has been the topic developed in the book so far. This chapter introduces dependability analysis concerns. Dependability analysis is carried out using either formal models or systematic methods, and this chapter provides an overview of the most common ones, which are compliant with current industrial standards (i.e., the International Electrotechnical Commission standards). Special attention is given to Fault Tree and Stochastic Petri Net formalisms, since they will be used later in Chap. 8 for the dependability analysis of the case studies.

Chapter 7

During the last two decades, several proposals have been developed to create dependability DSMLs (D-DSMLs). DAM, presented in Chap. 5, is an example of a D-DSML developed as a UML profile. Most of these proposals also accomplish the transformation of the D-DSML into proper dependability analysis models, as those from Chap. 6. This chapter presents and evaluates 36 proposals from the literature, most of them having in common that their D-DSML is based on UML.

Chapter 8

The objective of this chapter is to describe some proposals of interest for practitioners, selected from those presented in Chap. 7. The focus of interest is on how these proposals address the translation of a D-DSML into models for analysis. Concretely, the chapter focuses on availability and reliability proposals. We selected one from Bernardi et al., addressing availability, and the another from Pai and Dugan, addressing reliability. These two approaches are applied to the case studies developed in Chap. 5. Availability analysis is then applied to a secure distributed system case study, while reliability models are obtained for a mission avionics case study.

Chapter 9

Once the state of the art on dependability modeling and analysis of software systems has been presented, the last chapter discusses research issues that are still open and need additional effort.

Acknowledgments

Authors would like to thank Vittorio Cortellessa and Julio Medina, whose comments helped to substantially improve the book. Special thanks are due to the editor, Ralf Gerstner, for his advice in structuring the book and for his patience.

Zaragoza, Spain   Simona Bernardi, José Merseguer
Ottawa, Canada   Dorina Corina Petriu
2013

Contents

1   Dependability Assessment and Software Life Cycle 1

2   Dependability Concepts 9

3   Software Models 19

4   Dependability Domain Model 41

5   Dependability Modeling and Analysis Profile 51

6   Dependability Analysis Techniques 73

7   Proposals for Dependability Assessment 91

8   From Software Models to Dependability Analysis Models 105

9   Conclusions and Advanced Open Issues 133

A   The MARTE Profile 151

B   Classes in the Dependability Domain Model............................. 163

References... 175

Index.. 185

Acronyms

AADL	Architecture Analysis and Design Language
BPEL	Business Process Execution Language
BPMN	Business Process Modeling Notation
CTMC	Continuous Time Markov Chain
CGSPN	Concurrent Generalized Stochastic Petri Net
DAM	Dependability Modeling and Analysis
DFT	Dynamic Fault Tree
DSL	Domain-Specific Language
DSML	Domain-Specific Modeling Language
D-DSML	Dependability-DSML
DSPN	Deterministic and Stochastic Petri Net
ESPN	Extended Stochastic Petri Net
FFA	Functional Failure Analysis
FMEA	Failure Mode and Effect Analysis
FMECA	Failure Mode, Effect, and Criticality Analysis
FT	Fault Tree
GQAM	General Quantitative Analysis Model
GSPN	Generalized Stochastic Petri Net
HAZOP	HAZard and OPerability studies
IEC	International Electrotechnical Commission
MARTE	Modelling and Analysis of Real-Time Embedded systems
M2M	Model-to-Model
MCS	Minimal Cut Set
MDD	Model-Driven Development
MOF	Meta-Object Facility
MRSPN	Markov Regenerative Stochastic Petri Net
NFP	Non-Functional Property
OCL	Object Constraint Language
OMG	Object Management Group
PHA	Preliminary Hazard Analysis
PN	Petri Net

QoS&FT	UML profile for Modeling Quality of Service and Fault Tolerance Characteristics and Mechanisms
RAMS	Reliability, Availability, Maintainability, Safety
RBD	Reliability Block Diagram
SAE	Society for Automotive Engineers
SAN	Stochastic Activity Network
SoaML	Service oriented architecture Modeling Language
SPN	Stochastic Petri Net
SPT	UML profile for Schedulabibity, Performance and Time Specification
SRN	Stochastic Reward Net
SWN	Stochastic Well-formed Net
TPN	Time Petri Net
UML	Unified Modeling Language
SysML	Systems Modeling Language
VSL	Value Specification Language

Chapter 1
Dependability Assessment and Software Life Cycle

Anyone can build something that works when it works. But it's how it works when it doesn't work that counts. – Roy Maxion Computer Science Department, Carnegie Mellon University

Abstract This introductory chapter describes the need, importance, and benefits of assessing dependability of software systems. It also establishes the approach followed in the book for dependability assessment.

1.1 Introduction

The original definition of dependability is *the ability to deliver service that can justifiably be trusted.* As pointed out by Avizienis et al. (2004), this definition stresses the need for justification of trust. An alternative definition states the dependability of a system as *the ability to avoid failures that are more frequent and severe than acceptable.* In this case the definition provides the criterion for deciding if the service is dependable.

According to Avizienis et al. (2004) dependability encompasses five attributes:

- reliability, the continuity of correct service,
- availability, the readiness for correct service,
- maintainability, the ability to undergo modifications and repairs,
- integrity, the absence of improper system alterations,
- safety, the absence of catastrophic consequences on the users and environment.

1.1.1 Dependability as a Non-functional Property of Systems

System non-functional properties (NFP), or qualities, characterize the operation of the system, while functional properties refer to the description of the system

S. Bernardi et al., *Model-Driven Dependability Assessment of Software Systems*, DOI 10.1007/978-3-642-39512-3_1, © Springer-Verlag Berlin Heidelberg 2013

nominal behavior. Dependability is a non-functional property of the systems which is strongly related to other systems NFPs, such as security and performance. Figure 1.1 depicts the relationships among these NFPs: the Venn diagram in the figure is an example to understand these connections, since the definitions in the literature of the considered NFPs are multiple and often not overlapping.

Software security (Devanbu and Stubblebine 2000) and software safety share the need to assure that software will remain *dependable* under extraordinary conditions, that is those conditions which software was not intended to gracefully tolerate. What distinguishes security from safety is the origin of such extraordinary conditions for the software and the consequences if the software fails as a result. Extraordinary conditions that threaten the software safety are the hazards, reflecting the perception of accidental conditions. By contrast, extraordinary conditions that threaten software security are the attacks, indicating their malicious intent. According to Avizienis et al. (2004), security is sharing two attributes—availability and integrity—with dependability, and is adding one more—confidentiality. In the context of distributed systems, other security attributes have been considered (Sterbenz et al. 2010), that is authentication, authorization, and accounting (AAA).

Software performance is the degree to which the software system or component meets its objectives for timeliness. Smith and Lloyd (2003) emphasize two dimensions of software performance: responsiveness and scalability. The former can be quantified in terms or response time or throughput while the latter is the ability of a system to continue to meet its response time or throughput objectives as the demand for the software functions increases. Performability is a derived NFP, coined by Meyer (1980), that takes into account the level of performance of *degradable* software systems in the presence of faults over a specified period of time (Haverkort et al. 2001).

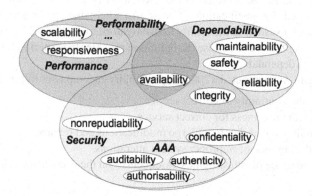

Fig. 1.1 Relationships among different NFPs

1.1.2 Dependability in the Software Life Cycle

Several classifications exist for NFP in the software field, e.g., the standard ISO/IEC-9126-1 (2001). NFPs, similar to functional properties, are managed throughout the life cycle of a software system. Software life cycle (also known as software development process) refers to the way in which a software product is developed. It consists of a set of sub-processes (each describing a variety of activities) by which a system is built, starting from the initial definition of the functional and non-functional requirements, and developing a system which will fulfill its requirements in a final deployment, which also will evolve in the life cycle. A typical software life cycle consists of the following stages: requirements, analysis, design, implementation, testing, deployment and operation. The actual development iterates through these stages in time, as the system is being built, maintained and/or evolved. NFPs are initially expressed as requirements of the system. As the project advances, NFPs evolve in the analysis and design models; eventually, they become to be considered as cross-cutting concerns in the implementation stage. The testing stage gives advice on the degree of NFP fulfillment, so before the deployment and operation of the system, it should be known whether the system really meets its NFPs.

Dependability, being a NFP, has to be managed throughout the software life cycle (IEC-60300-3-15 2009). According to the previous paragraph, this means that the developers need to capture the dependability requirements from the beginning, evolve them into design models and assess or advise on their fulfillment throughout the development process, in order to build and deploy a dependable system. This book is devoted to these challenges, namely how to express, assess, and manage dependability requirements throughout the software life cycle in order to develop dependable software. The approach we follow is model-based or model-driven (MDD), which means that the use of models is of primary importance for developing software, and in our case for achieving dependable software. We try to leverage model-driven techniques in benefit of software dependability. This basically consists of making an extra effort in the early life cycle stages (requirements, analysis and design) to develop software models that capture the dependability requirements. These models, following the model-driven paradigm, can be automatically converted into code, which will realize the dependability requirements. The next section describes different ways of achieving this objective. For example, we could use specific or general purpose modeling languages for constructing software models that also express easily dependability requirements.

In the model-driven paradigm, we identify two key activities for building dependable software, *modeling* (i.e., representing or expressing) and *analyzing* dependability attributes. These activities are carried out early in the software life cycle. Dependability modeling, in the context of the book, means to represent dependability requirements adequately in the software models. For example, we could model the parameters of a failure, such as its occurrence rate, consistency, or consequence. For applying model-driven techniques, an advantage is to integrate the description of dependability requirements in the very same software models that are used for development, i.e., in the models representing functional properties. In this way a software model can specify, e.g., the behavior of a component and, at the same time, the failures affecting such component. The advantage is, as previously indicated, that the code will also realize the dependability requirements.

Analysis of dependability attributes may imply quantitative and/or qualitative evaluation of the system, which is a research topic since the early times of computing. According to literature, dependability attributes are assessed either measuring the system while operation or using systematic methods (e.g., FMEA, HAZOP) or through formal dependability models of the system (IEC-60300-3-1 2003). Since this book is focused on model-driven techniques, the latter approach is closer to our goal. The use of models for dependability analysis is extensively recognized, e.g. by Lyu (1996) for reliability. However, the interest of the book is not on dependability models per se, but on modeling and analysis for dependability assessment in the context of software models used for software development.

Once dependability has been modeled and analyzed, we can say that the basis for assessment is already established. In the light of analysis results, assessment consists in checking whether the dependability requirements have been fulfilled. In case they are not, corrective actions should be carried out on input models.

1.2 Model-Driven Dependability Assessment

A *model* is an abstraction of the system for the purpose of understanding it before building it (Rumbaugh et al. 1991). In the book we are using three kinds of models:

(a) *software system model* represents the system under construction by using multiple views; in a broad sense we can distinguish between structural and behavioral software views, which together constitute the model of the system;

(b) *software model with dependability annotations* is obtained by extending model (a) with information related to dependability properties, which considers the abstractions needed to represent failures of the system and their consequences. This implies that, in some manner, this model needs to be related to the behavioral model of the system or at least to its abnormal behaviors.

(c) *formal models* such as fault trees, Markov chains, Petri nets, or Bayesian networks used for analysis; such models are too abstract for software development, but are supported by existing analysis methods and tools.

Consistently to the previous paragraphs, the task of developing models is known as *modeling*, while the task of analyzing quantitative or qualitative properties is known as *analysis*.

Two important research challenges addressed in the book are related to bridging the gap between these three kinds of models. The first challenge, related to dependability modeling, handles the transition from model (a) to (b). The second challenge, related to dependability analysis, addresses the model transformation from (b) to (c); the actual analysis of model (c) is performed with existing solvers for the formal model used in each case.

1.2.1 Domain-Specific Modeling Languages

Modeling software dependability means, in a broad sense, to identify properties, requirements, and measures of interest for reliability, availability, maintainability, safety, or integrity analysis. Such modeling activity produces the *dependability view* of the system. The dependability view, together with the structural and behavioral views, is what enables a software model for dependability analysis. Chapter 2 explains the properties, requirements, and measures for dependability and introduces the terminology for dependability used in the book.

The way explored in this book for specifying the system dependability view is through domain-specific modeling languages (DSMLs). A DSML (Graaf and van Deursen 2007) is a specification language that offers, through appropriate notations and abstractions, expressive power focused on a particular domain.

Nowadays, there are plenty of DSMLs, some of them have been recognized as international industry standards, such as SysML (2012) which is targeted at systems engineering applications, AADL (2009); AUTOSAR (2011), and MARTE (2011) in embedded software domain, or BPEL (2007); BPMN (2011), and SoaML (2012) in service-oriented business systems engineering, to cite a few well-known examples. DSMLs can be created by augmenting the modeling capabilities of a general purpose modeling language: this is the case, e.g., of SysML, MARTE, and SoaML that have been built on the Unified Modeling Language (UML2 2011).

UML is a general purpose modeling language that can be customized through the *profile* mechanism for creating DSMLs based on it. UML, standardized by the Object Management Group (OMG), is the most widely used modeling language for software development.

DSMLs for specifying dependability (D-DSML), or more precisely, for specifying the dependability view, offer a set of modeling constructs (either textual or graphical) that allow to specify the concepts of the dependability introduced in Chap. 2. For example, EAST-ADL2 (2010) refines EAST-ADL, an architectural language dedicated to automotive embedded electronic systems, to enable the specification of mainly safety requirements (e.g., safety integrity levels). Similarly, in the avionic domain, the Error Model Annex of AADL (2009) defines features to enable the specification of redundancy management and risk mitigation methods in an architecture, as well as to enable qualitative and quantitative assessments of system dependability properties.

For bridging the gap between dependability concepts and the modeling constructs offered by D-DSMLs, *domain models* are introduced. A domain model is a visual representation of conceptual classes or real-world objects in a domain of interest (Martin and Odell 1997). Chapter 4 develops a dependability domain model.

The approach for creating a D-DSML based on UML is presented in Chap. 5. In particular we develop DAM profile (Dependability Modeling and Analysis) for UML, which was initially introduced in (Bernardi et al. 2011c). A profile allows refining standard semantics in strictly additive manner using standard extension mechanisms (stereotypes, tagged-values,[1] and constraints; Selic 2007). A profile then customizes UML models for particular domains and platforms, in case of DAM for dependability. Chapter 3 explains the basis of UML modeling and its profile mechanism. UML models abstract not only the structure and behavior of the system but also the hardware platform where it will execute. So, the system can be described with great detail and a variety of diagrams. Class and object diagrams represent the system structure; use case, state machines, activity diagrams, and sequence diagrams the behavior; and component and deployment diagrams the platform.

DAM was constructed by extending the UML Profile for Modeling and Analysis of Real-Time and Embedded systems (MARTE 2011), which was standardized by OMG. MARTE addresses the issue of capturing requirements necessary for quantitative analysis to UML model elements, more specifically, for performance and schedulability analysis. MARTE was built on two previous OMG profiles: the Schedulability, Performance, and Time Specification (SPT 2005) and the profile for Modeling Quality of Service and Fault Tolerance Characteristics and Mechanisms (QoS & FT 2008).

It is worth to notice that it is possible to combine the use of multiple profiles for the same model, which would support consistent specification of different NFPs and their relationships, as well as the analysis of trade-off between different NFPs. So, a UML model together with the specification of NFPs by standard extension mechanisms represents a complete system model for carrying out the analysis of different NFP. However, so far no standard profile has been proposed or adopted that comprehensively addresses the dependability modeling and analysis.

This book reviews the approaches of D-DSMLs, published in the last decade, to support derivation of dependability analysis models. Chapter 7 concentrates on those approaches based on UML, they were the sources for constructing the DAM profile. Indeed, there is a large body of work extending UML with concepts required for carrying out quantitative and qualitative analysis of dependability. We have found approaches for reliability, availability, maintainability, and safety (RAMS) with UML. However, we apprise the reader that, although we have looked for UML extensions to model and analyze *integrity*, we have not found any. Among RAMS approaches, Chap. 8 recalls two interesting proposals, aimed to availability and reliability analysis.

---

[1]The term "tag value" was introduced in UML 1.X, for UML 2.0 tagged-values are standard metaattributes. The reader must be aware that we use the term "tag value" throughout the book as defined in UML 1.X, since most of the revised works conform to it.

1.2.2 Model-Driven Dependability Approach and Advantages

The book, as presented so far, is devoted to the integration of dependability modeling and analysis within the model-driven software development process (Schmidt 2006). Figure 1.2, inspired by the model processing paradigm in (SPT 2005), shows an ideal model-driven process that clearly separates the software domain and the

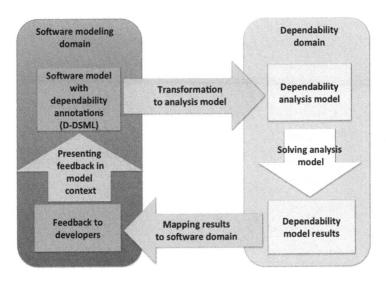

Fig. 1.2 Integrating dependability modeling and analysis in an MDD process

dependability domain. A D-DSML used by software developers is (automatically) transformed into a formal dependability model. The D-DSML is supposed to embed both the dependability specification and the functional requirements. The formal dependability model is solved using existing solvers and methods. Dependability results from the formal model are mapped to feedback to developers, expressed in terms of the D-DSML. The process bridges then two domains: the software modeling domain and the dependability analysis domain and is dealing with two categories of models and modeling languages: (a) for software development and (b) for dependability analysis.

A model-driven process offers advantages for assessment of system NFPs. Analyzing dependability based on design models allows developers to start verifying early in the life cycle whether the system under construction will meet its dependability requirements. It is less expensive to analyze different design alternatives and choose the best one at an early phase, when the investment in building the product has not been completely made yet. However, the verification may continue throughout the life cycle.

Chapter 2
Dependability Concepts

The cheapest, fastest, and most reliable components are those that aren't there. – Gordon Bell

Abstract This chapter introduces the dependability concepts used throughout the book. They are basic concepts for which no previous knowledge of dependability is required. Main sources for this chapter are the books of Lyu (1996) on reliability and Leveson (1995) on safety, and fundamentally the work of Avizienis et al. (2004) on dependability.

We start this chapter by giving a basic definition of dependability. So, we recall that dependability encompasses five attributes: reliability, availability, maintainability, integrity, and safety. Later, the threats of the dependability are defined: faults, errors, and failures. They establish a causal chain that threats the dependability of the systems. The means to attain dependability is the next topic addressed by the chapter: fault prevention, fault removal, fault tolerance, and fault forecasting. The last topic addressed is the model-based evaluation of the dependability. Being the book focused on the modeling and analysis of the dependability, we then introduce the concepts of measures, properties, and requirements of the dependability.

Definitions of dependability can be obtained from multiple sources. Here we mainly follow Avizienis et al. (2004) and Lyu (1996). Avizienis et al. (2004) surveyed the dependability terminology from a systemic point of view, while Lyu (1996) specifically addresses the software domain, focusing on reliability. Another source is Leveson (1995) for definitions of safety related concepts. Our intention is not to offer a comprehensive guide on the large number of existing dependability definitions and techniques, but to offer the basic conceptual framework of the book.

Dependability concepts addressed in this chapter are summarized in a checklist shown in Table 2.1. A label is assigned to each concept that will permit to pinpoint it in next chapters. In particular, Chap. 7 uses these labels to classify dependability approaches in literature.

S. Bernardi et al., *Model-Driven Dependability Assessment of Software Systems*, DOI 10.1007/978-3-642-39512-3_2, © Springer-Verlag Berlin Heidelberg 2013

2.1 Definition of Dependability

Avizienis et al. (2004) define dependability as the ability of a system to avoid failures that are more frequent and severe than acceptable. Dependability encompasses five attributes: reliability, availability, safety, maintainability, and integrity.

- *Reliability* (labeled **DA.R** in Table 2.1) ensures the continuity of correct service for a given system. In ANSI/IEEE (1991) is defined as the probability of failure-free software operation for a specified period of time in a specified environment.
- *Availability* (**DA.A**) is defined as the system readiness for correct service.
- *Maintainability* (**DA.M**) represents the systems ability to undergo modifications and repairs.
- *Integrity* (**DA.I**) is related not only to dependability but also to security. In a broad sense, integrity is the absence of improper system alterations. ANSI/IEEE (1991) defines it as the degree to which a system or component prevents unauthorized access to, or modification of, computer programs or data. In Biba (1977) integrity ensures that the system cannot be corrupted to perform in a manner contrary to the original determination.
- *Safety* (**DA.S**) emphasizes the absence of catastrophic consequences as a result of the system and/or the software usage, as defined by Leveson (1995).

Availability and maintainability are attributes of special significance for repairable systems, which were defined by Arnold (1973) as those that can be recovered after failure. The safety attribute applies to safety-critical systems.

All these basic definitions of dependability apply also to systems considering a component-based view. In Lyu (1996) a *component* is seen as an entity that interacts with other entities (hardware and/or software) and with the physical world. A component might be by itself a system made up of other components. Components interact through *connectors*. It is considered that the system or a component provides an expected *service* to the environment or the user, which is a sequence of outputs agreeing with a given specification.

2.2 Threats of the Dependability

Avizienis et al. (2004) refer *faults*, *errors*, and *failures* as threats to dependability (**DT**). They are seen as a causal chain (F-E-F) that threatens the dependability of a system in the sense that the chain completion leads the system to a state that reports incorrect service or outage. More specifically, in the F-E-F chain a fault is the cause of an error; in turn, the error is part of a state of the system that may lead to a failure (or service failure). In this causal view, an error is seen as an intermediate stage between failure and fault. Figure 2.1 depicts this causal chain.

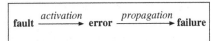

Fig. 2.1 The fundamental chain of dependability threats (from Avizienis et al. (2004))

2.2.1   Faults

Faults are the cause of the errors. Avizienis et al. (2004) provide a very rich and precise taxonomy of them. They classify faults according to eight basic viewpoints:

- Dimension. Where the fault originates or affects. There are *hardware* and *software* faults.
- Objective. Faults are introduced by humans with *malicious* or *non-malicious* objectives.
- Persistence (**DT.FP**). A *permanent* fault is assumed to be continuous in time. A *transient* fault is bounded in time.
- System boundaries. When the fault originates in the system boundary it is *internal*, otherwise it is *external* and may propagate errors into the system.
- Phenomenological cause. *Natural* or *human made* faults.
- Intent. *Deliberate* or *not deliberate* faults. Deliberate faults are the result of a harmful decision.
- Capability. Faults can be introduced inadvertently, i.e. *accidental* faults; or by *incompetence*, from lack of professional competence.
- Phase of occurrence (**DT.FO**). It refers to the phase of the life cycle in which the fault occurs. *Development* faults occur during development or maintenance, *operational* faults occur during the use phase.

Regarding the number of faults, there is a *single* fault or *multiple* fault assumption. The quantitative characterization of a single/multiple fault assumption distinguishes between the rate and probability of fault occurrences (**DT.FOQ**).[1] Consideration of multiple faults allows to distinguish between *independent* and *related* faults. The former are attributed to different causes while the latter to a common cause. To describe the *faulty behavior* (**DT.FB**) of components, connectors, and services means to identify the states of these elements in which a fault is active, according to Hawkings et al. (2003).

2.2.2   Errors

In model-based dependability, the *erroneous behavior* (**DT.EB**) characterizes error states for components, connectors, and services due to fault occurrences.

The quantitative characterization of an error (**DT.EQ**) might be the probability of its occurrence assuming that the fault has positively occurred (**DT.FOQ**).

On the other hand and due to the component-based assumption, sometimes a component raises an error that does not reach the system boundaries, which means that it does not cause a failure. This happens when the service delivered by the component is not in the system interface. However, such component may offer its service to another internal component; this may lead to *error propagation* between components. Figure 2.2 details the error propagation. The error propagation between two components can also be characterized, from a quantitative point of view, with a probability (**DT.EPQ**).[1] Cortellessa and Grassi (2007) accurately modeled this phenomena.

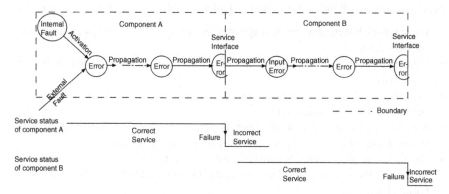

Fig. 2.2 Error propagation (from Avizienis et al. (2004))

2.2.3 *Failures*

Avizienis et al. (2004) define failures or service failures as events that occur when the delivered service deviates from correct service. The different ways in which the deviation is manifested are system's service *failure modes*, as in Powell (1992). The service failure modes characterize incorrect service according to four viewpoints:

- Domain (**DT.FMD**). The failure is classified as a *content* and/or *timing*. A content failure means that the service reports information that deviates from the one specified. A timing failure means that the service does not report the information when specified or with the expected duration, so it can be a "late" or "early" failure. When both content and timing are incorrect, then the failure can be a "halt" (the service is halted) or an "erratic" failure.
- Detectability (**DT.FMDet**). Failures are *signaled*, those in which the system sends a warning signal to the user, and *un-signaled*.

---

[1]Note that DT.FOQ and DT.EPQ are also dependability measures.

- Consistency (**DT.FMC**). Lamport et al. (1982) differentiate *consistent* from inconsistent or *byzantine* failures, depending on whether the failure is identically perceived by all the users or not.
- Consequences on the environment (**DT.FMSL**). The consequence of a failure grades it into *failure severity levels* (we will refer to this concept in Sect. 2.4 as a safety measure, concretely *safety level*). Different criteria can be used to define severity levels. For example, according to the standard MIL-STD-882d (2000) they are rated as catastrophic, critical, marginal, or minor.

Finally, failures can be *dependent* or *independent* (**DT.FMDep**). Failures are dependent when the affected components share the cause of the failure, i.e., the error is common to all of them. An example of multiple dependent failure is a "common failure mode" that typically occurs within a redundant structure.

"Failure behavior" (**DT.FailB**) of a component, connector, or service refers to the specification of failure events or conditions that lead to the failure states of the component, connector, or service, according to Bondavalli et al. (2001a).

2.2.4 Hazards

For safety-critical systems, the concepts of fault, error, and failure are supplemented with that of *hazard*. Leveson (1995) defines *hazard* as a state or set of conditions in a system that, together with other conditions in the environment of the system, will inevitably lead to an accident. An *accident* is an undesired and unplanned (but not necessarily unexpected) event that results in (at least) a specified level of loss.

For every possible hazard in the system it is important to know, at least, its *origin* (**DT.HO**) and main characteristics, i.e., *severity* (**DT.HS**) and *likelihood* (**DT.HL**). The hazard severity is defined by Leveson (1995) as the worst accident that could result from the hazard. As in the case of failures, the hazard severity can be graded by *severity levels* such as minor, marginal, critical, and catastrophic. The hazard likelihood can be defined quantitatively or qualitatively (e.g., frequent, probable, occasional, remote, improbable, or impossible). Severity and likelihood are combined to obtain the *hazard level*. Some safety-critical techniques, such as HAZOP (2000) (HAZard and OPerability study), use guidewords (**DT.HGW**) and parameters (specifics of the process in study) to identify hazards in the system. For example, the set of guidewords in HAZOP is: No, More, Less, As Well As, Reverse, and Other Than.

2.3 Means of the Dependability

The problem of achieving a dependable software system is usually addressed by applying four technical methods, also known as dependability means in Avizienis et al. (2004): fault prevention, fault removal, fault tolerance, and fault forecasting.

Table 2.1 Checklist for dependability concepts

L1	L2	Dependability concept or issue	Restriction
DA		Dependability attributes	
	R	Reliability	
	A	Availability	repairable system
	M	Maintainability	repairable system
	I	Integrity	
	S	Safety	safety-critical system
DM		Dependability measures	
	R	Reliability measures.	
	A	Availability measures.	repairable system
	M	Maintainability measures.	repairable system
		Integrity measures.	
	S	Safety measures and safety properties.	safety-critical system
	C	Software complexity measures.	design level
DR		Dependability requirements	
	BOUND	Upper/lower bound requirements on dependability measures.	
	S	Safety properties to be checked w.r.t. the system behavior.	safety-critical system
DT		Dependability threats (Fault)	
	FP	Fault persistence.	
	FO	Fault occurrence.	
		Other Fault classifications: hw/sw, development/-operational faults.	
	FB	Faulty behavior of components, connectors, services.	
	FOQ	Fault occurrence quantitative characterization.	
DT		Dependability threats (Error)	
	EB	Erroneous behavior (error states).	
	EQ	Error quantitative characterization.	
	EP	Error propagation.	
	EPQ	Error propagation quantitative characterization.	
DT		Dependability threats (Failure)	
	FMD	Failure mode w.r.t. the domain.	
	FMDet	Failure mode w.r.t. the detectability.	
	FMC	Failure mode w.r.t. the consistency.	
	FMSL	Failure mode w.r.t. the consequence (severity levels).	
	FMDep	Failure mode w.r.t. the dependency.	
	FailB	Component, connector or service failure behaviour.	
DT		Dependability threats (Hazard)	
	HO	Hazard origin.	safety-critical system
	HS	Hazard severity (severity levels).	safety-critical system
	HL	Hazard likelihood.	safety-critical system
	HGW	Hazard guide-words.	safety-critical system
FT		Fault tolerance	
		Error detection.	
	R	Recovery.	
M		Maintenance	repairable system
	M	Modifications.	
	R	Repair.	
R		Redundancy (A fault tolerance implementation)	
	T	Type.	
	L	Level.	
	F	Failures (max. number of tolerated failures).	
	R	Roles.	

Fault prevention encourages the use of techniques that prevent the system from faults (Chillarege et al. 1992). Formal methods are useful for performing automatic software verification that, together with software testing, are the common techniques for *fault removal* (Boehm 1984; Weyuker 1982). *Fault tolerance* techniques (Avižienis 1967; Lyu 1995) aim at avoiding failures despite the presence of faults after the software system is deployed. The last method, the *fault/failure forecasting* is carried out through the qualitative and quantitative evaluation of the system behavior with respect to faults/failures occurrences (Meyer 1980).

Common fault tolerance techniques to achieve failure avoidance are system recovery (**FT.R**) and error detection. *System recovery* tries to transform an erroneous or faulty system state into a correct one by using "error handling" and "fault handling" techniques. Error handling uses rollback, rollforward, and compensation, while fault handling relies on diagnosis, isolation, reconfiguration, and reinitialization.

Fault tolerance techniques can be implemented in different ways (e.g., redundancy, n-version, reflection, or self-checking component) (Avizienis 1985; Huang and Kindala 1996). *Redundancy* (**R**) implies to describe the:

- type (**R.T**): information, software, and hardware;
- level (**R.L**): number of components in a redundant structure;
- failures (**R.F**): maximum number of tolerated failures;
- roles played by the component within the fault-tolerant structure (**R.R**): replica, controller, adjudicator, voter, hot/cold/warm spare.

Finally, maintenance[2] is another means to achieve dependability. The distinction between fault tolerance and maintenance is that the latter is carried out by an external actor. Maintenance follows "fault handling" in the life cycle and refers to *repairs* (**M.R**) as well as *modifications* (**M.M**) for removing faults in the system during the use phase (ISO/IEC 14764 2006). Moreover, repair and fault tolerance are related concepts; actually, repair is sometimes seen as a fault tolerance activity.

2.4 Model-Based Evaluation of the Dependability

A *model* is an abstraction of the system for the purpose of understanding it before building it. A *software system model* describes a specific system view; in a broad sense we can distinguish behavioral and structural software views. A *dependability model* considers the abstractions needed to represent the failures of the system and their consequences. This implies that in some manner the dependability model needs to be related to the behavioral model of the system or at least to its abnormal behaviors. Models are developed using different kinds of languages and/or

---

[2]It is important to note the difference between maintainability (a dependability attribute) and maintenance (a technical method to achieve dependability).

notations, some of them with an underlying mathematical formalism supporting some kind of analysis (e.g., fault trees, Markov chains, Petri nets, or Bayesian networks). These are called *formal models*, analyzable models, or models for analysis.

During the first stages of the life cycle, when implementations are not yet available, dependability attributes can be evaluated by solving *formal dependability models*.

2.4.1   Dependability Measures, Properties, and Requirements

According to Hosford (1960), *dependability measures* (**DM**) represent a quantified estimation or calculation of a dependability attribute. However, not all dependability attributes can be quantified. For instance, in the safety analysis context, as pointed out by Leveson (1995), *safety properties* (**DM.S**) are not strictly measures, but rather qualitative indicators used to express the level of injury caused by system hazards or seriousness associated with system's unsafe states. Once an estimation of a dependability measure is obtained, e.g. by solving a formal dependability model, it has to be checked against the *dependability requirements* (**DR**) (Littlewood and Strigini 1993). A dependability requirement can be thought of as an upper or lower bound (**DR.BOUND**) of a specific dependability measure. However, in the case of safety, a requirement (**DR.S**) represents the satisfaction of a given safety property.

In model-based evaluation, the computation of reliability, availability, and maintainability measures basically means a *quantitative* evaluation of the formal dependability model, while safety properties imply the *qualitative* evaluation of the model (Billinton and Allan 1992). This does not necessarily mean that the nature of safety models has to differ from the others; e.g., fault-trees or Petri nets can be used to perform both forms of evaluation, while Bayesian networks aim just to quantitative evaluation. It is also true that safety properties can be checked without an underlying formal dependability model but using specific techniques such as HAZOP or Functional Failure Analysis (FFA).

2.4.2   Dependability Formulae

In the following we describe some important dependability measures, most of them used in this book. The measures for reliability (**DM.R**), availability (**DM.A**), and maintainability (**DM.M**) are usually defined with respect to time or the number of program runs (Lyu 1996; Trivedi 2001; Hosford 1960; Johnson 1989).

2.4.2.1 Reliability

The execution time or calendar time is appropriated to define the reliability as:

$$R(t) = Prob\{\tau > t\} \tag{2.1}$$

i.e., reliability at time t is the probability that the time to failure (τ) is greater than t or, the probability that the system is functioning correctly during the time interval $(0, t]$. Considering that $F(t) = 1 - R(t)$ (i.e., unreliability) is a probability distribution function, we can calculate the expectation of the random variable τ as:

$$\int_0^\infty t \, dF(t) = \int_0^\infty R(t) dt \tag{2.2}$$

This is called *MTTF* (Mean Time To Failure) (Johnson 1989) and represents the expected time until the next failure will be observed. Another measure is the *failure rate* (called also rate of occurrence of failures), which represents the probability that a component fails between (t, dt), assuming that it has survived until the instant t, and is defined as a function of $R(t)$:

$$h(t) = -\frac{1}{R(t)} \frac{dR(t)}{dt} \tag{2.3}$$

The *cumulative failure* function denotes the average cumulative failures associated with each point in time, $E[N(t)]$.

A key reliability measure for systems that can be repaired or restored is the *MTBF* (Mean Time Between Failure) (Johnson 1989), i.e. the expected time between two successive failures of a system. The system/service *reliability on-demand* is the probability of success of the service when requested. When the average time to complete a service is known, then it might be possible to convert between MTBF and reliability on-demand.

2.4.2.2 Maintainability

Maintainability is measured by the probability that the time to repair (θ) falls into the interval $(0, t]$ (Johnson 1989):

$$M(t) = Prob\{\theta \leq t\} \tag{2.4}$$

Similarly, we can calculate the expectation of the random variable θ as:

$$\int_0^\infty t \, dM(t), \tag{2.5}$$

that is called *MTTR* (Mean Time To Repair), and the *repair rate* as:

$$\frac{dM(t)}{dt} \frac{1}{1 - M(t)} \tag{2.6}$$

2.4.2.3 Availability

Availability is defined as the probability that the system is functioning correctly at a given instant (de Souza e Silva and Gail 1989):

$$A(t) = Prob\{\text{state} = UP, \text{time} = t\}.$$

In particular, the *steady-state* availability can be expressed as function of *MTTF* and *MTTR* (or *MTBF*):

$$Availability_\infty = \frac{MTTF}{MTTF + MTTR} = \frac{MTTF}{MTBF}.$$

2.4.2.4 Safety and Integrity Properties

Safety properties are traditionally expressed in qualitative terms, such as safety levels or risk factors associated with failures or hazards (Leveson 1995). Nevertheless, often they are defined in function of quantitative criteria. An interesting example is the safety integrity level (SIL) (IEC-61508 1998) that specifies the required protection against software or system failure and corresponds to an interval of the "average probability of failure to perform a safety function on demand" (IEC-61508 1998) (e.g., SIL1[10E-2, 10E-1), SIL2 [10E-3, 10E-2)). Other examples of safety properties are the probability of reaching (or of being in) a safe/unsafe state and the tolerable accident rate.

Integrity is a property common to dependability and security. Similar to SIL, the concept of integrity level was defined in Biba (1977) for security to grade damage caused by information sabotage. However, it is more common to use procedures to verify and ensure the integrity of the system than to use formally defined measures to compute grades of integrity. Clark and Wilson (1987) presented a formal model for integrity verification, while Sailer et al. (2004) developed an architecture for integrity measurement that relies on code measurement based on standards defined by TCG (2011).

Chapter 3
Software Models

*There are two ways of constructing a software design: one way
is to make it so simple that there are obviously no deficiencies
and the other way is to make it so complicated that there are no
obvious deficiencies. – C.A.R. Hoare, The 1980 ACM Turing
Award Lecture*

Abstract This chapter provides an overview of the features contained in languages
for software modeling. The main focus is on UML, a widely used modeling
language, adopted by both industry and academia, which has become the "lingua
franca" for software modeling. Besides the features for structural and behavioral
modeling, another important characteristic of UML will be discussed: its profiling
mechanism that provides the ability to extend UML by standard means, allowing
for the definition of domain-specific languages as light-weight extensions of UML.
The role of the UML diagrams in the development process is briefly described; the
emphasis is on diagrams used for dependability modeling and assessment, although
concrete proposals are not described yet. This chapter also presents briefly an
architecture-centric domain-specific modeling language, namely AADL, an SAE
standard used in particular application domains, such as automotive and avionics.

3.1 Unified Modeling Language

The Unified Modeling Language (UML) is a well-known modeling language
for software-intensive systems. It is widely used in the software development
process to specify, visualize, modify, construct, and document the artifacts of an
object-oriented software-intensive system under development. It is considered the
successor of several Object-Oriented Analysis and Design (OOA&D) methodologies developed in the late 1980s and early 1990s. In particular, it results from
the fusion of concepts derived from three widely-adopted object-oriented methods
at the time: the Booch method, Object Modeling Technique (OMT) and Object

S. Bernardi et al., *Model-Driven Dependability Assessment of Software Systems*,
DOI 10.1007/978-3-642-39512-3_3, © Springer-Verlag Berlin Heidelberg 2013

Oriented Software Engineering, developed by Grady Booch, Jim Rumbaugh, and Ivar Jacobson, respectively. Furthermore, other new concepts have been added in UML, such as the extension mechanisms (stereotypes, tagged-values, constraints).

The Object Management Group (OMG) takes care of the standardization process of UML since 1997 when the version 1.1 was issued. Over the years, UML underwent several minor revisions, with the purpose to clarify certain shortcomings and to fix inconsistencies detected through practical experience, followed by the UML 2.0 major revision (UML 2.0 was adopted by the OMG in 2005). UML 2.0 has brought significant changes, such as: better software architecture modeling by adopting a component-based approach, more appropriate models for workflows and business-oriented systems by enhancing the activity diagrams and more scalable behavioral models by allowing for horizontal and vertical decomposition of interaction diagrams. The current release of UML is version 2.4.1 (UML2 2011).

3.1.1   UML Metamodel

The UML architecture is based on a metamodeling structure that consists of four layers: (M0) user object, (M1) model, (M2) metamodel, and (M3) meta-metamodel. In principle, a *metamodel* constitutes an explicit set of constructs and rules needed to build specific models within a domain. In other words, a metamodel is a model of a modeling language, while a model expressed in that language is an instance of the metamodel.

More specifically, a metamodel defines the *abstract syntax* and *static semantics* of a modeling language, but not its *concrete syntax*. The abstract syntax defines the constructs (i.e., the model elements) and their relationships, describing thus the structure of the language. The static semantics of a language determines the criteria for well-formedness of a model expressed as constraints between the model elements (e.g., in UML, every object instance must have a class).

On the other hand, the concrete syntax defines the concrete form in which the constructs of the language are represented textually or graphically. The concrete syntax must be consistent with the metamodel and render it in an unambiguous way. A modeling language has only one abstract syntax (i.e., one metamodel), but may have more than one concrete syntax (for instance a graphical and a textual one).

The meta-metamodeling layer (M3) forms the foundation of the metamodeling hierarchy. Its primary responsibility is to define the language for specifying a metamodel. In the case of UML, the meta-metamodeling language is called the Meta-Object Facility (MOF). MOF is more compact than UML; it also has the ability to describe itself. In the major UML 2 revision, MOF has been aligned with UML, sharing a common design philosophy and constructs. Practically this means that MOF and UML use a common language subset, which is defining basic class diagrams.

The UML metamodel is described in the OMG specifications in a semi-formal manner, as a combination of formal language, graphical notation, and natural language (English). Formal definitions are given as MOF class diagrams defining the UML abstract syntax and as OCL constraints representing the well-formedness rules. The concrete syntax of UML is represented by the graphical notation for UML diagrams, which will be briefly presented in the Sect. 3.1.3.

3.1.2 UML Runtime Semantics

The UML *runtime semantics* refers to the execution of the model and is specified as a mapping of modeling concepts into corresponding runtime execution happenings. There are two fundamental assumptions regarding the nature of UML semantics. The first is that all behavior in a modeled system is ultimately caused by actions executed by the so-called active objects. The second is that UML behavioral semantics only deals with discrete *event-driven* behaviors (UML2 2011).

Figure 3.1 identifies the key semantic areas covered by the current standard and how they relate to each other. The items in the upper layers depend on the items in the lower layers. The basic layer is structural, reflecting the premise that all behavior

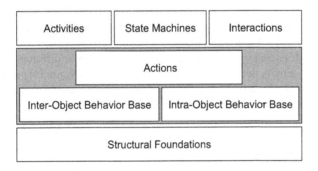

Fig. 3.1 A schematic of the UML semantic areas and their dependencies (from UML v2.1.4)

in UML is the consequence of the actions of structural entities. The middle layer (represented by the shaded box) is the *behavioral semantic base*, which provides the foundation for the semantic description of the higher-level *behavioral formalisms* (i.e., formalism for describing behavior, such as state machines, Petri nets, and data flow graphs).

The middle layer consists of three separate sub-areas arranged into two sublayers. The bottom sublayer consists of the *inter-object behavior base*, which deals with the communication between structural entities, and the *intra-object behavior base*, which addresses the behavior within each structural entity. The *actions* sub-layer defines the semantics of individual actions. Actions are the fundamental units of behavior in UML and are used to define fine-grained behaviors. Their resolution and expressive power are comparable to the executable instructions in traditional programming languages. Actions in this sublayer are available to any of the higher-level behavioral formalisms of UML: activities, state machines, and interactions.

The UML *causality model* specifies how things happen at runtime and is quite straightforward: objects respond to messages generated by other objects executing communication actions. When a message arrives, the receiving object eventually responds by executing the behavior that is matched to that message. The dispatching mechanism by which a particular behavior is associated with a given message depends on the higher-level formalism used and is not defined in the UML specification, i.e., it is a semantic variation point (UML2 2011).

3.1.3   UML Graphical Notation

As mentioned above, a modeling language has a single metamodel describing its abstract syntax and static semantics, but it may have more than one concrete syntax. For instance, UML has a standard graphical notation described in the OMG specifications, which represents its standard concrete syntax, but there were several attempts to define nonstandard textual concrete syntax for different diagram types. In this section we present briefly the UML standard graphical notation, which is implemented by the UML tools compliant with the OMG standard.

UML provides several types of diagrams which capture different aspects and views of the system. A detailed description of each UML diagram type is out of the scope of this book. We will give only a brief description, insisting on the diagrams and their features used in the rest of the book.

3.1.3.1   Class Diagram

Class Diagrams (CDs) describe the static structure of the system in terms of classes and their relationships. This UML notation comes from a melding of OMT, Booch and class diagrams of most other object-oriented methods. The Class Diagram depicted in Fig. 3.2 models an example of customer order. A *class* is a description of a set of objects with similar structure, behavior, relations, and semantics. At runtime, objects are created as instances of classes to store and process the program data. All objects of a class share the same list of attributes and operations. The scope of an attribute can be at instance level, in which case each object instance holds its own value for the attribute, or at class level, when there is just one value of the attribute for the entire class. A class is drawn as a rectangle with one or more sections: the upper part contains the class name, the middle part the attributes, and the lower part the operations. (The attributes and operations may be shown or not). Some classes are abstract, meaning that they cannot be instantiated; their names are written in italics (e.g., class *Payment*). Structural relations between two classes are specified by associations and generalizations. In particular, a binary *association* between two classes is represented by a line connecting the classes and an optional association name, e.g., association *sale* depicted in Fig. 3.2 represents a binary association between classes *Customer* and *Order*.

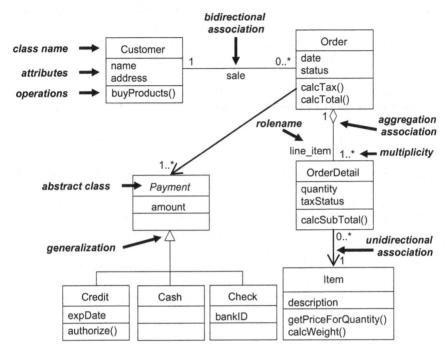

Fig. 3.2 Example of UML Class Diagram

The UML metamodel distinguishes the association itself from its ends: binary associations have exactly two association-ends. Different adornments specifying association properties, such as navigability, aggregation, role names, qualifier, and multiplicities, may be attached to the association-ends.

An association is *navigable* if, given an object at one end, it is possible to get to objects at the other end directly, usually because of the existence in the source object of some references to target objects. Navigability in one direction is graphically represented with an arrowhead attached to the end of the line representing the association (e.g., the association between *OrderDetail* and *Item* in Fig. 3.2); while a simple line without any arrows represents navigability in both directions.

A special kind of binary association is the *aggregation* that represents a *part-of* relationship. There are two forms of aggregation: (1) a weaker form, whose intended meaning is to distinguish the *whole* from a *part*, graphically denoted as a diamond attached to the association-end closer to the class representing the *whole*; and (2) a stronger form of aggregation, i.e., the composition, expressing that the *part* is strongly owned by the *composite* and may not be part of any other object. Composition association is graphically depicted as a filled diamond attached to the association-end closer to the composite class.

Another adornment that may be attached to an association-end is the *rolename* that indicates the role played by the class attached to the end of the path near the rolename. For example, in Fig. 3.2 the rolename *line_item*, attached to an association-end of the aggregation between classes *Order* and *OrderDetail*, allows to represent an order as an aggregation of lines, each line specifying in detail each ordered item. The rolename represents a pseudo-attribute of the source class and it provides a name for traversing from a source instance across the association with the target instance(s), e.g., by using the dotted syntax we can represent an order $o \in Order$ as a set of order details $o.line\_item = \{od_1, \ldots, od_n\}$.

An association-end may be characterized by a *multiplicity* specifying the number of target instances that may be associated with a source instance. The multiplicity is a range of nonnegative integers denoted as *lower-bound..upper-bound*. If a single integer value is specified, then the integer range contains exactly one value. In addition, the star character ("*") may be used for the upper bound to denote an unlimited upper bound; a star may also be used alone, in which case it has the same meaning as *0..**. For example, in Fig. 3.2 an order detail specifies a single item and, vice versa, a single item can be mentioned in zero or more orders.

Classes of a CD can be related by a *generalization/specialization* relationship, which is used to model inheritance between classes. The subclass inherits all the properties of the superclass, i.e., attributes, operations, associations. Moreover, additional properties can be specified in the subclass. Generalization is graphically represented as a solid line from the subclass to the superclass with a large hollow triangle at the end of the path, close to the superclass; e.g., in Fig. 3.2 classes *Credit, Cash*, and *Check* are subclasses of the class *Payment*.

3.1.3.2 Interaction Diagrams

There are four types of Interaction diagrams in UML 2.x (the first two were present in UML 1.x, while the last two are new to UML 2.x):

- Sequence Diagram (SD) is the main type of interaction diagrams. It focuses on the order in which the exchange of messages between the participants of an interaction takes place along the participants' lifelines.
- Communication Diagram (which used to be called Collaboration Diagram in UML 1.x) shows the messages passed among a set of participants, focusing on the structural relationship between participants.
- Interaction overview diagram combines the activity diagram and sequence diagram features: at a high level, it looks like an activity diagrams with activity nodes detailed as sequence diagrams.
- Timing diagram shows interactions with a precise time axis.

Sequence and communication diagrams can be used in two forms: the generic form and the instance form. The *instance form* describes a specific scenario in detail, documenting one possible interaction, without any conditions, branches or loops. The *generic form* describes all possible alternatives in a scenario; therefore, branches, conditions, and loops may be included.

SDs are more suitable for real-time specifications and for the representation of complex scenarios in which it is important to represent explicitly the temporal aspects. They have been used in a variety of Object-Oriented methods under the names of *interaction diagrams, message trace diagrams, event trace diagrams*, and, in general, they can be considered as successors of *message sequence charts* (ITU-TS 1995). An SD shows an interaction arranged chronologically: usually, the time is represented by the vertical axis of the SD and it proceeds downward while the participants are aligned horizontally.

In Fig. 3.3 an example of an interaction representing a scenario that may occur in an e-commerce application is represented by a sequence diagram. The scenario transfers the shopping cart content into a newly created order for a registered customer, executes a payment authorization, and returns a page with the details of the order to the user. Each object participating to the interaction modeled by an SD is represented by a vertical dashed line called *lifeline* together with a

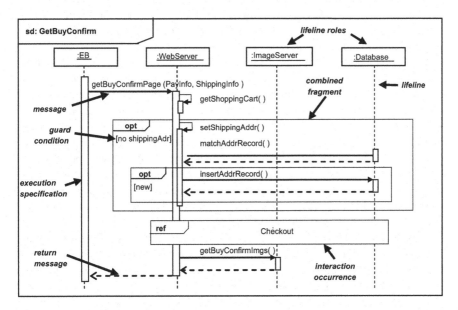

Fig. 3.3 Example of UML Sequence Diagram

rectangular box (i.e., *object symbol*) superscribed with the string: *Objectname "/" ClassifierRolename ":" Classifiername*, where *Objectname* is name of the object, *ClassifierRolename* is the name of the role played by the object in the interaction and, finally, *Classifiername* is the name of the class the object belongs to. In general, it is not required a complete specification of the above string for each participating object. For example, the name of the role can be omitted if there is only one role to be played by the objects of a given class, as well as the name of the object when it represents a generic object of a given class. In Fig. 3.3 the participants to the interaction are: *EB* represents the client web browser, and three components at the e-commerce site, *WebServer*, *ImageServer*, and *Database*.

A message exchanged between two objects in the SD is graphically represented by an arrow from the sender's to the receiver's lifeline. Depending on the type of action performed by the sender that caused the message to be sent the arrow corresponding to the message can be of different type. Messages caused by synchronous actions are drawn as filled solid arrowhead arrows, while messages caused by asynchronous actions are drawn as stick arrowhead arrows. Among the latter, messages representing return from procedure calls are further distinguished being depicted as dashed arrows. Moreover, message arrows can be either drawn horizontally, indicating the time required to send the message is "atomic" (instantaneous message), or slanted downward, indicating that the message requires some time to arrive (timed message). If an object is created following the execution of a create action, then the creation message arrow points to the created object symbol. If an object is destroyed as a consequence of the execution of a destroy action, then the destruction message arrow is followed by a large "X" along the lifeline of the destroyed object. Messages are labeled with the name of the *operation* to be invoked or with the name of the *signal* to be raised.

A new feature introduced in UML 2 called *combined fragment* is a logical groupings of model elements, represented by a rectangle which contain the conditional structures that affect the flow of messages. A combined fragment contains interaction operands and its type is determined by an interaction operator, which defines the semantics of a combined fragment and determines how the interaction operands are used. The operator defines the type of logical conditions to apply to the operands. For example, a combined fragment with an *alt* (alternative) operator acts like an if-then-else statement, choosing one of the operands depending on the guard conditions; an *opt* operator is like an if-then statement; a *loop* operator indicates a repetition of the operand; a *par* operator indicates that the operands should be executed concurrently, etc.

Another new feature in UML 2 allows for multiple SDs to share portions of an interaction. The common part is represented as a separate SD in its own frame. An SD referencing it contains a fragment called *interaction occurrence* marked with *ref* in the left corner (e.g., *Checkout* in Fig. 3.3).

The following operations are performed in the SD from Fig. 3.3:

- *EB* issues a synchronous request message to *WebServer* for the buy-confirm page;
- *WebServer* gets the corresponding shopping cart object;
- An *opt* fragment checks if the shipping address is not known; if the condition is true, a shipping address is obtained and *WebServer* tries to match it with information from the database;

- If no address record is found, insert a new address record (modeled as a nested *opt* fragment)
- The Checkout SD is invoked (modeled as an *interaction occurrence*;
- *WebServer* gets necessary images from *ImageServer*;
- *WebServer* constructs the html code for the buy/confirm page and returns it to *EB*.

3.1.3.3   StateCharts

Statecharts (SCs) are the graphical representation of UML State Machines, they are basically Harel (1987) statecharts with minor modification. The execution of a state machine is based on the *run-to-completion* algorithm in which an event instance can only be dequeued and dispatched if the processing of the previous current event instance is fully completed. In particular, a state machine is characterized by the following components: an *event queue* that holds incoming event instances until they are dispatched; an *event dispatch mechanism* that selects and dequeues event instances from the event queue and, finally, an *event processor* that executes dispatched events.

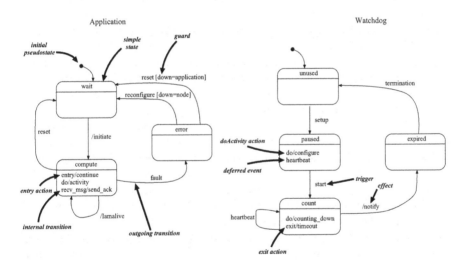

Fig. 3.4 Example of UML Statechart

SCs are used to model the behavior of class objects and they describe *possible sequences of states and actions through which objects can proceed during their lifetimes as a result of reacting to occurrence of discrete events (e.g., signals, operation invocations)* (UML2 2011). An example of two statecharts representing the behavior of an application process and its error detector (i.e., the watchdog mechanism), is depicted in Fig. 3.4.

An SC basically consists of states and transitions. States represent situations during the life of the object in which either it satisfies some condition or it performs some action or it waits for some event to occur. A simple state, such as states *wait, compute, error* in SC *Application* and states *unused, paused, count* and *expired* in SC *Watchdog* of Fig. 3.4, is drawn as a rectangle with rounded corners subdivided into two compartments separated by a horizontal line: the upper part contains the name of the state, the lower part may contain actions, that are performed while the represented object is in the state, deferred events and internal transitions. Initial states are instead special states (pseudo-states), and they are drawn as a small solid filled circle.

Actions within a state are denoted as *action_label / action_expression* where *action_label* allows to determine whether the action specified by *action_espression* is an *entry* action or a *do* action or an *exit* action. Entry actions are performed upon entry to the state (e.g., action *continue* in state *compute* in SC *Application*), do actions correspond to an ongoing activity performed as long as the object is in the state or until the computation specified by the action is completed (e.g., action *counting_down* in state *count* of SC *Watchdog*), exit actions are instead performed upon exit from the state (e.g., action *timeout* in state *count* of SC *Watchdog*).

The events received by an object are results of actions carried out either by the object itself or by other objects interacting with the former. In particular, deferred events are those events that do not cause a change of the state: they are simply retained to be processed subsequently. For example, in the SC *Watchdog* the event *heartbeat* in state *paused* is a deferred event, meaning that while the watchdog is in a pause state potentially can consume a heartbeat event but is not able to process it so that the event is retained to be processed when the watchdog is in another state.

A transition indicates that specific actions will be performed when a specified event occurs provided that a certain condition is satisfied. In general in an SC, a transition is labeled as *event_name (parameter-list) [guard-condition]'/ action_expression*. A transition is triggered by at most one event that represents the reception of either a signal or a request to invoke a specific operation, in this latter case a list of parameters are associated that conform to the operation's list of parameters. The guard provides control over the firing of the transition: it is represented as boolean expression and, when not explicitly specified, is assumed always true. When the transition fires, an action (or a sequence of actions) may be performed. When the transition has not an explicit trigger event is called *completion* transition and it fires only after all the events and actions present in the current state are processed and completed.

There are two main types of transitions: internal and outgoing. Internal transitions, as deferred events, do not cause a change of state when fire but, unlike deferred events, the event that triggers the transition is processed and, when specified, the associated action(s) are executed.

Firing of an outgoing transition causes an exit from the state and an entry into the target state, possibly the source state itself in case of self-transition. Self-transitions are different from internal transitions; indeed, while the firing of a self-transition causes the execution of entry and exit actions, the firing of an internal transition does not cause any execution of entry or exit actions.

StateCharts may represent other important constructs, such as synchronization states, stub states, composite states, sub-machine states, and pseudo-states mainly meant for a hierarchical definition of the underlying state machines, and for introducing concurrency inside a state machine or between different state machines. We omit to describe such features, since we have not dealt with them explicitly. We focus instead on the relationships between StateCharts and Class Diagrams and between Statecharts and Sequence Diagrams.

A CD defines attributes, operations, and relations for a class of objects: this static structure is fundamental for the inter-object behavior (represented by Sequence Diagrams) and for the intra-object behavior (represented by StateCharts).

Let us consider a set of StateCharts representing interacting objects; among the actions executed by an object there are some actions that invoke operations of the called object or that generate signals that can be perceived by other objects. The invocation of an operation (or generation of a signal) provokes one or more event occurrences that are perceived by other objects.

The interactions between StateCharts, and the relationships between StateCharts and Class Diagrams, can be exemplified by looking at two SCs of Fig. 3.4: the application, whose behavior is modeled by the SC *Application*, and the watchdog, whose behavior is modeled by the SC *Watchdog*, are two communicating processes. Both the application and the watchdog can be considered as two objects belonging to two different classes, e.g., *AP* and *WD*, respectively. In particular, let us assume that class *WD* is characterized by an attribute *timer* and two operations *init(timervalue)* and *confirm()*. A first type of interaction between the two objects occurs when, both the application and the watchdog are in their initial states (*wait* and *unused*, respectively) and, the application initializes the watchdog by setting the watchdog timer. This interaction is carried out through the call action *initiate* that invokes the operation *init(timervalue)* in order to set the *timer* attribute to the value *timervalue*. The invocation of such operation provokes the occurrence of a *setup* event in the watchdog and the processing of such event brings the watchdog in the *paused* state. Other interactions between the application and the watchdog occur either through the causal chain: action *continue*—operation *confirm()*—event *start*, when the application confirms the settings and the watchdog starts its count-down to expiration, or the causal chain: action *Iamalive*—signal *kick*—event *heartbeat*, when the application sends an "Iamalive" to the watchdog in order to reset its timer to the initial value.

On the other hand, a message exchanged between two objects in an SD is caused by the execution of an action (e.g., a call action when an operation is invoked, a send action when a signal is generated) that causes the reception of an event in the receiver object. Looking at the SCs of Fig. 3.4 we can represent their interactions with an SD showing the sequence of messages, generated by either call actions or send actions, exchanged between the application and the watchdog.

3.1.3.4   Use Case Diagrams

Use Case diagrams describe the system's functionality, i.e. what a system does
to satisfy the requests of its users. Use cases are implemented by collaborations
of classes. Use cases exist in a structural context, which includes the system and
associated actors. An *actor* is an object outside the scope of the system that interacts
with it. An actor may be the primary actor of a use case if it triggers it, or a secondary
actor if participates in the use case only. Actors may be human users of the system or
external systems interacting with the system. In real-time and embedded systems,
actors may be sensors, actuators, or timers. A given functionality (capability) of
a system represents a use case only if it returns a result visible to one or more
actors.

A use case may be realized by different scenarios, which describe the sequence
of actions performed inside the system when the use case is triggered in different
conditions. In other words, a scenario represents a specific interaction between
the object roles that collaborate to produce the system behavior corresponding to
the use case. A medium-size system will have up to a few dozen use case, and
each use case up to a few dozen scenarios of interest a use case may have a
primary scenario (happy path) and a lot of alternatives a scenario set is considered
complete when all of the operational requirements are covered in at least one
scenario.

Use Cases are typically used in the requirement specification phase of a software
system development but can also be used in the later stages of the software life
cycle, in particular during the validation and verification activities for test cases
generation. Scenarios, which are related to use cases, can be used early in the
analysis phase: a domain expert and the customers can walk the analyst through
dozens of typical system usage scenarios, in order to help uncover important facets
of the system behavior that were not mentioned in the initial problem statement.
This way, scenarios help uncover less obvious requirements. Figure 3.5 depicts an
example of Use Case diagram with an actor and three use cases.

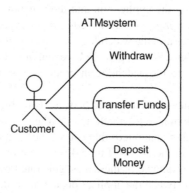

Fig. 3.5 Example of UML Use Case Diagram taken from UML2 (2011)

3.1.3.5   Activity Diagrams

The activity diagram specifies the control flow of a component, sub-system, or system. It is widely used for modeling business processes, workflows, or system low level processes. It features most of the common control flow structures such as decision, fork, join, loop, or merge. Figure 3.6 models a partial behavior of a reliable communication system (Bernardi et al. 2011c).

An interesting feature of activity diagrams is that the actions can be placed in *activity partitions*. An activity partitions groups actions according to a certain criterion, for instance who is responsible for the actions or where they take place.

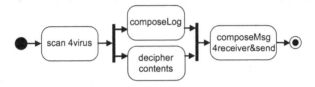

Fig. 3.6 Example of activity diagram

3.1.3.6   Component Diagrams

Component-based development is very popular in software engineering. A *component* is a modular part of a system that encapsulates its contents and defines its behavior in terms of *provided* and *required interfaces*. A component is intended to be a substitutable unit that can be replaced at design time or runtime by another component that offers equivalent functionality based on the compatibility of its interfaces.

In software engineering, components and classes are different concepts, but in UML 2, a component is very similar to a *structured class*. A structured class (or a structured classifier) is also based on the concepts of decomposition and encapsulation. It contains an internal collaboration structure of *parts*, which are instance roles linked together with *connectors*. A structured class representing the whole owns its parts and connectors and is responsible for their creation/destruction and coordination. Encapsulation is realized through ports and interfaces. A *port* specifies a distinct interaction point between a classifier and its environment or between a classifier and its internal parts. A port specifies the services provided by the classifier to its environment as well as the services required by the classier from its environment. The port fully isolates the object from its environment and may be associated with required or offered interfaces.

There is a clear difference between interfaces and ports. An interface is a collection of operations provided elsewhere; it has no behavior in and of itself and cannot be instantiated. On the other hand, a port is different from an interface, in the sense that it can be instantiated. A port instance is a connection slot into an instance of a class; the instance can identify which port has provided a message. A port may accept messages and either pass them to the owner instance for processing, or relay them to an internal part of that owner.

Component diagrams may be very useful for dependability specification and analysis, because many dependability attributes are associated with components. Figure 3.7 depicts an example of Component diagram with two components and interfaces.

Fig. 3.7 Example of UML Component Diagram taken from UML2 (2011)

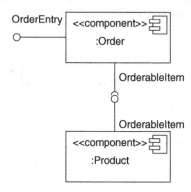

3.1.3.7   Deployment Diagrams

Deployment Diagrams allow to specify the physical configurations at runtime of the hardware and the allocation of software to hardware. Nodes represent the physical structure of a system; they may model execution environments in the form of layered platforms, as understood in MDA. Nodes may also represent devices, either processors (on which software executes) or non-processing devices (such as disks and different of I/O devices). Nodes are connected to other nodes via connections that may represent buses, links, or networks.

Artifacts are another model element in deployment diagram, which represent files containing software code of sub-systems and/or components that are deployed on nodes. Artifacts manifest instances of runtime components, which represent the runtime view of the software. Figure 3.8 shows a deployment diagram for the components of the e-commerce system whose interaction is represented in Fig. 3.3.

From the point of view of quantitative evaluation of the system, deployment diagrams can be used as suggested in Cortellessa and Mirandola (2000), to specify the features of communication means used by the interacting components (e.g., network bandwidth) that have an impact on the communication delays.

Fig. 3.8 Example
Deployment diagram

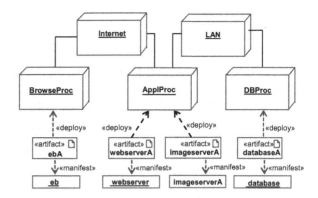

3.1.3.8 Package Diagrams

Packages allow developers to organize large UML models in order to reduce their complexity, to separate domains, and to enforce a cleaner structure. A package is a design-time model element that may contain lower-level packages, as well as other UML model elements (such as classes, but also use cases, sequence diagrams). Packages cannot be instantiated.

An important characteristic is that packages define namespaces. Some model elements inside a package can be related to other model elements defined in other packages, which creates in turn a dependency between the packages. Dependency relationships can be drawn automatically by most of the UML tools and packages can usually be exported/imported between models. Normally, packages are the basic configuration item for configuration management tools.

3.1.4 Object Constraint Language

Additional constraints among model elements can be specified by the modeler; constraint expressions can be written in any of the UML diagrams; e.g., in Class Diagrams to specify constraints among class objects, in Sequence Diagrams to specify timing constraints on messages, etc.

These constraints can be specified either in natural language or through the use of a predefined constraint language also standardized by OMG: the Object Constraint Language (OCL 2006). OCL provides a number of predefined data types like `Boolean`, `Integer`, `String` and `Set` and operations on these data to be used in the constraints for attributes, parameters, return values, etc. Besides these predefined types, all classes in the model can be used as types for OCL expressions and the OCL dotted-syntax allows to navigate along the associations of a class using the rolenames. There are also several reserved keywords to denote special part of the constraint, among them we report the ones that have been used in this book:

- **context**: it is used to declare the context for the constraint expression,
- **inv**: it is used to state an invariant for the corresponding context class,
- **self**: it is used as reference to an object of the context class.

An example of constraint written in OCL on the class *Order* of the CD shown in Fig. 3.2 is the following:

context Order **inv** :

self.paid_by $\rightarrow$ exists(p : Payment | p.amount > 0)

This expression evaluates to true if the amount of at least a payment related to the order is greater than zero.

3.1.5 UML Extension Mechanisms

UML 2 introduced the profile mechanism as a metamodeling technique to extend and adapt the language for different purposes. Reasons to extend UML are of different natures, for example to introduce terminology adapted to a given platform or domain, e.g., the EJB profile (UML-EDOC 2001), or to add semantics not already present in UML that can be used for model transformation purposes, e.g., the profile MARTE (2011) extends UML with concepts from the real-time and embedded systems domain, facilitating the derivation of performance or schedulability analysis models from UML + MARTE models. Since profiles are standard extension mechanisms, they are recognized by standard UML tools and can be exchanged among them.

Stereotypes and tagged-values are extension mechanisms used to define a profile. A stereotype extends one or more UML meta-classes and can be applied to UML model elements (classes, objects, attributes, states, transitions, etc.). For example, MARTE introduces a stereotype for a well-known concept from the real-time domain, that of "type of clock," which extends the UML meta-class "Class." Figure 3.9a depicts the definition of the stereotype "clockType." The stereotype can be applied to any Class instance in a UML+MARTE model by labeling it with "clockType," as shown in Fig. 3.9b. Last, tagged-values represent the attributes of the stereotypes; for instance, in Fig. 3.9a are listed the attributes of "clockType" stereotype (nature, unitType, and so on). Every time when the stereotype is applied to a class or instance, the stereotype attributes will be added to the respective model element, extending it with extra information. Appendix A presents the basic structure of the MARTE profile and describes its main stereotypes that are extended by the DAM profile in this book.

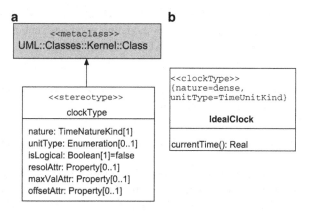

Fig. 3.9 Example of (a) stereotype definition and (b) application

3.2 Domain-Specific Language: AADL

Architecture Analysis and Design Language (AADL) is an architecture description language that has been adopted as an industry standard by the International Society for Automotive Engineers (SAE) in 2004. The language was developed to model the software and hardware of real-time embedded systems, including abstractions of software, computational hardware, and system components, as well as mapping of software onto hardware elements (AADL 2006). An AADL architecture model can then be used either as a design documentation, for analysis of non-functional properties (such as schedulability and reliability) or for code generation.

AADL is defined by a core language that supports the modeling of software and its runtime platform including hardware by using the same notation. Having a single representation for all system aspects facilitates the analysis of non-functional properties of the system. The language specifies system-specific characteristics using model elements properties.

The core language can be extended with the following methods:

- *User-defined properties*: users can extend the set of core AADL language properties and add their own to specify their requirements;
- *Supplemental language annexes*: the core language may be enhanced by annex languages that enrich the architecture description for different purposes. With the definition of a new annex, the AADL tool support has to be upgraded in order to be able to handle the newly introduced constructs and features. Examples of annex documents defined so far are:

   - *Behavior annex*: expressing component behavior with state machines
   - *Error-model annex*: specifies fault and propagation concerns enabling depend-ability analysis;
   - *ARINC653 annex*: defines modeling patterns for modeling avionics systems;

– *Data-model annex*: provides guidance on a standard way of associating data models expressed in other data modeling notations such as UML with architecture models expressed in AADL.

3.2.1   Core Language Capabilities

An important AADL abstraction is that of *component*, which can be used to represent software, hardware, or a combination thereof. A component is characterized by its identity, interfaces with other components, distinguishing properties and subcomponents and their interactions. In addition to interfaces and internal structural elements, other abstractions can be defined for a component and system architecture, such as abstract data or control flows (AADL 2006).

The AADL component abstractions are separated into three categories for representing software, execution platform, and systems:

1. *Application software:*

   (a) *thread*: active component that can execute concurrently and be organized into thread groups
   (b) *thread group*: component abstraction for logically organizing thread, data, and thread group components within a process
   (c) *process*: protected address space whose boundaries are enforced at runtime and may contain threads and thread groups
   (d) *data*: data types and static data
   (e) *subprogram*: a callable piece of source code.

2. *Execution platform (hardware):*

   (a) *processor*: schedules and executes threads
   (b) *memory*: stores code and data
   (c) *device*: represents sensors, actuators, or other components that interface with the external environment
   (d) *bus*: interconnects processors, memory, and devices

3. *Composite:*

   (a) *system*: design elements that enable the integration of other components into distinct units within the architecture.

System components are composites that can consist of software or hardware components, as well as of other systems.

AADL includes semantics for data exchange and runtime control, such as message and event passing, synchronized access to shared components, thread scheduling protocols, timing requirements, remote procedure calls.

AADL components interact exclusively through defined interfaces. A component interface consists of directional flow through: data ports for unqueued state data, event data ports for queued message data, event ports for asynchronous events, synchronous subprogram calls, and explicit access to data components.

Allocation of software elements to platform elements can be indicated by defining constraints for binding threads to processors, ports to buses, source code, and data to memory. The constraints can limit binding to specific processor or memory types, as well as prevent co-location of application components to support fault tolerance.

The concrete syntax of AADL is expressed as both a graphical notation and a textual representation. The graphical notation facilitates a clear visual presentation of a systems structural hierarchy and communication topology and provides a foundation for distinct architecture perspectives. Figure 3.10 shows a subset of the graphical notation for the main AADL model elements (AADL 2006).

3.2.2 Example of an AADL Model

The model of a surveillance system is represented in Fig. 3.11, which was presented in Cao et al. (2006). The customer wants to install a surveillance system to monitor three houses located far from the office. No local networks are available in those locations. The need to effectively prevent intruders leads to the requirement that the detection must be quick, for instance less than two seconds. This is an end-to-end response time of the entire system that should be verified in the architectural design phase.

A solution is to deploy three web cameras to monitor the houses. The video information from the cameras will be sent to the office computer wirelessly. However, not all video streams can be accommodated by the limited bandwidth of the wireless communication, which leads to the need for compressing the streams. A video processor will be embedded onto each camera to compress and preprocess the video data, but this may affect the end-to-end response time. With the help of an AADL model, several design alternatives (such as different hardware choices for the video processor, different compression, and intruder detection algorithms) can be evaluated and compared, by keeping the focus on satisfying the end-to-end response time.

The next step is to define the high-level system architecture, as shown in Fig. 3.11. The Video_Detection_System, which is the core system running at the main office is represented by the *system* construct, while the three video cameras and display are represented as *devices*. A *port group* and *connections* are used to model the communication between the remote video cameras, the core system and the display.

The software constructs *process, data, thread,* and *system* are used to model the internal view of the Video_Detection_System. The hardware constructs *processor, memory, bus,* and *device* are used to describe the system's physical features. More specifically, the execution platform in Fig. 3.11 is specified by the processor, memory, radio transceivers, wireless link and internal bus.

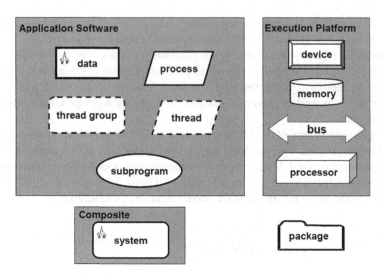

Fig. 3.10 AADL Graphical Notation (from AADL 2006)

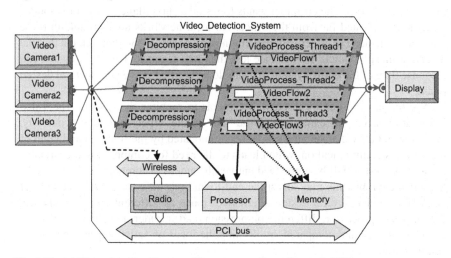

Fig. 3.11 AADL model of a video surveillance system (from Cao et al. 2006)

After defining the components, we need to specify how they interact. Component interactions use *ports* (data and event inputs and outputs), *port groups* (a collection of ports), *subcomponent access, subprogram calls, data exchange,* and *sharing.* These constructs define the functional interfaces and communication among components. In Fig. 3.11, input and output data ports (represented as triangles on the border of processes and threads) are used to describe the data exchange between the software elements and to represent the data flows corresponding to the three video cameras: VideoFlow1, VideoFlow2, and VideoFlow3. AADL offers the ability to model data and control flows in order to support end-to-end analysis, such as end-to-end response time, error propagation, and quality-of-service resource management. A flow defines sequential data or events through several components and connections.

Figure 3.11 shows also how the software is bound to the hardware platform. The core system communicates with the cameras over the wireless network, through the radio device; this is shown by binding the port group on the left-hand side of the system to the wireless bus (binding is shown as a dashed arrow). The software processes are bound for execution to the processor (plain arrows) in accord with scheduling properties. The video data processed by every thread are bound to memory for storage (shown as dotted arrows). The protocols are reflected as properties on a bus and feed through to analysis tools. Different bus types, such as PCI or VME can be defined, including the protocol and performance characteristics of those standards. It is also possible to define a customized bus, Wireless, which models the features of the CSMA/CA wireless link.

An important characteristic of AADL is the ability to model on the same diagram the structural view of the target system (composed of both hardware and software), as well as the data and control flows specifying the high-level behavior view of the system. This helps the modeler to specify and evaluate the overall properties of the complete system. In the example presented in Fig. 3.11, the choices of video cameras, radio transceivers, and processors directly affect the end-to-end response times defined along the three flows, VideoFlow1, VideoFlow2, and VideoFlow3, corresponding to the three houses surveyed by the system.

3.2.3 AADL Versus UML

The main differences between AADL and UML stem from the fact that the two languages have different purposes: UML was designed as a software modeling language intended to support software development and ultimately code generation from models (UML2 2011), while AADL is an architecture modeling language intended to model and analyze runtime architecture (de Niz 2007). Runtime architecture is concerned with representing the runtime system structure, composed of hardware (processors, memory, buses, devices) and software (processes, threads subprograms, data) as well as their interactions (event and message passing, access to shared components, subprogram call, flows). Runtime architecture provides the software system with specific quality attributes such as timeliness, fault tolerance, or security, and therefore AADL is able to support different types of analyses of runtime non-functional properties, such as performance and dependability. On the other hand, AADL is not concerned with the detailed specification of data types and functional structure of the software, nor with object-oriented structure and behavior specification. Therefore, AADL is not appropriate for supporting the entire software development process the way in which UML does, from requirements elicitation and analysis to design and code generation.

UML has the ability to represent software models at different levels of abstraction, from high-level architecture models (such as those represented in AADL) to detailed design models. In order to analyze a certain non-functional property of the software system under construction, the analysts are free to choose the appropriate UML model at the right level of abstraction, extend it with extra annotations describing the property of interest by using a UML profile, and then transform the annotated model into an analysis model using a suitable formalism. For example, the MARTE profile (MARTE 2011) can be used to extend UML models with information required to support performance and schedulability analysis, as mentioned at the beginning of the chapter.

Another difference between AADL and UML is the way in which the two languages support extensions to accommodate new modeling constructs. AADL provides an extension mechanism called *annex* to add new model elements for different kinds of analysis not covered with the core elements. The annexes are embedded in descriptions of the core language and can make references to core model elements. Along with the annex, tool support needs to be built to handle the analysis of the annex sub-models. Two examples of AADL annexes are the error annex and the behavioral annex. The error annex supports the specification and analysis of error propagation (transformed to a Markov chain) in order to enhance dependability analysis. The behavioral annex allows the description of functional behavior to enable formal verification in the style of model checking.

As opposed to AADL, the UML extension mechanism called "profile" (described in Sect. 3.1.5) has the advantage that it does not require additional tool support in order to handle the new model elements. A profile, once defined, is supported by any UML editor that conforms to the UML standard.

As already mentioned, in this book we selected UML as the modeling language for representing the systems whose dependability characteristics will be analyzed for a number of reasons: (a) UML is widely used and has become the "lingua franca" for software modeling; (b) the UML extension mechanism is flexible and does not require additional tool support; (c) there is a large body of work in dependability analysis of software system based on UML.

Chapter 4
Dependability Domain Model

Let's specify the dependability concepts with a model.

Abstract This chapter introduces a domain model for the dependability. The model describes core concepts of dependability while provides a vocabulary for it. The domain model bridges the gap between dependability concepts, introduced in Chap. 2, and the dependability profile, described in Chap. 5. The domain model defines information needed to create modeling constructs for dependability-specific modeling languages.

As stated in the Introduction of the book, modeling the dependability of a software system means to identify the properties, requirements, and measures of interest for reliability, availability, maintainability, safety, or integrity analysis. This modeling activity introduces the *dependability view* in the software model. The dependability view, together with the structural and behavioral views, is what enables a software model for dependability analysis.

A common way of specifying the dependability view is using a domain-specific modeling language (DSML) for dependability. DSMLs were defined in the Introduction as specification languages that offer, through appropriate notations and abstractions, expressive power focused on a particular domain (Graaf and van Deursen 2007). For example, SysML (2012) is a language for the specification of applications in the systems engineering domain. DSMLs can be created either from scratch or by augmenting the modeling capabilities of other general purpose modeling language. An example of the latter is the case for UML, which can be customized for specific domains using the *profile* mechanism. Hence, the goal of a dependability DSML is to offer a set of modeling constructs (either textual or graphical) that enable to specify the dependability view. These constructs, properly integrated in the software model, are assets that will allow to specify the concepts of the dependability introduced in Chap. 2.

S. Bernardi et al., *Model-Driven Dependability Assessment of Software Systems*,
DOI 10.1007/978-3-642-39512-3_4, © Springer-Verlag Berlin Heidelberg 2013

The goal of this chapter is to bridge the gap between dependability concepts and the modeling constructs for dependability DSMLs. The approach taken is that of the *domain model*, which is a visual representation of conceptual classes or real-world objects in a domain of interest (Martin and Odell 1997). The domain model presented in this chapter has been created considering:

- dependability concepts summarized in Chap. 2,
- standard techniques used for dependability analysis, discussed in Chap. 6, and
- a total of 43 papers from literature that propose DSMLs for dependability in the context of UML. These approaches are analyzed in Chap. 7.

All these sources guarantee that the proposed domain model is comprehensive enough to create dependability DSMLs for different purposes of dependability analysis, say availability, reliability, maintainability, or safety.

The dependability domain model is used in Chap. 5 for creating Dependability Modeling and Analysis (DAM), a dependability DSML. DAM is a dependability UML profile that extends UML with stereotypes for DAM. Moreover, DAM is built on another standard UML profile called MARTE (2011) (Modeling and Analysis of Real Time and Embedded systems). This chapter also discusses how the dependability domain model helps DAM to be integrated within MARTE.

4.1 Structure of the Domain Model

The left-hand side of Fig. 4.1 depicts the high-level organization proposed to present the models for the dependability concepts recalled in Chap. 2. This is a high-level view of the dependability domain model, which is organized into three packages: System, Threats, and Maintenance. The System package, see Fig. 4.1 right-hand side, is organized into another two packages: Core and Redundancy. The Redundancy depending on the Core. The Threats and Maintenance packages depend on the System. The criteria followed to organize the domain model have been: (a) the organization of the system and its redundancy and (b) the kind of threats that may affect the system and the maintenance actions that can be undertaken to attain system dependability.

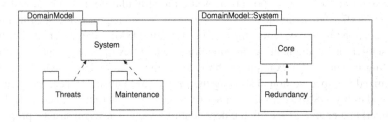

Fig. 4.1 Organization of the dependability domain model

- The *System* package provides concepts for a description of the system to be analyzed, according to a component-based view as in Avizienis et al. (2004) and Lyu (1996). These concepts appear in the *Core* package and refer to those explained in Chap. 2, Sect. 2.1. The *System* model includes also additional concepts to describe redundancy structures that may characterize a fault-tolerant system (Lyu 1995). They appear in the *Redundancy* package.
- The *Threats* package offers a model for the concepts of the causal chain introduced in Chap. 2, Sect. 2.2. Modeling threats is a necessary activity to carry out reliability and safety analysis. The concepts in this package and their relationships are related to those of the System (both the core concepts and the redundancy structure). Since the adopted terminology is slightly different in the reliability and safety domains, the package introduces the abstract concept of *impairment* that can be refined for the specific analysis to be carried out.
- The *Maintenance* package offers a model for some of the concepts introduced in Chap. 2, Sect. 2.3. These concepts are necessary to carry out availability analysis, basically the repair process from anomalous states. The model introduces maintenance actions undertaken in case of repairable systems (Avizienis et al. 2004; Lyu 1995). Avizienis et al. (2004) introduced the term *maintenance* to indicate not only repairs but also modifications of the system that take place during its usage. So, the package includes also concepts related to system reconfiguration. The concepts in the package are related to the concepts of the System.

4.2 System Core Model

Figure 4.2 depicts the *Core* package of the dependability domain model. This package, within the *System* package, represents the *context* where the dependability analysis is carried out. Actually, it provides a component-based description of the system to be analyzed. The system under analysis needs to specify both, its structural and behavioral views.

Observe that the different shadows assigned to the classes in Figs. 4.2–4.5 will be used in the Chap. 5 to describe the mapping of the domain model onto UML extensions. So, apart from the dark shadowed classes that represent MARTE domain concepts, the shadows are irrelevant in this chapter.

From the structural point of view, the system consists of a set of hardware and software *components* that are bounded together through *connectors*, i.e., logical or physical links, in order to interact. A component can be a sub-system consisting of sub-components. From the behavioral point of view, components provide and require *services*, hence the structure of the system is what enables to generate the behavior. The system then delivers a set of high-level services in response to user *service requests*. Each high-level service is part of the system behavior as perceived by its users and it is carried out by the interaction of

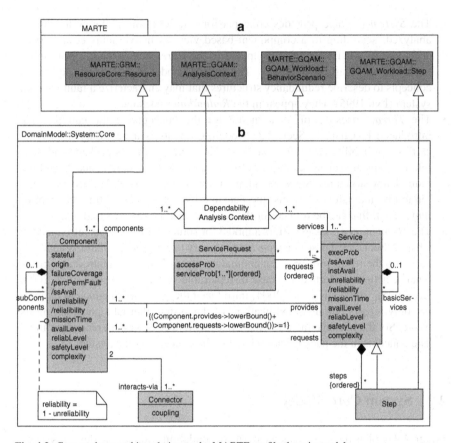

Fig. 4.2 Core package and its relation to the MARTE profile domain models

system components, which provide and request basic services to each other. A component must either provide or request at least one basic service. A service is implemented by sequences of *steps* that may represent component states and actions.

Table 4.1 shows an explanation of the attributes and association-ends of class *Component*. Some of the attributes represent measures, properties, or requirements according to Sect. 2.4. The explanation includes also references to works that use the corresponding attribute. Those attributes prefixed by a leading slash symbol are derived attributes, i.e., those that can be calculated from other attributes. On the other hand, associations can be subject to OCL constraints: a description of such constraints is also provided in Table 4.1. Table B.1 in Appendix B details the attributes and association-ends for the rest of the classes in this core model.

Table 4.1 Description of the attributes and association-ends of *Component*

Attribute	Description
stateful	(true) Faulty component can be characterized by an error latency, so it can be restored before failure. (false) Faulty component is considered as failed (Bondavalli et al (2001b); Majzik et al (2003)).
origin	Hardware or software component (Bondavalli et al (2001b); Majzik et al (2003)).
failureCoverage	Percentage of failure coverage (Pai and Dugan (2002)).
/percPermFault	Percentage of permanent faults (Bondavalli et al (2001b); Majzik et al (2003)). Derived from *fault* association-end and *persistency* attribute of Threats::Fault class.
/ssAvail	Steady state availability percentage (Sahner et al (1996); Bernardi et al (2004a)). Derived from *MTTF* (Threats::Failure) and *MTTR* (Maintenance::Repair) attributes.
unreliability	Probability that the time to failure random variable is less than or (equal to) the time t - time dependent (Sahner et al (1996)).
/reliability	Survival function (Evans et al (2000)): probability that the component is functioning correctly during the time interval $(0,t]$ - time dependent (Sahner et al (1996)).
missionTime	The maximum period of time for which a component can be used. After this time, it must be replaced. Mission time should be declared by the manufacturer of the component. Equivalent to *lifetime* (IEC-62061 (2005))
availLevel	Availability level associated to the nines of availability. E.g., very high corresponds to 99,9% of ssAvail, etc. (application specific).
reliabLevel	Reliability level (application specific).
safetyLevel	Safety level (application specific).
complexity	Complexity metric quantifies the component failure proneness (Bernardi et al (2004a); Jürjens (2003); Jürjens and Wagner (2005); Goseva-Popstojanova et al (2003)).
Association-end	Description
subComponents	A component may consist of a set of sub-components.
interacts-via	A component interacts with other components through one or more connectors.
provides/requests	A component may provide (request) services to other components. The OCL constraint states that a component cannot be isolated, i.e., it provides (or requests) at least a service to another component.

4.2.1 Integration Within MARTE Profile

As explained in the introduction of the chapter, the dependability domain model will be used in next chapter for defining DAM, a dependability UML profile. In particular, DAM will be integrated with MARTE (2011), an existing UML standard profile for schedulability and performance modeling and analysis. This core part of the dependability domain model is precisely the one meaningful for the integration with MARTE. Figure 4.2 depicts how the integration is carried out. In the MARTE domain model, there are four classes, see Fig. 4.2a, that are specialized by the core dependability concepts of *Dependability Analysis Context*, *Component*, *Service*, and *Step*.

4.3   System Redundancy Model

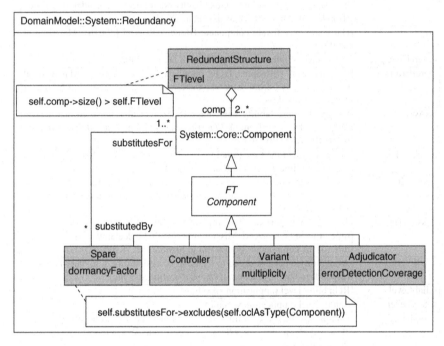

Fig. 4.3 Redundancy package

Figure 4.3 depicts the *Redundancy* package of the dependability domain model. This package, within the *System* package, is motivated by the objective of providing specific support for quantitative dependability analysis of fault-tolerant systems characterized by redundant structures. However, it is not in the scope of the package to provide full support for the modeling of fault-tolerant architectures; such issue has been tackled, e.g., by the standard UML profile QoS & FT (2008). The package represents the redundancy structures that may characterize a system. Software and hardware redundancy are the typical means used to add fault tolerance capabilities to software systems, e.g., by eliminating single points of failure. In the dependability analysis of fault-tolerant systems it is important to identify and evaluate the system under multiple dependent failure assumption (i.e., common mode failures).

The classes in Fig. 4.3 introduce the concept of *redundant structure* for characterizing the fault-tolerant system. A redundant structure is made at least of two components, of the kind described in the core package. Components can be *fault-tolerant components* (Lyu 1995), which can play different roles. In particular, *variants*, i.e., modules with different design that provide the same services, allocated over different *spares*. A *controller* that is responsible for the co-ordination of the variants, an *adjudicator* that either looks for a consensus of two or more outputs among the variants ("N-version software" scheme) or applies an acceptance test to the variant outputs ("recovery block" scheme). A spare may substitute for one or more components and, depending on the adopted fault tolerance strategy, can be unpowered until needed (*cold*), continually powered (*hot*), or partially powered in the standby mode until it is needed (*warm*). The type of spare can be specified by its *dormancyFactor*, which is the ratio between the spare failure rates in standby mode and in operational mode, respectively. For instance, a cold spare has a dormancy factor equal to zero, since it cannot fail in standby mode.

The redundant structure has the *fault tolerance level* attribute to specify the minimum number of components necessary to guarantee the service. The attached OCL constraint specifies that the fault tolerance level should be higher than the number of components within the redundant structure. The other OCL in the model, associated with the spare, indicates that a spare cannot substitute itself. Table B.2, in Appendix B, provides all details of this model.

4.4 Threats Model

Figure 4.4 depicts the *Threats* package of the dependability domain model. It represents the cause–effect relationships between the threats of the dependability, according to Sect. 2.2, and the relationships between the threats and the system concepts.

Classes in Fig. 4.4 include the threats that may affect the system, namely *faults, errors, failures* (Avizienis et al. 2004; Lyu 1996), and *hazards* (Leveson 1995). We have introduced an abstract concept of *impairment* that can be specialized depending on the type of analysis domain, i.e., failure for RAM analysis and hazard for safety. Then, a fault is the original cause of errors and impairments, and it affects system components. A *fault generator* concept represents a mechanism, used, e.g. by Bernardi and Merseguer (2006) and Pataricza (2000), to inject faults in the system and to specify the maximum number of concurrent faults. Errors are related to steps (i.e., states or actions) of the basic services provided by the faulty components. When an error affects an external state of a faulty component, that is the service interface of that component, then *error propagation* may occur from the faulty component to other components it interacts with, via the corresponding connectors. A series of error propagations may be interrelated, e.g. they may occur in a given order, as in Pai and Dugan (2002); ordered sequences of error propagations as well as nontrivial *error propagation relations* can be specified as logical expressions by means of the attribute *propagationExpr*. Errors may cause impairments at different system level: (1) at service step level, leading to *failure* or *hazard steps*, when the service provided by the component becomes incorrect; (2) at component level, when the component is unable to provide any basic service; (3) at system level, when the impairment is perceived by the system users. Finally, multiple dependent impairments can affect a redundant structure, such as when several redundant components fail in the same mode (i.e., *common mode failures* in Lyu 1995). Table B.3 in Appendix B details all the classes in this model.

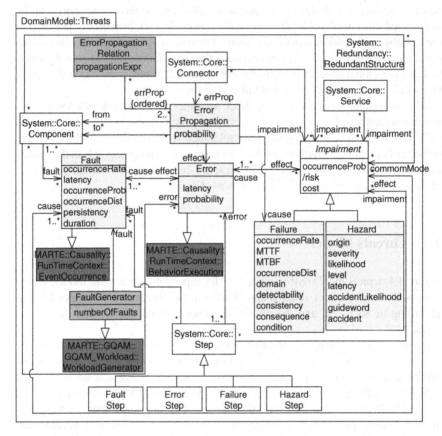

Fig. 4.4 Threats package

4.5 Maintenance Model

Figure 4.5 depicts the *Maintenance* package of the dependability domain model. The Maintenance model concerns repairable systems and includes concepts that are necessary to support the evaluation of system availability (Bernardi et al. 2011b, 2013). Indeed, during the execution of maintenance actions, the services provided by the system are either partially or entirely not delivered to the user, so the time to perform maintenance has an impact on the system availability.

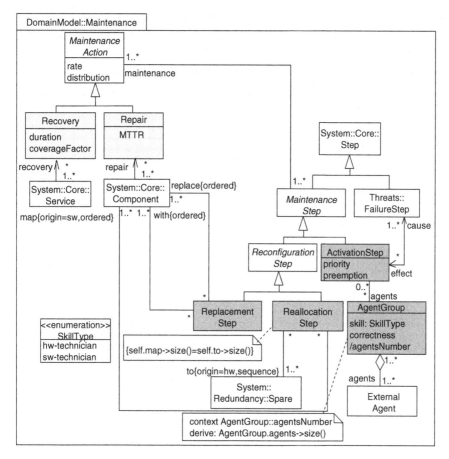

Fig. 4.5 Maintenance package

Classes in Fig. 4.5 include *maintenance actions* undertaken to restore the system affected by threats. The execution *rate* and the execution time *distribution* characterize maintenance actions from a quantitative point of view. According to Avizienis et al. (2004) and Lyu (1995), maintenance actions can be *repairs* of system components or *recovery* strategies, usually implemented in fault-tolerant systems. Both aim at transforming the system anomalous states into correct states. Maintenance actions are related to *maintenance steps*, which can be *reconfiguration steps* or *activation steps*. The former can be either *replacement* or *reallocation steps*. Replacement steps consist in actions in which a set of faulty components are replaced with other components (e.g., spares or variants). In *reallocation steps*, a set of software components is reallocated onto a collection of spares. To represent the new system reconfiguration, after the system recovery, the set of replaced/reallocated components and the spares must be ordered and have the same size. *Activation steps* are triggered by failure steps and they are related to the participation of groups of *external agents*, which carry out the maintenance repair actions. External agents, e.g., repairmen or test equipments, are *grouped* according to their skills.

Table B.4 in Appendix B details all the classes in this model.

Chapter 5
Dependability Modeling and Analysis Profile

UML + Dependability = DAM

Abstract This chapter presents a UML profile as an example of mapping the dependability domain model (Chap. 4) to UML, by using the standard UML extension mechanisms. The DAM profile relies on the standard OMG MARTE profile (Appendix A) and it consists of a set of UML extensions (i.e., stereotypes, tags, and constraints) that enable to annotate a UML model with dependability requirements, input parameters, and metrics for dependability analysis purposes. The chapter explains how to apply DAM extensions in UML-based system models. Two case studies, coming from different application domains, are presented.

According to Selic (2007), there are three main methods for defining a domain-specific modeling language (DSML). The first is to define a new modeling language from scratch: it provides the most direct and succint expression of domain-specific concept. On the other hand, a lot of effort is required to define it as well as to develop tool supporting its usage. The second method extends an existing modeling language by supplementing it with new domain-specific constructs. For example, the approaches that extend UML by using the Meta-Object Facility (MOF 2006) follow this second method. The third one consists in refining an existing more general modeling language by specializing some of its general constructs to represent domain-specific concepts. This is often the most practical and cost-effective solution that promotes the reuse of the tool frameworks of the base modeling language. The UML profiling is an example of lightweight approach that enables to define DSML by applying the standard UML extensions mechanisms, i.e, stereotypes, tags, and constraints.

This chapter presents a UML profile that enables the specification of dependability non-functional properties (NFPs) in UML model-based software systems. The UML profile supports also the dependability analysis of the latter, throughout the life cycle, by providing a common input DSML to the model-to-model (M2M)

S. Bernardi et al., *Model-Driven Dependability Assessment of Software Systems*,
DOI 10.1007/978-3-642-39512-3_5, © Springer-Verlag Berlin Heidelberg 2013

transformation techniques which either automatically or systematically produce formal dependability models from UML model-based specification.

The UML profile is not built from scratch, rather a systematic approach is followed (Selic 2007) to finally design a technically correct and effective profile which takes advantage of the UML2 (2011) profile mechanisms. The input specification is then the DAM domain model described in Chap. 4. The mapping of domain model concepts into UML standard extensions is an iterative process, in which each class is examined, together with its attributes, associations, and constraints, to identify the most suitable UML base concepts for it.

Since the objective is to introduce a set of stereotypes small yet expressive, that can be easily used by the software analyst, the guideline of Lagarde et al. (2007) has been used to select the subset of the domain classes that eventually are mapped to stereotypes. Moreover, several patterns proposed by Lagarde et al. (2007) (e.g., the *reference association* pattern) are applied that enable the creation of a profile from the domain model, while keeping it consistent with the UML metamodel. Finally, to keep track of the mapping between the domain model and the DAM profile, the best practice from the standard OMG MARTE profile (Appendix A) are adopted to name each introduced extension with the name of the mapped domain class prefixed by *DA*, namely Dependability Analysis.

5.1 Design of the DAM Profile

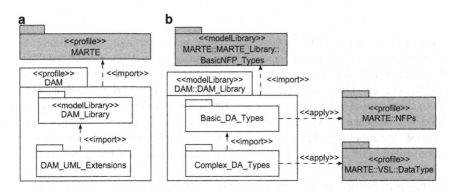

Fig. 5.1 (a) DAM profile and (b) DAM library

The DAM profile consists of two main packages, as shown in Fig. 5.1a: one includes the set of UML extensions (*DAM_UML_Extensions*) and the other is a model library (*DAM_Library*). The *DAM_UML_Extensions* package contains a set of dependability stereotypes, their attributes (also called tags), and constraints. Most of the DAM stereotypes specialize the ones of MARTE (2011).

The library, detailed in Fig. 5.1b, is made of basic and complex dependability types used to define the stereotype attributes. The DAM library uses basic NFP types, from the MARTE library. Moreover, the MARTE NFPs sub-profile is applied to the definition of new basic dependability types and the VSL sub-profile to the definition of the complex ones.

5.1.1 DAM UML Extensions

The DAM extensions package provides the domain expert with a set of stereotypes to be applied at model specification level, i.e., the stereotypes necessary to represent the dependability system view in a concrete UML model. Domain classes are natural candidates for becoming stereotypes. However, it is important to provide a small yet sufficient set of stereotypes to be actually used in practical modeling situations (Lagarde et al. 2007). Eventually, only a subset of the domain classes will be then mapped to stereotypes (i.e., the pale gray classes in Figs. 4.2–4.5). In order to maintain a traceable mapping, the name of each stereotype is the name of the domain class prefixed by *Da*, namely Dependability Analysis, as shown in Figs. 5.2 and 5.3.

In the process of selecting a minimum set of stereotypes, each package in the domain model is visited, characterizing their classes as *abstract, firm, uncertain*, or *parametric* (Lagarde et al. 2007). This criterion aims to clearly characterize the role of each DSML concept. *Abstract* classes refer to accessory concepts, *firm* classes are used as language constructs, *uncertain* classes sort indeterminate concepts, and *parametric* classes categorize concepts that can change depending on the sub-problem domain. For example, in the Core model package, the classes *Component, Connector, Service, ServiceRequest*, and *Step* as classified as *firm*, and are mapped to stereotypes (Fig. 5.2, pale gray), while the class *DepAnalysisContext* is regarded as *uncertain*. As for the classes regarded as *abstract*, e.g., *FT Component* (Fig. 4.3), they don't have to be mapped to stereotypes (Lagarde et al. 2007).

In the second stage, for each stereotype obtained from a *firm* class, suitable *extensions* are searched, i.e., the actual UML meta-classes to be extended by the stereotype. To facilitate the extension process, several proposals in the surveyed literature have been consulted, identifying the UML model elements annotated with the same dependability properties as the ones characterizing the stereotype. In other words, the general guidelines from Selic (2007) have been applied, based on the semantic similarity between the UML meta-classes and stereotypes. Finally, if a semantically equivalent stereotype exists in MARTE, then the DAM stereotype is defined as a sub-stereotype of the MARTE one (depicted in dark gray in Figs. 5.2 and 5.3).

For the final result of this stage, see Table 5.1 showing as an example the definition of the stereotype *DaComponent*. It specializes the MARTE stereotype shown in the "Generalization" row, it does not extend directly any UML meta-class (the "Extensions" row is empty) and extends indirectly the same UML meta-classes as the stereotype from which it inherits.

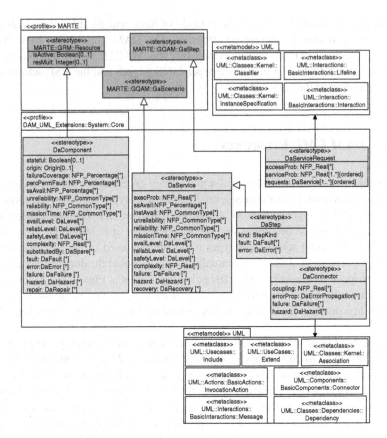

Fig. 5.2 DAM stereotypes from Core

The attributes of a stereotype, which characterize its properties, are obtained from the original class in the domain model, either from its attributes or from navigable association-ends. The type of the first kind of attributes is a basic UML type, a MARTE NFP type or a basic dependability type (described in Sect. 5.1.2.2). To define the type of the attributes obtained from association-ends, the complex dependability types are introduced (described in Sect. 5.1.2.1).

Since the mapping of association-ends is less trivial than that of attributes, the *reference association* pattern (Lagarde et al. 2007) is often applied. An example of such pattern is given in Fig. 4.4, where the *Component* class is associated with the *Fault* class through the association-end *fault*. The latter is used to define the attribute *fault* of *DaComponent* (with complex type *DaFault*, see Table 5.1). On the other hand, when an abstract class, e.g., *Impairment* in Fig. 4.4, is the target of associations ends, e.g., *impairment* from *Component*, then all the specialized classes (*Failure* and *Hazard*) inherit the associations ends but renamed. Thus, Table 5.1 shows *failure* and *hazard* as attributes of *DaComponent*. Finally, when defining the attribute multiplicity, the multiplicity values of the association-ends from the domain model are retained for the attributes.

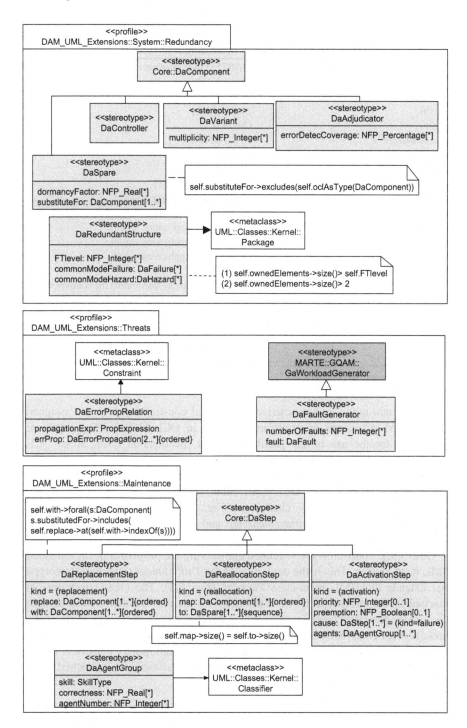

Fig. 5.3 DAM stereotypes from System Redundancy, Threats, and Maintenance

Table 5.1 Example of stereotype description

DaComponent maps the System::Core::Component domain class	
Generalization	MARTE::GRM::Resource
Extensions	none
Attributes	
stateful	Boolean[0..1]
origin	Origin[0..1]
failureCoverage	NFP_Percentage[*]
percPermFault	NFP_Percentage[*]
ssAvail	NFP_Percentage[*]
unreliability	NFP_CommonType[*]
reliability	NFP_CommonType[*]
missionTime	NFP_CommonType[*]
availLevel	DaLevel[*] - Application specific
reliabLevel	DaLevel[*] - Application specific
safetyLevel	DaLevel[*] - Application specific
complexity	NFP_Real[*]
substitutedBy	DaSpare[*] - Spares substituting the component
fault	DaFault[*] - Faults affecting the component
error	DaError[*] - Errors affecting the component
failure	DaFailure[*] - Failures affecting the component
hazard	DaHazard[*] - Hazards affecting the component
repair	DaRepair[*] - Repairs undergone by the component

The domain model is characterized by several constraints which are assigned to the DAM extensions as constraints written in OCL (2006). They represent constraints for the use of the profile at model specification level. Some OCL constraints are directly inherited in the profile, possibly by replacing the names of the domain classes with the name of the corresponding stereotypes. For example, compare the OCL constraints associated with the *Replacement Step* and *Reallocation Step* classes, in Fig. 4.5, with the ones associated, respectively, with the *DaReplacementStep* and *DaReallocationStep* stereotypes, in Fig. 5.3.

Other OCL constraints are redefined considering the properties of the extended UML meta-classes. This is the case, e.g., of the *DaRedundantStructure* stereotype that extends the UML meta-class *Package* (Fig. 5.3). The OCL constraint (1) attached to the stereotype is the redefinition of the one attached to the domain class *RedundandStructure* (Fig. 4.3), where the ownedElements property of the *Package* meta-class replaces the association-end comp. Finally, there are constraints extracted from the domain model. For example, the multiplicity constraint of the association-end comp (Fig. 4.3) is mapped to the OCL constraint (2) attached to the *DaRedundancyStructure* stereotype.

5.1.2   DAM Library

The DAM library—Fig. 5.1b—contains the basic and complex dependability types. The basic NFP types from the MARTE library are imported for the definition of these types. The MARTE NFPs sub-profile is applied to the definition of new basic dependability types and the VSL sub-profile is applied to the definition of the complex ones.

5.1.2.1   Complex Dependability Types

The complex dependability types are MARTE data types used to type DAM extensions. They are characterized by attributes, whose type can be a basic NFP type from the MARTE library, a basic dependability type, or a complex dependability type. The set of complex types is obtained by mapping classes which model threats or maintenance actions (i.e., the faint gray classes of Figs. 4.4 and 4.5). Table 5.2 describes the *DaFailure* complex dependability type.

Table 5.2 Complex dependability type description

DaFailure maps the Threats::Failure domain class	
Attribute	
occurrenceRate	DaFrequency[*]
MTTF	NFP_Duration[*]
MTBF	NFP_Duration[*]
occurrenceProb	NFP_Real[*]
occurrenceDist	NFP_CommonType[*]
domain	Domain[0..1]
detectability	Detectability[0..1]
consistency	Consistency[0..1]
consequence	DaCriticalLevel[*]
risk	NFP_Real[*]
cost	DaCurrency[*]
condition	FailureExpression[0..1]
causeF	DaFault[1..*]
causeE	DaError[1..*]

The mapping rules used to map domain classes to complex dependability types are the same as the one used to map domain classes to stereotypes. So, as for stereotypes, also complex dependability types are prefixed by *Da*. The attributes of complex dependability types can map either an attribute of the (mapped) domain class (e.g., *occurrenceRate* in *DaFailure*) or an attribute inherited from an abstract class (e.g., *occurenceProb*) or an association-end. Also the association-ends from the abstract classes are inherited and renamed, *causeF* in *DaFailure* maps the *cause* association-end between *Impairment* and *Fault* in Fig. 4.4.

5.1.2.2 Basic Dependability Types

Basic dependability types, see Fig. 5.4, can be either simple enumeration types or data types. An example of enumeration type is the *DaFrequencyUnitKind*, which includes a set of frequency units of fault/failure occurrence rates and of repair/recovery rates. An example of data type is the *DaFrequency* introduced to specify, e.g., a failure occurrence rate as a real value together with a failure frequency unit (e.g., 0.1^{-2} failures per hour).

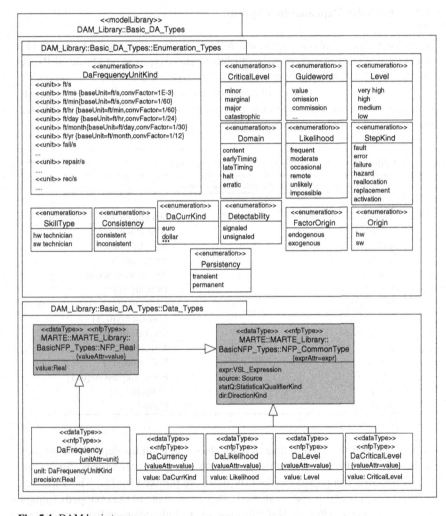

Fig. 5.4 DAM basic types

The data types specialize the *NFP_CommonType* from MARTE library, which enables to reuse several properties of the super-type then enriching the annotation capabilities at system model level. In particular, the *expression* property supports the specification of expressions using the Value Specification Language (VSL). The *source* property can be used to define the origin of the specification (*required*, a requirement to be satisfied; *estimated*, a metric to be computed; or *assumed*, an input parameter). The *statQ* property defines the type of statistical measure (e.g., maximum, minimum, mean). Finally, the *direction* (i.e., increasing or decreasing) defines the type of the quality order relation in the allowed value domain of the NFP, for comparative analysis purposes. Its usage will be exemplified in the first case study (Sect. 5.3).

5.2 Application of the DAM Profile

The DAM profile can be used, at system model level, to specify dependability requirements, input parameters, and metrics for dependability analysis purposes. In particular, the usage of the profile consists in stereotyping model elements and assigning tagged-values to the stereotype attributes of the stereotyped elements. The tagged-values, assigned to the stereotype attributes, obviously must conform to the attribute types and are specified with the VSL.

A DAM stereotype can be applied to a target model element provided that the latter belongs to a UML meta-class extended, either directly or indirectly through stereotype specialization, by that stereotype. For example, a *DaService* stereotype (Fig. 5.2) can be applied to a Use Case model-element. This is possible because the former specializes the *GaScenario* stereotype, from MARTE GQAM sub-profile, which in turn specializes the *TimedProcessing* stereotype, from MARTE TimeModels sub-profile. Since *TimedProcessing* extends the UML meta-class *Behaviour*, then *DaService* can be applied to a wide set of behavior-related elements such as Use Cases.

Although this is the "normal" way of usage, the DAM profile also provides support for the specification of nontrivial threat assumptions. In particular, three such examples deserve special attention: the state-based failure conditions, the common mode impairments of a set of redundant components, and the (sequence) dependencies of error propagation between components.

5.2.1 State-Based Failure Conditions

State-based failure conditions can be specified for either components or services. Indeed, both classes in the domain model have an association with the *Impairment* abstract class (Fig. 4.4). As shown in Table 5.1, the association-end *impairment* has been mapped to two attributes of the *DaComponent* stereotype, namely *failure* and *hazard* of complex types *DaFailure* and *DaHazard*, respectively.

Regarding *DaFailure* type (Table 5.2), its *condition* attribute (*FailureExpression* type) let us specify a logical expression that accounts for the state-based failure condition. The syntax is given in Table 5.3, where element term is a model element stereotyped as *DaComponent* (or *DaService* or their sub-stereotypes) and state term is a state associated with the element. The cardinality term is optional: it enables to specify the number of instances of the model element in the given state.

```
condition-value  ::=  '(' failure-body ')'
failure-body     ::=  fail-term | 'not' fail-term | 'not' '(' failure-body ')' |
                      ['('] fail-term logical-op fail-term [')'] |
                      ['('] failure-body logical-op failure-body [')']
fail-term        ::=  '(' 'element' '=' element ',' 'state' '=' state
                      [ ',' 'cardinality' = n_instances ] ')'
logical-op       ::=  'and' | 'or' | 'xor' | 'implies'
element          ::=  string
state            ::=  string
n_instances      ::=  integer
```

Table 5.3 BNF syntax for the specification of state-based failure conditions

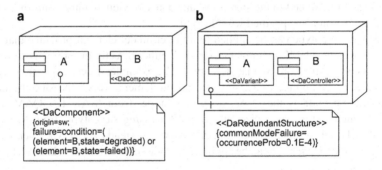

Fig. 5.5 State-based failure condition (a) and common mode failures: examples

For example, let us assume that the failure of component *A* depends on the state of component *B*, in particular when component *B* is either in state *degraded* or *failed*. Then, we can stereotype both components as *DaComponent* and annotate the failure condition on component *A*, as shown in Fig. 5.5a.

5.2.2 Common Mode Impairments

The stereotype *DaRedundantStructure* in Fig. 5.3 can be used to characterize the impairments affecting simultaneously the set of FT components belonging to a redundant structure; these impairments account for the failures and the hazards.

The association-end between the *RedundantStructure* and the *Impairment* classes (Fig. 4.4) is mapped to two attributes, *commonModeFailure* and *commonModeHazard*, respectively, belonging to the *DaRedundantStructure* stereotype. They enable to specify, among others, the common mode failure/hazard occurrence probability, i.e., the probability of failure/hazard of all the components belonging to the redundant structure. The annotation is then attached to a UML package, stereotyped as *DaRedundantStructure*, which includes the set of the components as exemplified in Fig. 5.5b.

5.2.3 Error Propagation Dependencies

The *DaErrorPropRelation* stereotype (Fig. 5.3) can be used to specify, through UML constraints, nontrivial error propagations between system components. This is achieved by assigning proper values to the attributes *errProp* (*DaErrorPropagation* type) and *propagationExpr* (*PropExpression* type). The value of the former is a declaration and initialization of an (ordered) set of variables: each variable is set to an error propagation term, which indicates the probability of error propagation from a source component to a target component (stereotyped as *DaComponent* or as *DaComponent* sub-stereotypes). The set should contain at least two variables. The value of the latter is a logical expression on the set of variables declared in the *errorProp* tagged-value. The syntax used for the specification of error propagation dependencies is given in Table 5.4. The BNF syntax allows specifying a wide range

```
propagationExpr−value ::= ['('] term logical−op term [')'] |
                          ['('] propagationExpr−value logical−op
                                propagationExpr−value [')'] |
                          'not' '(' propagationExpr−value ')' |
                          'ordered' '(' setOfTerms ')'
logical−op             ::= 'and' | 'or' | 'xor' | 'implies'
setOfTerms             ::= term ',' term | setOfTerms ',' term
errorProp−value        ::= '(' errorProp−body ')'
errorProp−body         ::= term '=' errorProp−term [';' errorProp−body]
errorProp−term         ::= '(' 'probability' '=' prob ','
                               'from'        '=' component ','
                               'to'          '=' component ')'
term                   ::= '$' string /* variable name */
prob                   ::= NFP_real
component              ::= string
```

Table 5.4 BNF syntax for the specification of error propagation dependencies

of cause–effect relationships. Besides the logical operators AND, OR, XOR, NOT, and IMPLIES, a sequence enforcing order for error propagation can be also annotated (ORDERED), then enabling the modeling of complex phenomena such as cascading failures which often occur in critical infrastructures. On the other hand, the basic term of an expression states the unconditional probability of error propagation from a source to a target component. Then, for example, we cannot annotate for a given source component different error propagations according to its failure modes. Figure 5.6a exemplifies the usage of the *DaErrorPropRelation* stereotype in a UML class diagram, where each class is stereotyped as *DaComponent*. The constraint is stereotyped as *DaErrorPropRelation* and specifies, with the syntax of Table 5.4, that the error is propagated to component B from the components A and C, only if the propagations occur in order (i.e., first A->B then C->B). Figure 5.6b shows a semantically equivalent constraint in terms of dynamic fault tree gates (Chap. 6, Fig. 6.3).

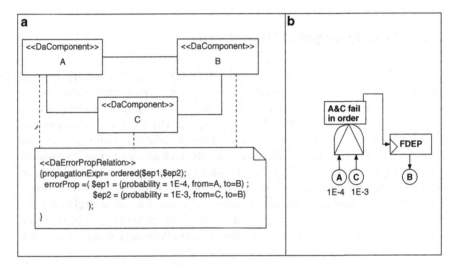

Fig. 5.6 Error propagation dependencies: an example

Besides the expressive power of the BNF syntax in Table 5.4, from the modeler point of view, the main difficulty in applying such annotation constraints is the complexity of error propagation phenomena which are studied and discovered through the use of dependability analysis techniques—either formal techniques, such as Fault Tree or Markov Analysis, or systematic methods, such as FMEA/FMECA (see Chap. 6). Then, complex error propagation expressions should be rather the result produced by the dependability analysis and fed back to the UML system model than an input specification to an M2M transformation to get a dependability analysis model from a MARTE-DAM annotated model.

5.3 Case Study 1: An Intrusion-Tolerant Message Service

We first consider the case study of a Message Redundancy Service (MRS) that was originally presented in Bernardi et al. (2011c). The MRS aims at improving the dependability of distributed systems, which have to provide their services even in the presence of malicious attacks. In particular, the goal of the MRS is to enhance distributed systems with *intrusion-tolerance* capabilities. The MRS ensures delivering only uncorrupted messages to the target destination. For this purpose, some well-known fault tolerance mechanisms are applied, such as hardware and software redundancy and voting (Lyu 1995). By using these mechanisms we attain a fault-tolerant MRS, it should be able to mask software faults that otherwise could lead to service failures. Usually, these mechanisms are implemented along with *recovery* strategies that restore the system services. For the sake of simplicity, we will not consider *recovery* here.

5.3.1   Modeling with UML

The UML specification of the MRS is shown in Figs. 5.7–5.9. The Use Case Diagram (UCD) shows the main use case, which is realized by the service scenario given by the Sequence Diagram (SD) in Fig. 5.8 as follows. MRS receives messages from Clients, specifying the target receiver and the file to deliver. A Message Replicator (MR) is an interface agent, which creates for each message another agent, the Redundancy Manager (RM). RM is in charge of the actual delivery. RM creates N replicas (*software redundancy*), called Payloads, which scan and decipher the file. Each Payload sends back to RM a result that can be of approval, if the file

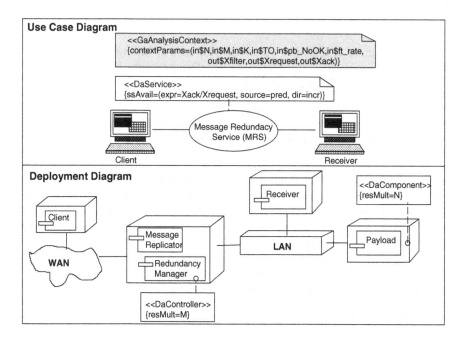

Fig. 5.7 Message Redundancy Service: Use Case and Architecture

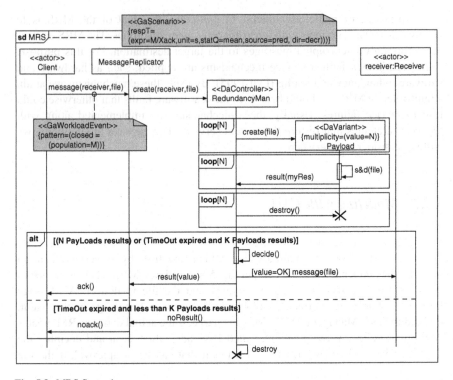

Fig. 5.8 MRS Scenario

was found clean, or of rejection, otherwise. RM ends up killing the Payloads and deciding, with a majority *voting* algorithm, to deliver or not the message to its final receiver. In any case, MR is informed about the service outcome:

- the message has been correctly delivered (`value=OK`),
- the message has been detected as corrupted (`value` with others values),
- a time-out exception occurred and no decision was taken by the RM, then producing a `noResult` message.

The Deployment Diagram (DD) specifies the system architecture. The Payloads, when created, will be deployed on N different nodes to improve dependability (*hardware redundancy*), while the unique MR and the RMs execute on the same node to avoid transmission delays. The local area network (LAN) is a secured one, so the messages can be trustily delivered.

The State Machines (SMs) specification in Fig. 5.9 provides a better understanding of the MRS behavior. MR processes requests through transition `message` (`receiver,file`). It also receives service outcomes from RM, in both cases, not only when the service successes (`result(value)`) but also when the service fails due to a time-out exception (`noResult()`). MR ends up either acknowledging (`ack()`) or not (`noack()`) the Client about the delivery of the

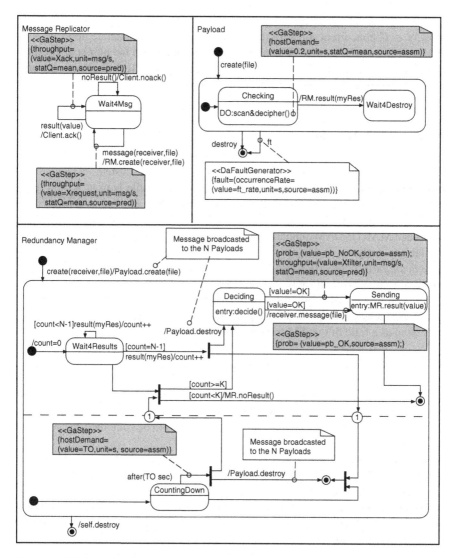

Fig. 5.9 MRS State Machines

message. Observe that MR sends an `ack` to the Client even if the file had been considered corrupted. After processing the `message`, MR creates an RM that, in turn, creates the *N* Payloads and sends the file to them for analysis. RM sets then a time-out and, concurrently, waits for the Payloads to reply. Just in case the *N* Payloads answer before the time-out expires, the RM destroys them, aborts the time-out, and starts deciding. On the other hand, if the time-out is raised while RM is still waiting for results from the Payloads, then the latter are destroyed and RM checks if at least *K* Payloads have sent the results ([count>=K]). In a positive case, RM is allowed to decide about the integrity of the file. Therefore, the MRS can mask at most $N - K$ concurrent software faults, i.e., the service can tolerate up to $N - K$ Payloads down per message. When the time-out expires and the number of results received from the Payloads is less than K (`[count<K]`), RM does not take any decision and sends a message `noResult()` to MR.

5.3.2   DAM Annotation

The DAM profile uses the UML diagrams to annotate system dependability properties, measures, and requirements. The MARTE profile is used to introduce performance properties in the UML diagrams. The DAM annotation appears with white notes, in Figs. 5.7–5.9, while the MARTE appears with gray notes. The combined MARTE-DAM annotations will allow in Chap. 8 (Sect. 8.1.4) to perform availability analyses. In this case study, we are interested in computing the *steady-state availability* of the MRS (see `DaService` annotation in Fig. 5.7(UCD)). Here, the *steady-state availability* is interpreted as the percentage of messages that the system can process (not only those delivered but also those detected as corrupted) out of all messages requested by the clients. So, the *steady-state availability* is expressed as a ratio of two SM transition throughputs:

$$Xack/Xrequest.$$

These two parameters, being quantitative, are annotated using the GQAM, concretely the `GaStep` stereotype (see the MR state-machine in Fig. 5.9). Note that these throughputs are output parameters, i.e., measures to be computed, as indicated by the modifier `source=pred`.

The deployment diagram, in Fig. 5.7, defines the type of the resource and its multiplicity. There are M software controllers, as many as the number of client requests, N replicated nodes (hardware redundancy) where the Payloads are running on. The Payloads are software variants and their multiplicity is specified in the MRS scenario for a concrete service request (Fig. 5.8). On the other hand, we need to define the system fault assumption in terms of:

1. which MRS components can be affected by faults and in which states,
2. the fault occurrence rate, and
3. the maximum number of faults that can concurrently affect the MRS.

Payloads are components where faults can occur. Consequently, a new transition is introduced in the Payload State Machine (Fig. 5.9) that is stereotyped as `DaFaultGenerator`. Such transition identifies the states where the fault can lead to a failure. The fault occurrence rate (`ft_rate`) is also specified as input parameter (*source=assm*). Finally, an explicit annotation for the maximum number of faults is not needed, since the design *per se* allows to mask up to $N - K$ software faults.

The rest of the annotations (gray ones) concern the quantitative MARTE stereotypes needed for carrying out the analysis. The sequence diagram supports the workload definition, which is closed with population M, i.e., the number of requests from clients. The sequence diagram is stereotyped as GaScenario, where the scenario mean response time is specified. The response time accounts for the elapsed time since the client requests until a positive ack is replied. The timing duration of the activities are annotated in the state machines with the hostDemand tag (GaStep stereotype). For the GaStep activities, we have specified either constant durations, e.g., the time-out, or mean duration, e.g., scan & decipher. The GaStep stereotype is also used to specify the probability of execution in case of guarded transitions (prob tagged-values). Moreover, to evaluate the robustness of the MRS, we annotate in the MR state machine the throughput (Xfilter) of the GaStep transition [value!=OK]. This measure corresponds to the number of corrupted files per second the service can detect. All the input and output parameters are gathered in the analysis context of the UCD.

Finally, it is worth to note that some input parameters, such as the fault occurrence rate (ft_rate) and the time-out (TO), will enable to carry out sensitivity analysis by assuming different values during the analysis. For sensitivity analysis purposes, an increasing direction (dir=incr) has been assigned to the steady-state availability (i.e., a higher steady-state availability is obviously better) and a decreasing one has been assigned to the response time (i.e., a lower response time is preferred).

5.4 Case Study 2: A Mission Avionic System

The Mission Avionic System (MAS) case study is an example of mission & safety-critical embedded system, which has been designed to be highly redundant (both software and hardware redundancy) and reconfigurable. It has been presented in Pai and Dugan (2002) to illustrate a method for deriving, automatically, *Dynamic Fault Tree* (DFT) models from UML-based system specification: the approach of Pai and Dugan (2002) will be described in Chap. 7.

The MAS consists of five sub-systems: the crew-station control (*CrewStnA, CrewStnB*), the scene and obstacle control (*S&OA,S&OB*), the local path generation (*PathGenA, PathGenB*), the system management (*SysMgtA, SysMgtB*), and the vehicle management (*VM1A,VM1B,VM2A,VM2B*). The block diagram of MAS representing the sub-systems and their interconnection is shown in Fig. 5.10.

Each sub-system consists of software modules running on dedicated processors. There are primary processing units (postfixed by *A*) and hot spare backup units (postfixed by *B*) that take over control from the former if a failure or error is detected. For example, *S&OA* represents the scene and obstacle control sub-system primary processing unit, while *S&OB* is its hot spare backup unit. The vehicle management sub-system requires the use of two processing units: each of these units has its associated hot spare backup.

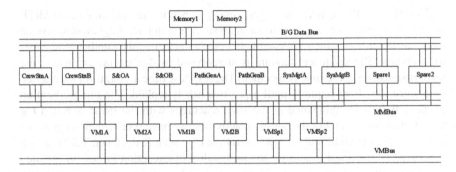

Fig. 5.10 MAS block diagram from Pai and Dugan (2002)

Additionally, there is a pair of cold spare backups (*Spare1, Spare2*) associated with the first four sub-systems and another pair (*VMSp1,VMSp2*) for the vehicle management sub-system. Each pair is used as backup in the case of simultaneous occurrence of two failures in any of the sub-systems is associated with. The mission management bus (*MMBus*) interconnects the sub-systems and is triplicated; the vehicle management system has its own duplicated bus (*VMBus*), and there are two memory units (*Memory1, Memory2*) connected to the first four sub-systems by a triplicated background data bus (*B/G Data Bus*).

The system fails if any one of the sub-systems cannot function correctly, or both the memories fail, or all the buses in any of type fail. Beside system redundancy, reconfigurability is incorporated to the MAS. In particular two of the sub-systems, that is the scene and obstacle control and the local path generation, have alternate minimal software versions that provide reduced functionality and require fewer computing resources. In particular, the minimal versions require only one processor to execute, while the full versions require two.

5.4.1 Modeling with UML and DAM

UML Class, Component, Deployment, Package diagrams can be used to model the MAS architecture. In Fig. 5.11 a package diagram is shown: it is an abstraction of the block diagram in Fig. 5.10, where each sub-system is represented by a package. Packages are related through dependencies, representing low level associations between the classes contained in the former. Only few packages are detailed with their contents, that is the classes modeling the components with similar functionalities. For example, the SM package includes two classes: the primary (SysMgtA) and spare (SysMgtB) components of the system management sub-system. We apply the DAM profile to specify the system redundancies and the reliability input parameters (i.e., component failure rates, error propagation probabilities).[1]

---

[1] For readability reasons, only a subset of DAM annotations are shown.

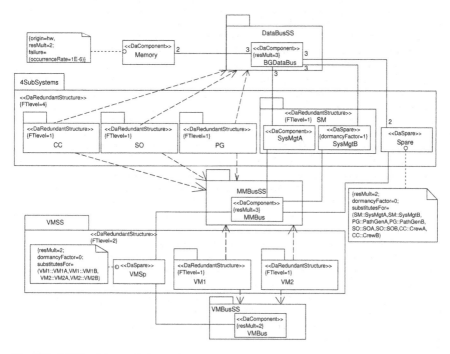

Fig. 5.11 MAS architectural view

The MAS is characterized by several redundancies:

1. There are replicated resources, such as the buses and the memories. The classes representing them are stereotyped as *DaComponent* to specify the number of instances though the *resMult* tagged-value. For example, the BGDataBus is a triplicated bus (i.e., *resMult=3*) and the Memory is a duplicated memory (i.e., *resMult=2*).

2. Each sub-system is a redundant structure. The packages modeling the sub-systems are then stereotyped as *DaRedundantStructure* to annotate the sub-system fault tolerance level (*FTlevel* tagged-value), that is the minimum number of components of the redundant structure required for successful system operations. Each stereotyped package contains two classes: the primary component (*DaComponent*) and the spare one (*DaSpare*). The type of spare is specified by the *dormancyFactor* tagged-value. The sub-system spares are all hot spares (i.e., *dormancyFactor=1*).

3. There are cold spare components (i.e., Spare and VMSp) that may substitute for primary components belonging to different sub-systems. Since *DaSpare* stereotype is a sub-stereotype of *DaComponent*, all the tags of the latter or inherited by the latter can be used in *DaSpare* stereotyped elements (such as *resMult*). Moreover, to indicate the components that can be replaced by the spare in case of failure, the *substitutesFor* tag is used: its value is the list of such components.

The input parameters annotated in the class diagram of Fig. 5.11 are the component failure rates. The failure rates are specified using the *occurrenceRate* tagged-values and attached to the classes stereotyped as *DaComponent* or *DaSpare*.

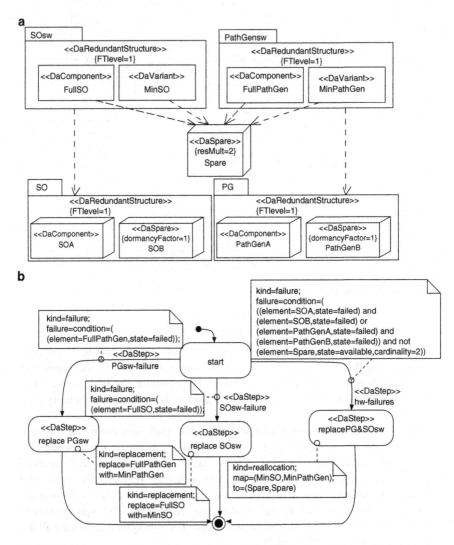

Fig. 5.12 MAS structural (a) and behavioral (b) reconfiguration

The system reconfiguration is modeled using both structural and behavioral diagrams. Concretely, Fig. 5.12 shows a deployment diagram (a) and a state machine diagram (b) representing the MAS reconfiguration. The deployment diagram (Fig. 5.12a) is used to specify the mapping between software and hardware resources: there are two software versions for the scene and obstacle control sub-system and the path generation sub-system. The minimal versions (*MinSO* and *MinPathGen*) have reduced functionalities with respect to the full versions (*FullSO* and *FullPathGen*, respectively). Since the deployment diagram provides a structural view of the reconfiguration, all the software versions are statically mapped to both the primary and spare processors. The software to hardware dynamic mapping can be captured by the behavioral view. The DAM profile is applied to the deployment diagram to emphasize the redundancies of the two considered sub-systems: in particular, the software versions are stereotyped as *DaVariant* and included into a *DaRedundantStructure* package. Observe that the hardware redundancies were already specified in the class diagram of Fig. 5.11: in the deployment diagram can be specified as well, since *DaComponent* and *DaSpare* stereotypes can be applied also to nodes.

The state machine of Fig. 5.12b represents the reconfiguration activities to be carried out when failures occur in the full versions of the two sub-systems. The minimal software versions are switched in, to replace the correspondent full versions when either the modules fail (*software failure scenario*) or the two processors, i.e., the primary and the hot spare components, fail (*hardware failure scenario*). The software failure scenario leads to the states `replacePGsw` and `replaceSOsw`, where the replacement activities are carried out. The hardware failure scenario leads instead to the state `replaceSO&PGsw` where, irrespective of whether one full version is still functioning, both the full versions are replaced with their minimal versions running on a single spare processor if the two spares are not available. We use the DAM profile to specify failure conditions which trigger the reconfiguration activities and the replacement/reallocation of the system components. In particular, the transitions leading to the reconfiguration states are stereotyped as *DaStep* of *failure* type, while the reconfiguration states are stereotyped as *DaStep* of either *replacement* or *reallocation* type. The failure conditions are attached to the transitions and they are specified using the BNF grammar of Table 5.3. The software replacement is annotated using the *replace* and *with* tagged-values, while the dynamic mapping of the minimal versions to the spares is specified using the *map* and *to* tagged-values.

Chapter 6
Dependability Analysis Techniques

Prediction is very difficult, especially if it's about the future.
— Anonymous

Abstract An overview of the techniques traditionally used in dependability analysis that are compliant with current industrial standards (i.e., the International Electrotechnical Commission standards) is provided. In particular, the focus is on those techniques that are chosen as target formalism of model transformations (described in Chap. 7), that is Fault Tree analysis and Petri Net analysis.

6.1 Introduction

Many analysis techniques have been applied by the engineers to assess the system dependability during the last four decades. Such techniques are used for the prediction, verification, and improvement of dependability properties, mainly reliability, availability, maintainability, and safety. They help in answering the questions that are most pressing to an engineer, such as: Is the flight control system able to tolerate N simultaneous equipment failures? When a shutdown occurs, how long does it take to recover the system? Is the system able to provide the service to the user during a given time period? And so on.

A list of the primary techniques, recommended by the international standard (IEC-60300-3-1 2003) for the dependability assessment, is shown in Table 6.1: they are mainly used early in the software life cycle, that is during the requirement and design activities. It is worth to mention that the list is a coarse classification provided by the standard of the primary dependability techniques: for example, the Petri Net analysis technique encompasses all the Petri Net semantics together with the correspondent solution methods.

There is no a general rule for the selection of the best technique to be applied for assessing the dependability of a specific system. Nevertheless, the IEC standard provides several guidelines to support the engineer in the choice of the most appropriate ones. Herein, we summarize the main criteria that should be considered for the technique selection.

Table 6.1 Primary dependability analysis techniques IEC-60300-3-1 (2003)

Technique	Other standards
Event Trees Analysis (ETA)	IEC-62502 (2010)
Failure Mode and Effect Analysis (FMEA)	IEC-60812 (1985), MIL-STD-1629a (1980), ANSI/IEEE-STD-352 (1987), SAE-ARP-4761 (1996); BS-5760-5 (1991)
Failure Mode, Effect, and Criticality Analysis (FMECA)	IEC-60812 (1985); MIL-STD-1629a (1980); BS-5760-5 (1991)
Fault Trees Analysis (FTA)	IEC-61025 (2006), ANSI/IEEE-STD-352 (1987), SAE-ARP-4761 (1996)
Functional Failure Analysis (FFA)	SAE-ARP-4761 (1996)
HAZard and OPerability studies (HAZOP)	IEC-61882 (2001)
Markov analysis	IEC-61165 (2006), ANSI/IEEE-STD-352 (1987)
Petri Net analysis (PN)	ISO/IEC-15909-1 (2004)
Preliminary Hazard Analysis (PHA)	MIL-STD-882c (1993), MIL-STD-882d (2000)
Reliability Block Diagrams analysis (RBD)	IEC-61078 (2006), ANSI/IEEE-STD-352 (1987)
Truth table	ANSI/IEEE-STD-352 (1987)

6.1.1   Applicability in the Life Cycle

The techniques in Table 6.1 are typically applied during the requirement and design stages of the software development process, and their applicability depends on the available system specification.

The *early* stages techniques (e.g., PHA, FFA, HAZOP) are used in the requirement analysis or at the very beginning of the design process and they focus on the analysis of the abstract concepts of the system. They enable to identify potential system failure modes then providing a feedback to the engineer for the definition of the system architecture.

The *late* techniques (e.g., Markov analysis, PN, Truth tables) are used when the detailed design specification becomes available. Such techniques allow to evaluate system reliability/availability and to perform trade-off analysis on different design alternatives. Finally, there are techniques (e.g., ETA, FMEA, FMECA, FTA, RBD) that can be used *across* different stages: initial models are constructed during the requirement analysis and, then, refined to a more detailed level as data become available in order to make decisions and trade-offs.

6.1.2 Aim of the Analysis

The aim of the analysis can be either *qualitative* or *quantitative*, in turn, we can use the same criteria to classify the supporting techniques. In particular, there are techniques that only support qualitative analysis, such as PHA, HAZOP, and FFA, while most of the remaining ones in the list can be used for both qualitative and quantitative analyses. The main objectives of the qualitative analysis are the identification of the component failure modes, their consequences at system level, and the cause–effect paths, as well as the determination of possible repair/recovery strategies. The quantitative analysis aims at defining numerical reference data to be used as input parameters of reliability/availability models, estimating availability/reliability metrics, under probabilistic or stochastic assumptions, performing component criticality and sensitivity analysis.

6.1.3 Bottom-Up/Top-Down

Bottom-up methods mainly deal with the effects of single faults and the starting point of the analysis is the identification of the faults at component level. Each component fault is considered separately and its effects at the next higher system level are studied. The analysis is iterated to discover the effects at all functional levels up to the system level (e.g., the user-service level). On the other hand top-down methods enable to analyze the effects of multiple faults. The analysis starts by considering a failure mode at the highest level of interest and then proceeds backward by identifying the causes of the failure.

In practice, to ensure the completeness of the analysis, combinations of bottom-up and top-down techniques are often applied. For example, cause-consequence analysis is carried out by using both ETA and FTA, where the root of the event tree is the top event of a fault tree; the FTA is applied to analyze the causes of a failure, while ETA is applied to analyze the consequence of initiating events.

6.1.4 Cause–Effect Relationships Exploration

This criterion, proposed by Mauri (2000) for safety analysis techniques, classifies the techniques depending on how they explore the relationship between causes and effects. There are different ways to proceed: *deductive* techniques start from known effects to seek unknown causes (e.g., FTA, FFA), *inductive* techniques start from known causes to forecast unknown effects (e.g., ETA, FMEA, FMECA), while *exploratory* techniques relate unknown causes to unknown effects (e.g., HAZOP, PHA).

## 6.1.5	Dependencies Modeling

An important criterion to be taken into account when selecting a dependability analysis technique is the capability of modeling time or sequence-dependent behavior as well as state-dependent events. For example, after failure, the system operates in degraded mode (time-dependency); the system fails only if event A is preceded by B and not vice versa (sequence-dependency); different failure or repair characteristics depending on the system state (state-dependency). A similar criterion is provided by Nicol et al. (2004) considering quantitative analysis techniques, where the latter are classified into combinatorial and state-based. Combinatorial techniques, such as FTA and RBD, do not enumerate all possible system states to obtain a solution and dependability measure are computed by adopting simpler approaches. However, they do not easily capture the aforementioned types of dependencies and imperfect coverage. On the other hand state-based techniques, such as Markov analysis and PN, are more comprehensive and they enable explicit modeling of complex relationships.

Table 6.2 Characteristics of the dependability analysis techniques IEC-60300-3-1 (2003)

Technique	Life-cycle	Aim	Bottom-up/ Top-down	Cause-effect relationship exploration	Dependencies modeling
ETA	across	ql./ qn.	bottom-up	inductive	yes
FMEA	across	ql.	bottom-up	inductive	no
FMECA	across	qn.	bottom-up	inductive	no
FTA	across	ql./ qn.	top-down	deductive	no
FFA	early	ql.	bottom-up	deductive	no
HAZOP	early	ql.	bottom-up	exploratory	no
Markov analysis	late	qn.	top-down	NA	yes
PN	late	ql./ qn.	top-down	NA	yes
PHA	early	ql.	bottom-up	exploratory	no
RBD	across	ql./ qn.	top-down	NA	no
Truth table	late	ql./ qn.	NA	inductive	no

NA: the criterion is not applicable with respect to this technique

Table 6.2 summarizes the characteristics of the primary dependability analysis techniques (Table 6.1) according to the aforementioned criteria: the applicability in the life cycle (second column); the aim (third column), i.e., qualitative (ql.) vs/ quantitative (qn.); bottom-up vs/ top-down (fourth column); the type of exploration of the cause–effect relationship (fifth column); and, finally, whether they support the modeling of dependencies (sixth column).

In the rest of this chapter, we focus on those analysis techniques that are the target of the transformation approaches considered in Chap. 7, namely FTA (Sect. 6.2) and PN analysis (Sect. 6.3). Other techniques and software tools will be briefly presented in Sects. 6.4 and 6.5, respectively.

6.2 Fault Tree Analysis

A Fault Tree (FT) is an acyclic graph with internal nodes that are logic gates (e.g., AND, OR, K-of-M), external nodes that represent component/sub-system faults (basic events, undeveloped events) and, possibly, transfer gates. The latter are used to indicate that the rest of the tree is developed in another part or page of the diagram; they are suitable for the construction of models following a hierarchical approach, then enhancing the readability as well as the reusability (e.g., the same sub-tree can contribute to the occurrence of different failure modes, then it can be reused in different fault-tree models).

FTs are used to represent and analyze the component faults whose combined occurrence causes a system failure to occur. It is a top-down technique, then the FT construction begins by considering a system failure mode—the *top event*—and terminates when either the basic events which provoke such a failure are all identified or the desired level of detail is reached. When several failure modes need to be investigated, then different FTs should be generated, one for each failure mode.

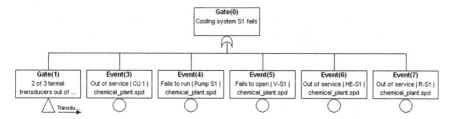

Fig. 6.1 Failure of the cooling system

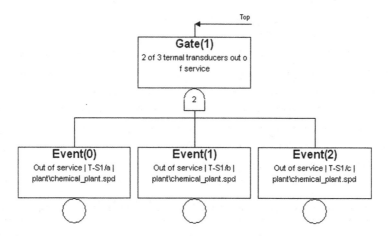

Fig. 6.2 Failure of 2-out-3 thermal transducers

Figure 6.1 shows an example of FT modeling the cooling system failure in a chemical power plant (Contini et al. 1999). The top event (*Gate(0)*) is caused by one of the events at the lower level, which are then connected with an OR gate. The *Event(i)* ($i = 3, \ldots, 7$) are basic events, while *Gate(1)* is a transfer gate that refers to the Fault Tree of Fig. 6.2. The latter represents the failure of a redundant component. Indeed, there are three thermal transducers and the failure occurs when at least two of them are out of service: then the basic events *Event(i)* ($i = 1, 2, 3$) are connected with a 2-of-3 logic gate.

Originally, in FT only independent basic events could be modeled. Later, to enhance the modeling capabilities, FTs have been extended to include various types of gates. In particular, *Dynamic Fault Trees* (DFT), defined by Dugan et al. (1992), include special purpose gates capturing sequence dependencies which frequently arise when modeling fault tolerant computer systems. Such special gates are: *functional dependency* gate, for modeling situations where one component's correct operation is dependent upon the correct operation of some other component; *spare* gate, for modeling cold, warm, and hot pooled spares; and *priority-AND* gate, for modeling ordered *AND*-ing of events. Figure 6.3 summarizes the basic event

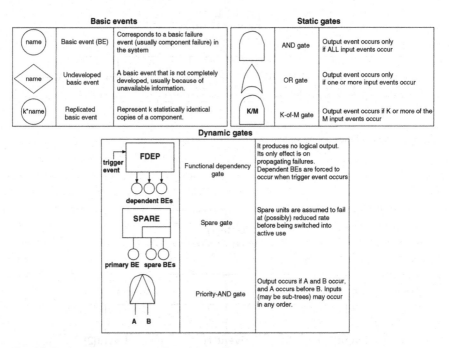

Fig. 6.3 Basic event construct, static and dynamic gates

constructs and the static gates common to both FT and DFT, as well as the dynamic gates of DFT.

Once an FT model is built, both qualitative and quantitative analyses can be carried out. The qualitative analysis is aimed at identifying all the combinations of basic events that cause the top event to occur. Combinations are called *cut sets* and they are ranked according to the number of basic events, since the smaller the number of events that cause the top event, the less resilient to failure is the modeled system. A *minimal cut set (MSC)* is a cut set that does not contain any subset of basic events that is still a cut set. The list of all the *MSCs* provides a valuable information to the analyst since it enables the identification of the potential weak points of the system, an essential step to initiate the corrective actions. Table 6.4 lists the MCSs (second column), ordered by rank, of the FT example.

The main objectives of the quantitative analysis are the evaluation of the probability of occurrence of the top event, considering the system mission time, and the identification of the MCSs which contribute most significantly to the system failure. The probability may correspond to the unreliability or unavailability metrics, computed at a given time instant, associated with the system (see Chap. 2); observe that, for non-repairable systems, the two metrics are equivalent.

The FTA assumes that the basic events, i.e., the component faults and, in case, the component repairs are statistically independent events. Many FT tools accept as input parameters constant fault/repair rates, thus implicitly assuming that the failure and repair times of each component are exponentially distributed and restricting the analysis to this case. Table 6.3 shows the input parameters of the FT example, where all the components are repairable. There exist several FT solution algorithms,

Table 6.3 Input parameters of the FT example

Events	Fault rate [1/hours]	Repair rate [1/hours]
Event(0), Event(1), Event(2)	$2.4 \cdot 10^{-5}$	$2.5 \cdot 10^{-1}$
Event(3)	$8.9 \cdot 10^{-5}$	$1.25 \cdot 10^{-1}$
Event(4)	$3.7 \cdot 10^{-4}$	$8.3 \cdot 10^{-2}$
Event(5)	$8.1 \cdot 10^{-5}$	$8.3 \cdot 10^{-2}$
Event(6)	$2.4 \cdot 10^{-5}$	$4.1 \cdot 10^{-2}$
Event(7)	$9.1 \cdot 10^{-5}$	$4.1 \cdot 10^{-2}$

mainly based on sums of disjoint products (Rai et al. 1995) and binary decision diagrams (Rauzy 1993; Zang and Trivedi 1999). The former rely on the computation of the MCSs and they are less efficient than the latter. The binary decision diagram techniques are normally used for solving very large fault trees. Concerning DFTs, when a dynamic gate is part of a model then the latter is solved via a Markov chain, rather than by using traditional methods.

Table 6.4 shows the results of the FT analysis of the example, computed for a given mission time, using the StarsStudio-Astra tool (Contini et al. 1999); in particular, the unavailability of each MCS (third column) and the cumulated unavailability (fourth column). The MCSs are ordered according to their unavailability, from the highest to the lowest. The cumulated unavailability at the ith row of the table corresponds to the probability of failure of at least one of the first i MCSs, i.e., $Pr\{MCS_1\ OR\ MCS_2\ OR\ \ldots\ OR\ MCS_i\}$. The cumulated unavailability at the last row corresponds to the unavailability of the top event.

Table 6.4 The MCSs of the example and analysis results (mission time 8.760 hours)

N	MCS	Rank	Unavailability	Cumulated Unavail.
1	Event(7)	1	$3.986 \cdot 10^{-1}$	$3.986 \cdot 10^{-1}$
2	Event(3)	1	$1.949 \cdot 10^{-1}$	$5.158 \cdot 10^{-1}$
3	Event(4)	1	$1.850 \cdot 10^{-1}$	$6.054 \cdot 10^{-1}$
4	Event(6)	1	$1.051 \cdot 10^{-1}$	$6.469 \cdot 10^{-1}$
5	Event(5)	1	$4.050 \cdot 10^{-2}$	$6.612 \cdot 10^{-1}$
6	Event(2), Event(0)	2	$1.473 \cdot 10^{-2}$	$6.662 \cdot 10^{-1}$
7	Event(1), Event(2)	2	$1.473 \cdot 10^{-2}$	$6.711 \cdot 10^{-1}$
8	Event(0), Event(1)	2	$1.472 \cdot 10^{-2}$	$6.759 \cdot 10^{-1}$

6.3 Petri Net Analysis

Petri Net analysis relies upon the use of Petri Nets (PN) as modeling formalism, defined by C.A. Petri in 1962 as part of his thesis dissertation. A PN is a bipartite directed graph, where P and T are the disjoint sets of nodes, namely *places* and *transitions*. The former, signified by circles, are used to model conditions; the latter, graphically depicted by bars, represent events/activities that may occur in the system. The directed arcs $A = (P \times T) \cup (T \times P)$, shown by arrows, describe which places are pre- or post-condition for which transitions, they are called, respectively, input and output places. Places may contain tokens (drawn as black dots) and a token assignment over the set of places is called *marking*.

The PN behavior is governed by the transition enabling and firing rules. A transition is *enabled* in a given marking, when all of its input places contain at least one token. An enabled transition may *fire* and, upon firing, it removes one token from each of its input places and add one token in each of its output places, causing a change of marking (i.e., a change of state).

Given an initial marking of a PN, it is possible to compute the set of all the markings reachable from the initial one by transition firings (i.e., reachability set), provided that every place of the net is bounded. The reachability graph associated with a PN is a directed graph whose nodes are the markings in the reachability set and each arc connecting a marking M to a marking M' represents the firing of a transition enabled in M and leading to M'.

Since the Petri's original proposal, many classes of PN have been proposed in the literature in order to enhance their modeling and analysis capabilities. In particular, Stochastic Petri Nets (SPN) are of interest when dependability analysis is a concern; they are defined as extensions of un-timed PN, where each transition is characterized by a random variable exponentially distributed, modeling its firing time.

SPN is a modeling formalism at higher level of abstraction with respect to Continuous Time Markov Chains (CTMCs). An SPN is usually solved by deriving the underlying CTMC, which is isomorphic to its reachability graph, and then by using the wide variety of available techniques for CTMCs. Nevertheless, such techniques suffer the well-known state space explosion problem, then for large complex models alternative techniques are more suited, such as discrete-event simulation (Kelling 1996), approximation techniques and bound techniques based on the solution of linear programming problems (Campos and Silva 1992).

Several extensions have been proposed to the basic SPN formalism, they include: arcs with multiplicity, immediate transitions that fire with zero time delay (depicted by thin black bars), transition priorities, inhibitor arcs from places to transition that provide the zero-test capability (depicted by a small circle arrow-end). The most popular variant of SPN are Generalized Stochastic Petri Nets (GSPN—Ajmone-Marsan et al. 1994). Other extensions allow the modeler more flexible firing rules, such as Stochastic Activity Networks (SAN—Sanders and Meyer 2001). Similarly, Stochastic Reward Nets (SRN—Muppala et al. 1993) and Stochastic Well-Formed Nets (SWN—Chiola et al. 1993) include guards and enabling functions.

On the other hand, there have been several proposals on relaxing the "exponential distribution transition firing time" assumption, then making the stochastic process associated with the SPN not still a CTMC. For example, Extended Stochastic Petri Nets (ESPN—Dugan et al. 1985) are SPN where transitions can be characterized by general firing time distributions. Their underlying process is a semi-Markov process when certain restrictions are met. Deterministic and Stochastic Petri Nets (DSPN—Lindemann 1998) have immediate, exponential, and deterministic transitions. The stochastic process associated with a DSPN is a Markov regenerative process. Markov Regenerative Stochastic Petri Nets (MRSPN—Choi et al. 1994) and Concurrent Generalized Stochastic Petri Nets (CGSPN—Vita et al. 1995) are generalizations of DSPNs and still have a Markov regenerative process associated. Numerical techniques, based on the solution of the underlying stochastic process, have also been proposed for the aforementioned SPN variants.

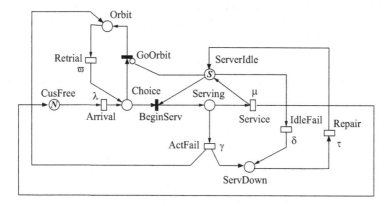

Fig. 6.4 GSPN model of multiserver retrial system with dependent breakdowns

Figure 6.4 shows the GSPN model of a multiserver retrial system (from Gharbi and Dutheillet 2011) with N customers (initial marking of place *CusFree*) and a service station characterized by S identical and parallel servers (initial marking of place *ServerIdle*). Each customer is either free (place *CusFree*), under service (*Serving*) or in orbit (*Orbit*). On the other hand, each server can be either operational—idle (*ServIdle*) or busy (*Serving*)—or non-operational (*ServDown*). Customer requests are assigned to operational idle server randomly. If there is an idle server at the moment of the request arrival, then the latter is processed immediately. Otherwise, if all the servers are not available (i.e., busy or down), the customer joins the orbit. These two alternative conditions are modeled by the two conflicting immediate transitions *BeginServ* and *GoOrbit*, respectively. All the timed transitions are characterized by exponentially distributed firing times (the firing rate parameters are shown near the transitions). Observe that it is possible to model a state-dependent breakdown discipline: indeed, the server can fail either in idle state or in busy state with different failure rates (i.e., $\delta \neq \gamma$).

The SPN models can be used both to verify qualitative properties and to compute metrics. In the dependability context, qualitative analysis may consist in verifying the unreachability of unsafe states, e.g., by using model checking techniques on the SPN reachability graph, and validating the model consistency via structural analysis techniques (which are based on the property of the SPN as a graph).

From the quantitative analysis point of view, SPNs are used to compute dependability metrics, under transient or steady-state assumptions. In transient analysis, the model behavior is observed during a finite time interval, while steady-state analysis assumes the observation of the model behavior during a *sufficiently large* period, such that the SPN state variables, and then dependability metrics, are time-independent. Typically, reliability/unreliability and instantaneous availability metrics are computed under transient analysis assumptions while mean value metrics, such as MTTF, steady-state availability and failure rate can be estimated under the steady-state assumption. The input parameters of an SPN model boil down to transition firing rates/weights and, possibly, place initial markings: Table 6.5 shows the input parameters of the GSPN model in Fig. 6.4.

Table 6.5 Input parameters of the GSPN example

Transition	Rate Param.	Value [1/s.]	Place	Marking Param.	Value
Arrival	λ	4	CusFree	N	50
Service	μ	10	ServerIdle	S	5
Retrial	ϖ	1			
ActFail	γ	$5 \cdot 10^{-2}$			
IdleFail	δ	$1 \cdot 10^{-1}$			
Repair	τ	$5 \cdot 10^{-1}$			

Dependability metrics of an SPN model can be defined as reward functions, considering the associated underlying CTMC (Goseva-Popstojanova and Trivedi 2000). For example, let

$$r_M = \begin{cases} 1 & \text{if } M \in O \\ 0 & \text{if } M \in F \end{cases}$$

a state reward that partitions the set of reachable markings $RS(M^0)$ of the SPN into two subsets of markings: O that represents the set of operational system states and F that represents the system failure states.

The most simplest availability measures are based on such a reward:

$$A(t) = \sum_{M \in RS(M_0)} r_M \sigma_M(t) = \sum_{M \in O} \sigma_M(t)$$

$$A_\infty = \sum_{M \in RS(M_0)} r_M \sigma_M = \sum_{M \in O} \sigma_M$$

$$\bar{A}(t) = \frac{1}{t} \sum_{M \in RS(M_0)} r_M \int_0^t \sigma_M(\tau) d\tau = \frac{1}{t} \sum_{M \in O} \int_0^t \sigma_M(\tau) d\tau$$

where $A(t), A_\infty, \bar{A}(t)$ are, respectively the instantaneous, steady-state and interval availability metrics, and $\sigma_M(t) = Pr\{X(t) = M\}, \sigma_M = \lim_{t \to \infty} \sigma_M(t)$ are the transient and steady-state probabilities of the marking process associated with the SPN being in marking M at time instant $t \geq 0$. Similar reward functions can be defined for reliability metrics.

Considering the GSPN model in Fig. 6.4, several dependability metrics can be computed depending on the definition of the set of operational states (i.e., the subset O). We can compute, e.g., the steady-state availability of at least $0 < N_A \leq S$ servers, by defining the subset O as follows:

$$O = \{M \in RS(M_0) \mid M(ServerIdle) + M(Serving) \geq N_A\}.$$

Table 6.6 shows the results computed using the GreatSPN (2002) tool.

Table 6.6 Steady-state availability of at least $0 < N_A \leq S$ servers	N_A	A_∞
	1	0.999988
	2	0.999464
	3	0.990342
	4	0.911475
	5	0.573473

6.3.1 Non-stochastic Petri Nets

Besides SPN, other classes of non-stochastic Petri Nets, enhanced with timing specification capabilities, have been proposed in the literature. The most well-known are Time Petri Nets (TPN—Berthomieu and Diaz 1991), where each transition is characterized by an earliest and a latest firing time $[a, b]$. The latter are relative to the instant at which the transition was last enabled. Hence, if the transition has been last enabled at time τ, then it may not fire before $\tau + a$ and it must fire before or at $\tau + b$, unless it is disabled before by the firing of a conflicting transition. Most of the analysis techniques are enumerative, i.e., they are based on the construction of the state space associated with the TPN model. TPN have been applied mainly for the verification of timeliness properties. However, there are also some proposals for the safety assessment (Leveson and Stolzy 1987) and the timing failure risk assessment (Bernardi et al. 2011a).

6.4 Other Techniques

In the following, the other standard techniques considered in Tables 6.1 and 6.2 are briefly presented: for an in-depth analysis, we suggest the reader to refer to the standards indicated in Table 6.1 and to the bibliography at the end of the book.

6.4.1 Event Tree Analysis

Event Tree analysis (ETA) is an inductive technique used to evaluate the consequences of an initiating event and the probability of each of the possible sequences that can occur.

The Event Tree (ET) is a logical structure suitable to model the consequences of the initiating event (e.g., a node breakdown), identifying the states (success or unsuccess) of all the mitigation systems; the result is a set of different possible scenarios, each associated with an occurrence probability.

The Fault Tree analysis is generally used to calculate the probabilities of event occurrences. Indeed, each event (branch) in the ET can be interpreted as the top event of an FT: the value thus computed represents the conditional probability of the occurrence of the event, given that the events which precede on that sequence have occurred. Multiplication of the conditional probabilities for each branch in a sequence gives the probability of that sequence.

In the case of structural dependencies it is possible to combine ET and FT techniques in a profitable way, linking one FT to each ET branch. This combined technique is called *ET with boundary conditions* (Stapelberg 2008) and consists in decomposing the system so as to identify the supporting part or functions upon which some components and systems are simultaneously dependent. The supporting parts thereby identified appear explicitly as system event tree headings, preceding the dependent protection systems and components. Since the dependent parts are extracted and explicitly treated as boundary condition in the ET, all the conditional probabilities are made independent and the probability of the accident sequences can be computed by simple multiplications.

6.4.2 FMEA and FMECA

Failure Mode and Effect Analysis (FMEA) is an inductive analysis technique used to study the effects of component failure modes on a system. FMEA starts from knowledge of component failure modes and considers the effects of each failure on sub-systems and the system. It implies the study of all the components in a system and is often applied to higher-level assemblies and systems. FMEA helps to check whether the components, with their known failure modes, fulfill system level safety requirements. The results of the FMEA may be to accept the proposed components or, perhaps, to issue recommendations for maintenance checks, or to ask for components to be replaced.

It is common to use FMEA to determine the presence or absence of single points of failures in a system design. FMEA is basically a qualitative technique; Failure Mode, Effect and Criticality Analysis (FMECA) extends FMEA by introducing a criticality analysis to verify whether failure modes with severe effects have sufficiently low occurrence probability. Both the techniques produce tabular outputs.

6.4.3 Functional Failure Analysis

FFA techniques is applied to the early system design in order to identify hazards from a functional perspective. Indeed, the objective of FFA is the identification of the system functions that contribute to hazards, and thus assigning them a criticality level. It is a deductive technique that considers three types of failure condition: (1) function not provided when requested; (2) function provided when not required; and (3) malfunction. The output is a set of tables which give for each function, for each failure condition, and for each operational state, a description of effects, mitigation procedures, and often the type of analysis that has to be performed to have the system accepted by regulatory authorities.

6.4.4 HAZard and OPerability Studies

HAZard and OPerability study (HAZOP) is a structured and systematic examination of a planned or existing process/operation in order to identify and evaluate hazards to personnel, equipment, or operation. It was initially developed to analyze chemical process systems in the early 1970s but has later been extended to other types of systems, including software systems in the early 1990s.

HAZOP is a qualitative technique based on guidewords and it is often carried out by a multidisciplinary team during the early stages of the system life cycle (i.e., requirement analysis, high-level design) to anticipate hazards. A guideword (e.g., none, more of, less of, part of, more than, other) describes a hypothetical deviation from the normally expected characteristic of a process flow. Driven by these guidewords, failure causes and their effects are listed. Each effect is then considered and actions are proposed either to mitigate it or to decrease the likelihood of the failure cause. The information gathered with HAZOP is represented in tabular form.

6.4.5 Markov Analysis

Markov analysis is a stochastic technique that enables to specify the dependence of failure or repair characteristics of individual components on the state of the system. It is a technique suitable for the dependability evaluation of complex system structures and complex repair and maintenance strategies. It should be observed that Markov analysis often represents the basis of some previously introduced formalisms, such as SPN and DFT.

The simplest Markov model is a Markov chain, that is a Markov process with a discrete state space. A Markov chain can be defined for a discrete set of times (i.e., discrete-time Markov chain—DTMC) or for time taking nonnegative real values (i.e., continuous time Markov chain—CTMC). For dependability applications, the normal reference model is the CTMC. A lot of literature exists on the topic, the interested reader may refer, for example, to Papoulis (1965), Cox and Miller (1965), Kulkarni (1995), Trivedi (2001).

Let $Z(t)$ be a stochastic process defined over the discrete state space Ω. $Z(t)$ is a CTMC if, given any ordered sequence of time instants $(0 < t_1 < t_2 < \ldots < t_m)$, the probability of being in state $\mathbf{x}^{(m)}$ at time t_m depends only on the state occupied by the system at the previous instant of time t_{m-1} and not on the complete sequence of state occupancies. This property, which is usually referred to as the *Markov property*, can be rephrased by saying that the future evolution of the process only depends on the present state and not on the past. Formally, the Markov property may be written as:

$$P\{\, Z(t_m) \,=\, \mathbf{x}^{(m)} \mid Z(t_{m-1}) \,=\, \mathbf{x}^{(m-1)} \,,\ldots,\, Z(t_1) \,=\, \mathbf{x}^{(1)}\}$$
$$= P\{\, Z(t_m) \,=\, \mathbf{x}^{(m)} \mid Z(t_{m-1}) \,=\, \mathbf{x}^{(m-1)}\}.$$

6.4.6 Preliminary Hazard Analysis

PHA, a qualitative technique, is used early in the system life cycle (i.e., requirement analysis and early design) and is aimed at identifying the safety critical areas, providing an initial assessment of hazards and defining requisite hazard controls and subsequent actions. It is not a formal technique, typically consists in brainstorming with the use of checklists to help in the identification of hazards. The technique produces tabular output.

6.4.7   Reliability Block Diagram Analysis

A Reliability Block Diagram (RBD) is a graphical representation of the system's components and connectors. An RBD consists of blocks and lines: the blocks represent system components (generally, hardware components), the lines describe the connections between components. If any path through the system is successful, then the system succeeds, otherwise it fails.

It is assumed that connectors have reliability one (i.e., do not fail) and that both the system and its components are in one of two states: either up or down. Hence, in an RBD, each component can be seen as a switch that is closed when the component is up and open when the component is down. The system will be up only when a path exists between the input and output nodes.

An RBD can always be constructed as connected groups of three basic patterns: (a) components in series; (b) components in active redundancy; or (c) components in standby redundancy. Components in series is the simplest form where if one or more of the components are down then the system is down.

When the system contains redundant structures, then not all of the components belonging to a redundant structure are required to be up for successful operation of the system. An "m/n redundant group" is a group of n components where only (any) m of them has to be up for the group to be considered up. There are two forms of redundancies: active and standby redundancy.

In the case of active redundancy all the n components in the group are active when the system is operating, but only m components are necessary to be up for the group to be up. In a standby redundancy, only m components are required to be in an active state and the remainders $(n - m)$ are in passive state. When an active component fails then one of the passive components is switched on in its place. The failure time distribution associated with a component depends on whether the latter is in an active or passive state (the failure rate of a component in an active state is generally much larger than its failure rate when it is in a passive state).

RBD is both a qualitative and quantitative (stochastic) technique: in the latter case, it can be used to evaluate the system reliability or availability, given the reliability, availability of the individual components. The failures/repairs of the components are assumed statistically independent.

6.4.8   Truth Table

The truth table methods consists of listing all possible state combinations (operating state, failed state) for the various components that make up a system and studying their effects. The first steps in the application of the method are similar to those of a FMECA. The failure modes of the components as well as their failure states should be listed once the system has been broken down into a manageable size. The system state is represented by a state vector that is a combination of component states, each component being represented by either its operating state or its failed state. The truth table is completed by analyzing the effect of all the component state vectors: a system failure state is labeled as 0 (zero) and a system operational state is labeled as 1 (one). The probability of the system failed state is computed by summing the occurrence probability of each state vector resulting in the system failed state. The truth table method is difficult to apply to complex systems since the number of state increases exponentially.

6.5   Tools Overview

Software tool support is essential to perform dependability analysis and many tools exist. In the following, we present a not exhaustive list (Table 6.7), focusing on those supporting Fault Tree (FT) or Stochastic Petri Net (SPN) formalisms and their variants. Most of them enable the application of several dependability analysis techniques, besides FT and SPN.

Table 6.7 Dependability tools

Tool	ETA	FMECA	FTA	HAZOP	Markov	SPN	RBD
SHARPE		✓			✓	✓	✓
SURF-2					✓	✓	
GreatSPN						✓	
TimeNET						✓	
Möbius		✓			✓	✓	
DEEM						✓	
Galileo		✓					
StarsStudio-Astra	✓	✓	✓	✓			
FaultTree+	✓		✓		✓		

- *SHARPE* (Sahner and Trivedi 1987; Trivedi 2002)—Symbolic Hierarchical Automated Reliability and Performance Evaluator— is a toolkit for specifying and analyzing performance, reliability, availability, and performability models. It supports combinatorial modeling, with FTs, Reliability Block Diagrams and product-form queueing networks, and state-based modeling, with Markov and semi-Markov reward models and generalized SPNs. From the analysis point of view, steady-state, transient, and interval-based measures can be computed. SHARPE is a multi-formalism tool that enables hierarchical model composition by combining results from different kinds of models.
- *SURF-2* (Béounes et al. 1993) enables modeling with Markov chains and generalized SPNs. The tool provides support to the RAMS comparative analysis of different system architecture designs. Reward structures can be added to the

model to get QoS measures in terms of dependability, performance, and cost. SURF-2 supports both transient and steady-state analyses.

- *GreatSPN* (Baarir et al. 2009)—GRaphical Editor Analyzer for Timed and Stochastic Petri Nets—enables modeling with generalized SPNs, stochastic Well-Formed nets (SWNs), Deterministic and SPNs (DSPN), and SPNs with general (not exponentially) distributed timed transitions. It also provides support to net composition by using the package *algebra* (Bernardi et al. 2001). GreatSPN includes both transient and steady-state solvers: numerical techniques, based on the solution of the underlying Markov chain, are available for transient and steady-state analyses, while simulators can be used only for steady-state analysis.

- *TimeNET* (Zimmermann 2012) has been designed especially for models with non-Markovian SPNs. It supports Deterministic and SPNs (DSPN), Extended DSPNs (EDSPNs), colored SPNs, discrete-time SPNs, and hierarchically structured models. Transient and steady-state analyses are available for DSPNs, steady-state analysis only for EDSPNs with no concurrently enabled deterministic transitions, steady-state approximation for DSPNs with concurrently enabled deterministic transitions, transient and steady-state simulation for non-Markovian SPNs, and discrete-time analysis for DSPNs with concurrently enabled deterministic transitions. TimeNET also provides functionalities for the steady-state analysis and simulation of colored SPNs.

- *Möbius* (Clark et al. 2001)—Model-Based Environment for Validation of System Reliability, Availability, Security, and Performance—provides an infrastructure to support multiple interacting modeling formalisms and solvers. Several modeling formalisms are supported: Stochastic Activity Networks, FTs, Buckets and Balls (a generalization of Markov chains), and PEPA (a process algebra). Möbius allows combining (atomic) models to form composed models through replication and join operators and customizing measures of system properties (e.g., reliability, availability, performance, and security). Measures can be computed at specific time instants, over periods of time or when the system reaches steady state. Parametrized models can be constructed and sensitivity analysis is supported by the tool. Möbius solvers include distributed discrete-event simulators and Markov chain numerical solvers.

- *DEEM* (Bondavalli et al. 2004)—Dependability Modeling and Evaluation of Multiple Phased Systems—is a tool for dependability model-based evaluation of multiple phased systems. It enables the MPS modeling through deterministic and SPNs. DEEM solvers implement efficient analytical solution techniques based on the separability of the Markov regenerative process underlying the deterministic and SPN: both steady-state and transient analyses are supported. Dependability measures are defined through the general mechanism of marking-dependent reward functions.

- *Galileo* (Sullivan et al. 1999) is a software tool for dynamic FT modeling and analysis. Dynamic FT models can be created in either a textual or a graphical representation. Galileo includes a dynamic FT solver based on an efficient algorithm that first modularizes an FT into statistical independent sub-trees, which are then solved using either a dynamic sub-tree solver or a static sub-tree solver (Dugan et al. 1997).

- *StarsStudio-Astra* (Contini et al. 1999) is a software package that supports several dependability modeling and analysis techniques: FTA, ETA, FMECA, and HAZOP. The tool allows to apply ET and FT techniques in a combined manner (i.e., Event tree with boundary condition technique) by linking one FT model to each ET branch. The FMECA and HAZOP analysis can be carried out by filling FMECA/HAZOP tables; besides the tables, the tool can generate histograms, which contain the number of FMECA failure modes or HAZOP items versus severity, frequency and risk classes, and risk tables, which summarize the situation of all the FMECA failure modes or HAZOP items with respect to the risk.
- *FaultTree +* (Isograph 2012) is a software package that allows dependability modeling and analysis with FTs, ETs, and Markov models. The tool computes reliability and availability metrics, minimal cut sets in FT models. It enables to define different types of distributions for failure events and includes failure data libraries (NPRD11 2011; IAEA-478 1988) for a wide variety of component types including mechanical, electromechanical, and electronic assemblies.

Chapter 7
Proposals for Dependability Assessment

*So far so good. Now, how to bridge the gap between UML &
dependability analysis ?*

Abstract During the last two decades, several dependability domain-specific
modeling languages (D-DSML) have been proposed. This chapter surveys 36
proposals of D-DSML in literature. Most of the proposals are based on UML and
a good number also accomplish the transformation of the D-DSML into proper
dependability analysis models, as those presented in Chap. 6. DAM, presented in
Chap. 5, is an example of D-DSML developed as a UML profile.

Software system modeling for dependability analysis has received a growing interest
during the last two decades. In particular, significant efforts have been focused
on defining dependability DSMLs (D-DSMLs) and transformations of D-DSML
specifications into different types of dependability analysis models used to obtain
dependability measures or to validate dependability properties.

In this chapter, we consider 36 representative proposals that have been developed
in a total of 49 papers: Table 7.1 lists the papers that gather the proposals, ordered
according to their presentation throughout the chapter. These proposals have in
common the modeling approach, i.e., all of them develop a proper D-DSML starting
from a standard software specification language.

Most of the contributions define the D-DSML by extending UML with annotations; however, only a few of them use the standard profiling mechanism explained
in Chap. 2. DAM, discussed in Chap. 5, has been built on the UML-based proposals
considered in Table 7.1. The reader interested in a comprehensive evaluation of
the proposals based on UML can refer to the survey of Bernardi et al. (2012).
Besides UML, there are proposals that consider also other specification languages
such as SysML (David et al. 2009; Cancila et al. 2009), BPEL (Zarras et al. 2004;
Bocciarelli and D'Ambrogio 2011a), BPMN (Bocciarelli and D'Ambrogio 2011b),

S. Bernardi et al., *Model-Driven Dependability Assessment of Software Systems*,
DOI 10.1007/978-3-642-39512-3_7, © Springer-Verlag Berlin Heidelberg 2013

AADL and its extended Error Model annex (Bozzano et al. 2011; Rugina et al. 2007, 2008, 2011).

Table 7.1 List of dependability proposals

Attribute	Approach name	Papers
Reliability	D'Ambrogio	(D'Ambrogio et al, 2002)
Reliability	Yacoub	(Yacoub et al, 2004)
Reliability	Rodrigues	(Rodrigues et al, 2005)
Reliability	Singh	(Singh et al, 2001)
Reliability	Cortellessa	(Cortellessa and Pompei, 2004)
Reliability	Pai	(Pai and Dugan, 2002)
Reliability	Grassi	(Grassi et al, 2005, 2007)
Reliability	Bocciarelli	(Bocciarelli and D'Ambrogio, 2011a,b)
Reliability	David	(David et al, 2009)
Availability	Bernardi-a	(Bernardi and Merseguer, 2006)
Maintainability	Genero	(Genero et al, 2003, 2007)
Safety	Allenby	(Allenby and Kelly, 2001)
Safety	Johannessen	(Johannessen et al, 2001)
Safety	Hansen	(Hansen et al, 2004)
Safety	Iwu	(Iwu et al, 2007)
Safety	Liu	(Liu et al, 2007)
Safety	Hawkings	(Hawkings et al, 2003)
Safety	Pataricza	(Pataricza et al, 2003)
Safety	Ober	(Ober et al, 2006)
Safety	Zoughbi	(Zoughbi et al, 2006, 2007)
Safety	Cancila	(Cancila et al, 2009)
Safety	Lu	(Lu and Halang, 2007)
Safety	Goseva	(Goseva-Popstojanova et al, 2003)
Safety	Hassan	(Hassan et al, 2005)
Reliability, Availability	Bondavalli	(Bondavalli et al, 2001a; Majzik et al, 2003; Pataricza, 2000)
Reliability, Availability	DeMiguel	(DeMiguel et al, 2001)
Reliability, Availability	Leangsuksun	(Leangsuksun et al, 2003)
Reliability, Availability	DalCin	(Dal Cin, 2003)
Reliability, Availability, Maintainability	Addouche	(Addouche et al, 2004, 2006)
Reliability, Availability, Maintainability	Bernardi-b	(Bernardi et al, 2004a,b)
Reliability, Safety	Mustafiz	(Mustafiz et al, 2008; Mustafiz and Kienzle, 2009)
Reliability, Safety	Zarras	(Zarras et al, 2004)
Reliability, Safety	Jürjens	(Jürjens, 2003; Jürjens and Wagner, 2005)
Reliability, Availability, Maintainability, Safety	Bernardi-c	(Bernardi et al, 2011c; Merseguer and Bernardi, 2012)
Reliability, Availability, Maintainability, Safety	Bozzano	(Bozzano et al, 2011)
Reliability, Availability, Maintainability, Safety	Rugina	(Rugina et al, 2007, 2008, 2011)

Some of the proposals consider translations from the D-DSML to a dependability analysis model or technique, and most of them tackle the dependability analysis.

The proposals consider the evaluation of reliability, availability, maintainability, and safety (RAMS) properties, and, often, they are supported by a software tool. However, we have not found proposals in the integrity field.

7.1 Criteria for Proposals Presentation

Table 7.2 shows six criteria for evaluating the 36 approaches. These criteria will guide the subsequent presentation of the approaches. Criteria are based on the dependability concepts presented in Table 2.1 and discussed in Chap. 2. Besides, we have added two other important concerns, the *analysis type* and the *analysis model*.

(*C1*) *Dependability attribute*. Dependability includes several properties (*attributes*): each proposal deals with a subset of them. This criterion refers to the attributes of the dependability dealt by an approach. In Table 2.1 the label associated is **DA**, so, reliability **DA.R**, availability **DA.A**, maintainability **DA.M**, and safety **DA.S**.

(*C2*) *Analysis type*. The nature of the dependability analysis may be either *quantitative* or *qualitative* (IEC-60300-3-1 2003). This strongly constraints the type of specification as we later discuss. For quantitative analysis we have found approaches that follow either *stochastic* analysis or *not stochastic*. For the sake of simplicity, "stochastic" and "probabilistic" are considered synonymous. In general, qualitative analysis aims to prove dependability properties, while quantitative analysis aims to estimate dependability measures.

(*C3*) *Analysis model*. There exist a variety of dependability models and/or techniques used for dependability analysis. A few of them, like stochastic Petri nets (Ajmone-Marsan et al. 1994), are useful for both quantitative and qualitative analyses. However, others are exclusively targeted to qualitative analysis, such as HAZOP (2000), and others to quantitative analysis such as Bayesian models or Markov models.

The analysis, either quantitative or qualitative, of a dependability model requires a proper specification of the input parameters, output parameters, or measures to be calculated and requirements, as explained below:

(*C4*) *Input parameters*. The input dependability parameters required by the approach to effectively carry out the proposed analysis. They support the specification of dependability characteristics. In Table 2.1, such characteristics are classified as: dependability metrics associated with system components (**DM**), i.e., MTTF; dependability threat assumptions (**DT**), i.e., probability of error propagation; fault tolerance assumption (**FT**), i.e., recovery activities; maintenance assumptions (**M**), i.e., MTTR; redundancy assumptions (**R**), i.e., specification of spare components and type of spares.

(*C5*) *Dependability measures.* The kind of dependability measures or properties the approach evaluates. In Table 2.1 the label associated is **DM**.

(*C6*) *Dependability requirements.* The kind of requirements the approach supports. In Table 2.1 the label associated is **DR**: a requirement can be expressed with a bound (**DR.BOUND**), e.g., the minimum availability required for a system service is 99 %, or it can be specified as a property, e.g., the system will never reach an unsafe state (**DR.S**).

Observe that, both criteria *C4* and *C5* reference the dependability measure item in Table 2.1 (**DM**). Indeed, an approach may require dependability measures as input parameters. For example, the Mean Time To Failure (MTTF) of system components is needed to evaluate the MTTF of the overall system.

In the following we present the approaches according to the dependability attribute they address (criterion *C1*), i.e., reliability, availability, maintainability, or safety. Firstly, approaches dealing with only one attribute are addressed. Later, approaches focused on more than one dependability attribute will be presented.

Table 7.2 Presentation and evaluation criteria

Dependability characteristics		
Code	Criterion	Values (according to Table 2.1)
C1	Dependability attribute	DA.R (reliability); DA.A (availability); DA.M (maintainability); DA.S (safety)
C2	Analysis type	qualitative; quantitative (stochastic; non stochastic)
C3	Analysis model	FMEA; HAZOP; Fault trees; stochastic Petri nets, ...
C4	Input Parameters	DM (dependability measure); DT (dependability threats), FT (fault tolerance), M (maintenance), R (redundancy)
C5	Dependability measures	DM.R (reliability); DM.A (availability); DM.M (maintainability); DM.S (safety); DM.C (software complexity measures)
C6	Dependability requirements	DR.BOUND (upper and lower bounds); DR.S (safety properties)

7.2 Reliability

All the proposals surveyed in this section, but David et al. (2009), aim at providing support to a quantitative evaluation (*C2*) of software systems reliability. David's proposal addresses qualitative analysis and uses, besides UML, also SysML as input specification language. Bocciarelli's proposal considers BPMN as input specification language and provides model-to-model transformations to BPEL and UML. All the contributions focus on the early stages of the software life cycle; in particular, software architecture (D'Ambrogio, Yacoub and Rodrigues) and design (Singh and Cortellessa, Pai, Grassi, David, Bocciarelli). Only Bocciarelli provides support to the specification of the reliability requirements to be assessed with the proposed approaches.

D'Ambrogio's proposal is focused on the software architecture of the system. The approach defines a transformation of UML sequence and deployment diagrams into Fault-tree models (*C3*) to predict the system failure rate (*C5*—**DM.R**). Although no UML extension standard mechanisms are used, several UML model elements whose failure (basic events in Fault-tree models) can lead to the system failure (top event in Fault-tree models) are identified, such as failure of nodes and communication paths, call/return actions, and operations. MTTF is assigned to such elements as input parameter (*C4*—**DM.R**).

Yacoub and Rodrigues' proposals aim at calculating the system reliability on-demand (*C5*—**DM.R**) as a function of the component/ connector reliability (*C4*—**DM.R**) and the scenario execution probabilities. Yacoub considers also the probability of error propagation between components (*C4*—**DT.EPQ**). To compute the measure, Yacoub constructs a probabilistic model, called Component Dependency Graph (CDG), from sequence diagrams and develops an algorithm, based on the CDG. Instead, Rodrigues uses Labeled Transition Systems to synthesize sequence diagrams and interpret them as Markov models (*C3*). These approaches are also focused on the software architecture.

Singh and Cortellessa's Proposals use the Bayesian framework (*C3*) to derive a probability distribution of system reliability (*C5*—**DM.R**) from UML use case and sequence diagrams. Cortellessa improves Singh's proposal by considering also deployment diagrams and the connector failures, beside the component failures, and the use case execution probabilities (*C4*—**DM.R**). These approaches are focused on the software design stage of the life cycle.

Pai's Proposal uses dynamic Fault tree as target formalism (*C3*) to evaluate the system unreliability (*C5*—**DM.R**) of fault-tolerant software systems at design stage. Unlike D'Ambrogio's approach, Pai introduces a set of stereotypes and tags to enrich UML system models with information needed for the reliability analysis. In particular, tags are used to define input parameters, such as failure rate of system components and error propagation probability (*C4*—**DM.R, DT.EPQ**). The approach supports the modeling and analysis of sequence error propagations (*C4*—**DT.EP**) that lead to dependent failures (*C4*—**DT.FMDep**), redundancies, and reconfiguration activities (*C4*—**FT.R**). Several stereotypes are defined to represent different kinds of dependencies between system components and to model the type of spare components, e.g., hot, cold, and warm spares (*C4*—**R.T**).

Grassi's Proposal defines a model-driven transformation framework for performance and reliability analysis of component-based systems at design stage. Grassi builds an intermediate model that acts as bridge between annotated UML models and analysis-oriented models. In particular, discrete-time Markov process models (*C3*) can be derived for the computation of the service reliability (*C5*—**DM.R**). The proposal uses the UML extensions in Cortellessa and Pompei (2004) and complements them, by associating failure input parameters with both hardware and software components and by considering both atomic failures and failure probability distributions (*C4*—**DM.R**).

Bocciarelli's Proposal introduces an extension of BPMN (2011), namely PyBPMN (Performability-enabled BPMN), for the specification of performance and reliability properties in business processes. Unlike UML, the BPMN metamodel does not have a profiling mechanism so Bocciarelli extends the BPMN metamodel by adding new meta-classes which represent performance and reliability concepts (*C4*—**DM.R, DT**, *C5*—**DM.R**, *C6*—**DR.BOUND**) defined in MARTE (2011) and DAM (Bernardi et al. 2011c) profiles, respectively. This extension approach has the disadvantage that one needs to extend the tool support, as existing tools do not understand the new meta-classes.

Two transformations of PyBPMN models are also provided to obtain on one side BPEL (2007) documents and, on the other side, UML activity diagrams annotated according to the SoaML (2012) and MARTE profiles. The outputs of such transformations represent the specification of abstract business processes. Concrete business processes are derived through a set of steps that include (1) service discovery, considering the property of interest and (2) quantitative analysis to select the service configuration that provides the best predicted QoS, in terms of performance or reliability attributes. In particular, Bocciarelli and D'Ambrogio (2011b) provide a method to derive concrete business processes considering reliability metrics, such as the time to failure or the number of failures over a time interval. The reliability prediction is carried out by an algorithm that implements a global optimization strategy.

David's proposal focuses on the identification of behavioral failure modes, e.g., with respect to their detectability (*C4*—**DT.FMDet**), in system design using Failure Mode and Effects Analysis (FMEA) technique (*C3*). Besides UML, SysML (2012) is considered as modeling notation for specifying system functional behavior. A drawback of the approach is that a *Dysfunctional Behavior data-base*, which organizes the knowledge about possible elementary failure modes of components, needs to be constructed and maintained to support an automated reuse of the method.

7.3 Availability

To the best of our knowledge, Bernardi-a is the only proposal that tackles, exclusively, software availability. It devises a method to evaluate, from a quantitative point of view (*C2*), the quality of service of fault-tolerant distributed systems design specifications under late-timing failure assumption (*C4*—**DT.FMD**). A QoS measure is defined as a function of two non-functional requirements (*C6*—**DR.BOUND**): one related to the system availability, i.e., the time to detect an error and isolate it (*C4*—**FT.ED**), and the other related to the cost of the fault-tolerant strategy, i.e., communication overhead. Bernardi-a proposes a transformation of UML sequence, state-chart and deployment diagrams, annotated with SPT (2005) profile, to a performability Generalized Stochastic Petri Nets (GSPN) model (*C3*). The latter is then analyzed via simulation to evaluate, under different system configurations, the considered QoS measure. State-charts are also proposed for the quantitative characterization of faults (*C4*—**DT.FOQ**) as well as for the behavioral specification of different types of fault with respect to their timing persistency (*C4*—**DT.FP**).

7.4 Maintainability

Genero is the only proposal that addresses specifically the maintainability of UML specifications during the design stage of the software life cycle. It is a quantitative, not stochastic, approach (*C2*) that relies on a software quality standard ISO/IEC9126-1.2 (2001) and proposes a set of measures as good predictors of two maintainability sub-characteristics, that is understandability and modifiability (*C4*—**M.M**). The set of measures includes both typical size measures (e.g., number of classes, attributes and methods) and structurally complexity ones (e.g., number of aggregations, dependencies and generalizations)—(*C5*—**DM.C**)—which can be applied on UML class diagrams. An empirical analysis is carried out to evaluate correlation between metrics and maintainability characteristics.

7.5 Safety

Safety modeling and analysis issues have been addressed by several proposals that together cover all the stages of the software life cycle, from requirements elicitation throughout software architecture and design specification to implementation. Traditionally, system safety has been assessed from a qualitative point of view, mainly by verifying properties (Leveson 1995). Accordingly, most of the proposals presented in this section support qualitative analysis (*C2*) with the exception of Ober, Cancila, Goseva, and Hassan's proposals. In particular, Ober and Cancila provide support to non stochastic analysis, while Goseva and Hassan's approaches rely on stochastic analysis. All the proposals are based on UML, Cancila's approach also consider SysML to define its D-DMSL, namely SOPHIA.

Allenby and Johannessen's proposals address safety requirements elicitation and they are application domain-specific. Both proposals use Use Case diagrams to identify system level functionalities of aerospace software (Allenby) or in automotive domain (Johannessen). They are both compliant with safety-standards (ARP-4754 1994; ARP-4761 1995; IEC-61508 1998) and provide systematic methods to identify failure modes with the help of guidewords (*C4*—**DT.HGW**). In particular, Allenby applies a subset of HAZard OPerability guidewords (*C3*) to pre- and post-condition, guard condition, and scenario sections of use case descriptions to identify failure modes considering the domain and their consequence (*C4*—**DT.FMD, DT.FMSL**) and to derive safety requirements related to use cases (*C6*—**DR.S**). Instead, Johannessen adopts Functional Failure Analysis guidewords (*C3*) and failures are classified according to their consequence (*C4*—**DT.FMSL**). Unlike Allenby, Johannessen provides also support to analyze the consequence of combined failures (*C4*—**DT.FMDep**). Both approaches are characterized by a low degree of automation.

Hansen and Iwu's proposals use HAZard OPerability guidewords (*C3,C4*—**DT.HGW**) to identify hazards in software architecture specification. Both works address specific application domains (automotive in Hansen et al. 2004 and embedded systems in Iwu et al. (2007)). While Iwu adopts an approach similar to Allenby (i.e., use case-based), Hansen considers each model element in package, class, component, object, sequence, and deployment diagrams. Then, the main drawback of Hansen's proposal is the limited scalability that, when applied to a real system, may result in a time-consuming activity.

Iwu uses also Fault tree analysis to combine faults that give rise to identified hazards (*C3*). Such faults are related to UML model elements (e.g., classes in class diagrams, messages in sequence diagrams) and are used to establish derived safety requirements. Safety requirements and healthiness properties (*C6*—**DR.S**, *C5*—**DM.S**) are specified using Practical Formal Specification state machines; a tool support is provided to check their consistency and completeness.

Liu's proposal addresses safety analysis on the variations in software product lines proposing a five-step approach. In the first step, common and variability analysis is carried out to identify requirements for the entire product line and for specific product members. Hazard analysis is then performed by using software Fault tree analysis customized to product-line domain (*C3*). The root node of the tree is typically a negation of a safety requirement, or it can be identified from preexisting hazard lists (*C4*—**DT.HGW**), while the leaf nodes are labeled with a commonality or variation, previously identified. In the third step, such leaf nodes are mapped into architectural components, whose behavior is then modeled with a UML state-chart. Safety requirement and failure scenarios are then derived from the fault tree (*C6*—**DR.S**) and, finally, behavioral safety properties (*C5*—**DM.S**) are checked in state-based models (*C3*) through scenario-guided execution or animation. The safety properties that can be automatically checked include ordering logic and relative timing of failures of events while, due to the tool limitations, the verification of exact time values is not supported.

Hawkings' proposal addresses the preliminary system safety assessment of UML design. A Fault tree is constructed (*C3*) where hazardous basic events are related to classes and operations in UML class diagrams. Then, the behavior of the classes—represented by UML StateCharts—is analyzed in order to derive detailed safety requirements. Beside the normal behavior, the faulty behavior (*C4*—**DT.FB**) is modeled by adding extra transitions in the StateCharts with the help of hazard guidewords (e.g., omission, commission and value) (*C4*—**DT.FMD, DT.HGW**). A reachability analysis of the mutated StateChart is performed to check whether the introduced faulty behavior can lead to unsafe states. The derived safety requirements restrict the hazardous behaviors and are specified with OCL as contracts on classes/operations (*C6*—**DR.S**).

Pataricza's proposal enables the modeling of the normal and faulty behavior of a system component in a single state machine (*C4*—**DT.FB**). The objective of the approach is to provide support to the identification of error propagation paths leading to catastrophic failures in railway control software (*C5*—**DM.S**). Pataricza defines UML stereotypes for erroneous states and correcting transitions in UML State Machines (*C4*—**DT.EB, DT.EP, FT.R**).

Ober's proposal presents a technique for the verification of safety properties of real-time and embedded systems via model checking (*C5*—**DM.S**). A UML profile (OMEGA) is defined to specify timing constraints in the UML design (Class Diagrams and State Machines) as well as dynamic and time-dependent safety requirements (*C6*—**DR.S**). In particular, the latter are expressed by *observers* UML classes, whose behavior is described as a State Machine characterized by error or invalid states (*C4*—**DT.EB**). Both design and requirements are then transformed into communicating extended timed automata (*C3*) and the design is verified against the requirements using model checking techniques.

Zoughbi's proposal defines a UML profile for specifying safety concepts of aerospace software systems in the design phase, so to support automated generation of certification-related information. The proposed UML extensions are compliant with the airworthiness standard RTCA (1992), they are used to record safety-related design decisions—e.g., failure consequence/ hazard severity (*C4*—**DT.FMSL, DT.HS**), roles within replicated structures (*C4*—**R.R**), safety/confidence levels (*C5*—**DM.S**) and complexity metrics (*C5*—**DM.C**) for collaboration, class, operation and relationship—and trace them back to the requirements. The approach is based on a rigorous definition of the profile (through a safety domain model) and an exhaustive completeness/consistency assessment with respect to the considered safety standard. The main weakness is the use of dynamic concepts (through the profile) that extend typically static concepts, then leading to mixed static/dynamic views in the same UML class diagram.

Cancila's proposal considers software architecture and design specifications of railways transport systems and propose a UML profile (SOPHIA) for safety concerns. SOPHIA relies on MARTE (2011) and SysML (2012) to express safety measures (tolerable accident rate, i.e., TAR, and frequency of an accident *C5*—**DM.S**), requirements (i.e., maximum TAR *C6*—**DR.BOUND**), and characteristics (accident severity, accident severity/frequency table, accident frequency *C4*—**DT.HS, DT.HL**). Cancila also proposes an algorithm for the automatic generation of derived safety attribute values (i.e., TAR) in design model.

Lu's proposal addresses the design of safety-critical distributed embedded real-time systems and the automated code derivation from UML design, considering PEARL as target programming language and Function Blocks (IEC-61131-1 1992) to support the code reusability. A set of PEARL code structures are proposed as suitable for building applications which have to meet safety integrity level requirements (IEC-61508 1998) (*C6*—**DR.BOUND**). The SIL-related PEARL constructs are represented as UML stereotypes and the Object Constraint Language (OCL) is used to specify constraints (i.e., pre- and post-conditions, invariants) on the expected execution of stereotyped components. Lu defines UML extensions also for representing Function Block diagrams as UML component diagrams.

Goseva and Hassan's proposals focus on the risk assessment step within the system safety analysis process. They both consider software architectures specified with UML. Goseva estimates the scenario risk factor (*C5*—**DM.S**) from risk factors associated with software components and connectors by constructing and solving a Markovian model (*C3*). The component/connector risk factor is computed as the product of two safety metrics: the severity level (*C4*—**DT.FMSL, DT.HS**) and the complexity/coupling associated with the component/connector. The severity is obtained using FMEA technique (*C3*), while the component complexity and connector coupling are estimated considering the UML dynamic specifications—State Machines and Sequence Diagrams—(*C5*—**DM.C**). Hassan addresses the problem of evaluating the failure severity based on UML specification. The proposal integrates different severity techniques (FFA, FMEA and FTA—*C3*) to identify and relate system level hazards and component/connector failure modes (*C4*—**DT.HO, DT.HL, DT.HGW**). A cost of failure graph is then constructed to evaluate the cost of failure (*C5*—**DM.S**) of system execution scenarios, software components/connectors. The costs of failure are reported in the UML models with the use of notes. Finally, the scenario and component/connector severity (*C4*—**DT.FMSL, DT.HS**) are obtained from the estimated costs of failure using a nonlinear mapping. Both the approaches rely on the US military standard for safety critical systems (MIL-STD-1629a 1980).

7.6   Reliability and Availability

The proposals considered in this section use UML as software specification modeling language and provide support for a quantitative stochastic analysis (*C2*) of reliability and availability. Unlike the proposals addressing only reliability analysis, the reliability and availability proposals define D-DSMLs that also enable the specification of repair/recovery characteristics, such as repair rate or MTTR, in order to support the evaluation of availability metrics.

Bondavalli's proposal is the most comprehensive approach, among the surveyed ones, for reliability and availability analysis of software architectures specified using UML. UML standard extension mechanisms (i.e., stereotypes and tags) are used for annotating dependability properties of software systems on UML specifications. Through a rigorous graph transformation process, Timed Petri Net models (*C3*) are derived via an intermediate model that captures the relevant dependability information from the annotated UML models. Several input parameters are defined for hardware and software components, such as fault occurrence rate (*C4*—**DT.FOQ**), percentage of permanent faults (*C4*—**DT.FP**), error latency for components with an internal state (*C4*—**DT.EQ**), and repair delay (*C4*—**DM.M**). The approach also supports the specification of error propagation between components (*C4*—**DT.EPQ**) by assigning a probability to the model elements representing either relationships (e.g., associations) or interactions between such components (e.g., communication paths, messages). The set of dependability measures that can be evaluated (*C5*—**DM.R,DM.A**) includes the reliability probability distribution function, MTTF, the steady-state and the immediate availability. Concerning the type of failures with respect to their dependency, both independent and dependent failures can be specified (*C4*—**DT.FMDep**). In particular, it is possible to assign common failure mode occurrence tags to redundant components belonging to complex FT structures (*C4*—**R.L, R.R**). Failures can be discriminated also with respect to the domain (*C4*—**DT.FMD**). Extensions for states and events of state machines representing the behavior of *redundancy manager* components are introduced, in order to discriminate normal and failure states and events (*C4*—**DT.FailB**). Such extensions are used to analyze the failure conditions of the FT structures. The Bondavalli's approach is supported by the model transformation framework VIATRA (Csertan et al. 2002) based on metamodeling.

DeMiguel's proposal considers the software architecture and detailed design of distributed real-time systems. Simulation models are generated automatically from UML models, annotated with dependability input parameters—e.g., object and network error occurrence, object time to failure and repair (*C4*—**DT.EB, DT.EQ, DM.R, DM.M**). In particular, the tool OpNet (1999) is used as simulation kernel. The approach supports the evaluation of several dependability measures, such as object and network availability, object failure distribution (*C5*—**DM.A, DM.R**), and different type of statistics can be computed (i.e., mean, variance, distribution).

Leangsuksun's proposal derives from UML deployment diagrams, normally used during the late software design and deployment stages, Fault tree and Markov chain models (*C3*) for the analysis of the reliability and availability, respectively. UML diagrams are annotated with node failure rate and repair rate parameters (*C4*—**DM.R, DM.M**). The method supports computation of reliability (i.e., survival function) and the steady-state availability (*C5*—**DM.R, DM.A**), under hardware failure independence assumptions.

DalCin's proposal defines a UML profile for designing dependability mechanisms, that is hardware/software components to be implemented or integrated in a real-time system to ensure fault tolerance (*C4*—**FT.ED, FT.R, R.R**). The proposed profile is aimed at supporting the quantitative evaluation of the effectiveness of the fault-tolerant strategy adopted, in terms of reliability and steady-state availability (*C5*—**DM.R, DM.A**). It provides a language (i.e., SQIRL) for specifying stochastic reliability and availability requirements of such mechanisms (*C6*—**DR.BOUND**).

7.7 Reliability, Availability, and Maintainability

The following two approaches deal, as the previous ones, with reliability and availability of UML-based system models, besides they address also maintainability (*C1*). Both proposals are aimed at providing support to quantitative analysis (*C2*): Addouche's proposal enables stochastic analysis, while Bernardi-b's approach is not stochastic.

Addouche's proposal defines a profile compliant with General Resource Modeling package in SPT (2005). UML extensions are used to annotate UML models with QoS characteristics (*C4*—**DM.R, DM.M**) and to derive probabilistic time automata

(C3) for the verification of dependability properties via temporal logic formulas and model checking (*C5*—**DM.R, DM.A, DM.M**). A pair of stereotypes is also defined to include probabilistic aspects of functioning and malfunctioning. The static model of the system is enriched with new stereotyped classes that are associated with each class representing a system resource. Such new classes are used to specify, via their attributes, failure conditions and possibly degraded/failure states of the resources (*C4*—**DT.FailB**). This mechanism can be used by the analyst to specify state-based conditional failures of components (*C4*—**DT.FMDep**).

Bernardi-b's proposal defines a UML Class Diagram (CD) framework to collect dependability and real-time requirements of distributed control automation systems and to support the design of fault tolerance strategies. It proposes a systematic method for the derivation of dependability analysis models, such as TRIO (Ghezzi et al. 1990) temporal logic models (*C3*). The CD framework enables to specify input and output parameters (*C4,C5*—**DM.R, DM.A, DM.M**), upper/lower bound requirements (*C6*—**DR.BOUND**). It also includes the fault-error-failure (FEF) chain (Avizienis et al. 2004) and fault tolerance mechanisms. In particular, fault classes have attributes that characterize the fault timing persistency and occurrence rates (*C4*—**DT.FP, DT.FOQ**) in system components. Error classes allow to quantify error latencies, error probability, and bit error rates (*C4*—**DT.EQ**) in automation functions. Finally, failures are classified according to their impact on the automation system in halting, degrading and repairing failures (*C4*—**DT.FMD**). From the analysis of TRIO temporal logic models it is possible to visualize traces of the system execution that concentrate on the predicates of interest. The requirement specification and analysis approach is compliant with the standard dependability management process (IEC-60300-3-1 2003).

7.8 Reliability and Safety

The reliability and safety proposals considered in this section enable the quantitative analysis (*C2*) through the derivation of either stochastic (Mustafiz and Zarras) or non stochastic (Jürjens) models. The Zarras' proposal assumes, besides UML, also BPEL as input specification language.

Mustafiz's proposal devises a requirement engineering process (DREP) for elic-itation, specification, and analysis of reliability and safety requirements. Mustafiz extends use cases to discover exceptional situations that can interrupt the system normal behavior and to define derived requirements to handle such situations. Use cases are mapped to DA-Charts, a type of state-charts where probabilities are associated with success/failure transitions (*C4*—**DT.FailB, DM.R**). A Markov chain is then constructed from a DA-Chart (*C3*) to compute the reliability on-demand and the probability of reaching safe states from the initial system state (*C5*—**DM.R, DM.S**). The dependability analysis produces information to the designer on the maximal achievable reliability and safety (*C6*—**DR.BOUND**), considering only the failures of the system environment (e.g., how sensor failures) and assuming the system under development be reliable.

Zarras's proposal addresses reliability and safety analysis of composite web services; availability is also dealt, but as secondary dependability property. Zarras considers BPEL (2007) as software architecture specification language and proposes a UML representation of environment through stereotypes. UML extensions are also defined to express the parameters needed for dependability analysis. In particular, they include: reliability, safety, and availability measures (*C5*—**DM.R, DM.S, DM.A**) to be computed, fault characterization of objects (*C4*—**DT.FP, DT.FO, DT.FOQ**)—e.g., fault rate, fault persistency, phase of occurrence, boundary and nature—the failure domain and consistency (*C4*—**DT.FMD, DT.FMC**), and redundancy schema within the devised FT techniques (*C4*—**R.L, R.F, R.R**)—e.g., the type of adjudicators in error-detection mechanisms, the redundancy level and FT level of a redundant schema. The UML annotated models are then transformed into Block Diagrams and Markov models which enable the dependability evaluation of the composite web services (*C3*).

Jürjens' proposal defines safety and reliability checklists, using UML stereo-types and tags, to support identification of failure-prone components (*C5*—**DM.S, DM.C**) in the software design. UML extensions are used to specify requirements on communication—e.g., maximum probability of message loss, safety/reliability level (*C6*—**DR.BOUND, DR.S**)—and failure assumptions (*C4*—**DM.R**) of communication links/nodes as a function of the failure domain (*C4*—**DT.FMD**) and of the type of voters within redundancy structures (*C4*—**R.R**). A precise semantics is provided to check the design, via temporal logic formulas (*C3*), against the requirements and constraints specified with the proposed UML extensions.

7.9 Reliability, Availability, Maintainability, and Safety

The proposals of Bernardi-c, Bozzano and Rugina enable the evaluation of RAMS properties. While Bernardi-c's proposal is based on UML and does not address a specific application domain, the Bozzano and Rugina's ones rely on AADL and apply to automotive/aereospace domain. Both Bernardi-c and Bozzano provide support to qualitative and quantitative RAMS analysis, while Rugina allows the evaluation of RAMS properties through quantitative stochastic analysis (*C2*).

Bernardi-c's proposal develops DAM (Dependability Analysis and Modeling), a UML profile that specializes (MARTE 2011). The profile supports dependability analysis in early phases of the software life cycle. DAM definition is based on a thorough analysis of most of the approaches presented in this chapter, consequently DAM builds on them. The main objective of the work has been to homogenize terminology and concepts for different dependability aspects (*C4, C5, C6*—**DM, DT, FT, M, R, DR**) under a common consistent dependability domain model. DAM reuses best practices and choices reported in literature on model transformation to generate formal dependability analysis models. In Merseguer and Bernardi (2012),

DAM profile is used for annotating UML State Machines (UML-SM). A formal translation of this software model is proposed to obtain an analysis model (*C3*), concretely a Deterministic and Stochastic Petri Net (DSPN). The formal model is used for availability assessment (*C3*—**DA.A**).

Bozzano's proposal considers real-time embedded systems and proposes a component-based modeling method centered around (AADL 2009). The nominal (i.e., not erroneous) system behavior is specified with AADL and the erroneous behavior is modeled using the AADL Error Model Annex (AADL-EM 2006). Bozzano et al. (2011) define a formal semantics of AADL and its Error Model Annex through the use of network of event-data automata and probabilistic finite state-machines. The integration of nominal and erroneous behaviors is then obtained by product construction of the two formal models. The proposed formal semantics enables various types of system analysis, both qualitative and quantitative, including the validation of RAMS properties (*C5*—**DM.R, DM.A, DM.M, DM.S**). In particular an integrated toolset, COMPASS, has been developed which takes as input a model specified with the proposed formal semantics and a set of properties to validate (*C5,C6*). The toolset generates several artifacts as output, such as FMEA tables and probabilistic Fault trees, and the validation of the system properties are based on symbolic model checking techniques (*C3*).

Rugina's proposal is a structured and stepwise approach for building dependability models from AADL (2009) specifications. The approach is modular and allows the analyst to progressively validate the RAMS properties (*C5*—**DM.R, DM.A, DM.M, DA.S**) of complex systems characterized by different kinds of dependencies: structural, functional, those related to the fault tolerance (*C4*—**FT**) and those associated with recovery and maintenance policies (*C4*—**M**). The AADL architectural model is annotated with dependability-related information, such as faults, failure modes, repair policies, and error propagation (*C4*—**DT**) through the standardized AADL Error Model Annex (AADL-EM 2006).

A set of transformation rules are provided to automatically obtain a Generalized Stochastic Petri Net (*C3*) from AADL models amenable to dependability analysis. Such rules have been implemented in the ADAPT tool which interfaces the open source tool OSATE (2012), on the AADL side, and the SURF-2 tool (Béounes et al. 1993), on the Generalized Stochastic Petri Net side.

Chapter 8
From Software Models to Dependability Analysis Models

I hear and I forget, I see and I remember. I do and I understand.
– Chinese proverb

Abstract The objective of this chapter is to describe some proposals, of interest for practitioners, from those in Chap. 7. The focus of interest is how these proposals address the translation of a D-DSML into models for analysis. Concretely, the chapter focuses on availability and reliability proposals. We selected one from Bernardi et al., addressing availability and the other from Pai and Dugan, addressing reliability. These two approaches are applied to the case studies developed in Chap. 5. Availability analysis is then applied to the secure distributed system case study, while reliability models are obtained for the mission avionics one.

The first part of the chapter, Sect. 8.1, addresses availability assessment following the proposal in Bernardi and Merseguer (2006); Merseguer and Bernardi (2012), it was coined as Bernardi-c in Chap. 7. As explained in Chap. 7, this proposal addresses reliability, availability, maintainability, and safety. However, here we will use it only to illustrate availability assessment. The section comprehensively presents the work developed in Merseguer and Bernardi (2012) for gaining availability analysis models from software models annotated using DAM profile. The work in Merseguer and Bernardi (2012) is applied to the Message Redundancy Service (MRS) presented in Sect. 5.3.

The second part of the chapter, Sect. 8.2, addresses a proposal in the reliability field, concretely that appearing in Pai and Dugan (2002), it was coined in Chap. 7 as Pai-Dugan proposal. This proposal considers UML structural and behavioral diagrams. UML diagrams are then mapped into Dynamic Fault Trees (DFT), then enabling reliability analysis. This section presents the algorithms developed by Pai-Dugan to carry out such a mapping. Originally, these algorithms took as input not only UML diagrams but also UML extensions, proposed by Pai-Dugan, for introducing reliability properties in the software model. However, instead of

S. Bernardi et al., *Model-Driven Dependability Assessment of Software Systems*,
DOI 10.1007/978-3-642-39512-3_8, © Springer-Verlag Berlin Heidelberg 2013

such extensions we have here considered their equivalents in DAM. In fact, the original extensions of Pai-Dugan inspired some DAM stereotypes. This section ends by applying these algorithms to the mission avionic system (MAS) in Sect. 5.4. Consequently, a DFT is obtained for the MAS and reliability analysis can be carried out using the DFT.

We have considered these two proposals because they complement each other in the following aspects. Bernardi-c proposes a formal definition of UML diagrams and a mapping, based on rules, from the formalized UML diagrams to Deterministic Stochastic Petri Nets (DSPN). Instead, Pai-Dugan propose a translation based directly on algorithms. The proposals also differ in the kind of analysis model obtained: in the first case DSPN, while in the second DFT. The type of dependability analysis that can be carried out obviously depends on the target modeling formalism: actually, both DSPN and DFT support availability and reliability analysis. Here, we illustrate the Bernardi-c approach to carry out availability analysis and the Pai-Dugan approach to perform reliability analysis.

8.1 Availability Analysis and Assessment with DSPN

Bernardi-c proposal uses DAM profile, which was presented in Chap. 5, as D-DSML. Therefore, it can be applied to all kinds of UML diagrams. The formalism used for availability analysis is Deterministic and Stochastic Petri nets (DSPNs). DSPNs are introduced and formally defined in Sect. 8.1.1. Among the UML diagrams, Bernardi-c proposal addresses UML state machines (UML-SMs) for availability modeling. UML-SMs basic concepts are then formally introduced in Sect. 8.1.2. Once introduced the languages for availability modeling and analysis, UML-SMs and DSPNs, respectively, Sect. 8.1.3 proposes a formalization of the operational semantics of UML-SMs in terms of DSPN. This formal translation is the basis for developing software tools that automate the process. Finally, Sect. 8.1.4 applies this translation to the case study in Sect. 5.4, analyzes the resulting DSPN, and obtains availability figures that are used for assessment.

8.1.1 Dependability Formalism for Analysis

Stochastic Petri nets (SPNs) were defined in Chap. 6 as a formalism for modeling software systems and for analyzing their dependability. Deterministic and Stochastic Petri nets (DSPNs) (Ajmone Marsan and Chiola 1987; Lindemann 1998) is an extension of SPNs, where timed transitions can be either exponentially distributed or deterministic. The possibility of including deterministic transitions in a model makes DSPN suitable for modeling some kinds of systems, e.g., real-time systems. In the following, the definition of a DSPN is re-called.

Definition 8.1. A DSPN is a tuple $\mathscr{N} = (P, T, I, O, H, M^0, \Phi, \Lambda)$ where:

- P is the set of places,
- $T = T_I \cup T_D \cup T_E$ is the set of transitions, divided into *immediate* (T_I), *deterministic* (T_D), and *exponential* (T_E) transitions,
- $I, O, H : P \times T \rightarrow \mathbb{N}$ are, respectively, the input, output, and inhibitor arc multiplicity functions,
- $M^0 : P \rightarrow \mathbb{N}$ assigns the initial number of tokens in each place,
- $\Phi : T \rightarrow \mathbb{N}$ assigns a priority to each transition: timed transitions (deterministic and exponential) have zero priority, while immediate transitions have priority greater than zero,
- $\Lambda : T \rightarrow \mathbb{R}$ assigns to each immediate transition a weight, and to each timed transition a firing time delay. The firing time delay is a constant for a deterministic transition, while for an exponential one represents the mean value of the negative exponential distribution.

The operational semantics of a DSPN is based on the transition enabling and firing rules. A transition is *enabled* in a marking M if both the following conditions occur: (1) its input places contain at least as many tokens as the corresponding arc multiplicities and its inhibitor places contain less tokens than the corresponding arc multiplicities; (2) its priority is greater or equal to the one of the transitions t' also satisfying condition (1) in M. A transition t, enabled in marking M, may fire then leading to a new marking M', according to the equation: $M'(p) = M(p) + O(p, t) - I(p, t), p \in P$.

The UML-SM formalization considers labeled DSPNs (Donatelli and Franceschinis 1996), that is DSPNs provided with transition and place labeling functions:

Definition 8.2. A labeled DSPN (LDSPN) is a triplet $\mathscr{LN} = (\mathscr{N}, \lambda, \psi)$, where $\mathscr{N}$ is a DSPN, as in definition (8.1); $\lambda : T \rightarrow 2^{L^T}$ and $\psi : P \rightarrow 2^{L^P}$ are the transition and place labeling functions, respectively, that assign to a transition/place a set of labels (or the empty set).

The DSPN labeling feature is used both to keep track of the translation from UML SMs to *component* DSPNs and to compose the latter over either *synchronization* transitions or *event mailbox* places, to get the final dependability DSPN model. Composition of DSPNs is then a key feature in the formalization.

8.1.1.1   Composition of DSPNs

In general, more than one label can be associated with a transition (place). However, here, in the composition of two nets, at most one label per transition (place) is actually considered: with this restriction a simplified version of the composition operator originally defined by Donatelli and Franceschinis (1996) can be used.

Definition 8.3. Given two LDSPN $\mathscr{L}\mathscr{N}_1 = (\mathscr{N}_1, \lambda_1, \psi_1)$ and $\mathscr{L}\mathscr{N}_2 = (\mathscr{N}_2, \lambda_2, \psi_2)$, their composition over the sets of labels L_P and L_T results in a new LDSPN:

$$\mathscr{L}\mathscr{N} = \mathscr{L}\mathscr{N}_1 \underset{L_P, L_T}{||} \mathscr{L}\mathscr{N}_2.$$

$\mathscr{L}\mathscr{N} = (\mathscr{N}, \lambda, \psi)$ is constructed as follows.

Let $E_P = L_P \cap \psi_1(P_1) \cap \psi_2(P_2)$ and $E_T = L_T \cap \lambda_1(T_1) \cap \lambda_2(T_2)$ be the subsets of L_P and of L_T, respectively, comprising place and transition labels that are common to the two LDSPNs, P_1^l (T_1^l) be the set of places (transitions) of $\mathscr{L}\mathscr{N}_1$ that are labeled l and $P_1^{E_P}$ ($T_1^{E_T}$) be the set of all places (transitions) in $\mathscr{L}\mathscr{N}_1$ that are labeled with a label in E_P (E_T). Same definitions apply to $\mathscr{L}\mathscr{N}_2$.

- $P = P_1 \backslash P_1^{E_P} \cup P_2 \backslash P_2^{E_P} \cup \bigcup_{l \in E_P} \{P_1^l \times P_2^l\}$,
- $T = T_1 \backslash T_1^{E_T} \cup T_2 \backslash T_2^{E_T} \cup \bigcup_{l \in E_T} \{T_1^l \times T_2^l\}$,
- Functions $F \in \{I(), O(), H()\}$ are equal to:

$$F(p,t) = \begin{cases} F_1(p,t) & \text{if } p \in P_1 \backslash P_1^{E_P}, t \in T_1 \backslash T_1^{E_T} \\ F_1(p,t_1) & \text{if } p \in P_1 \backslash P_1^{E_P}, t \equiv (t_1, t_2) \in \bigcup_{l \in E_T} \{T_1^l \times T_2^l\} \\ F_1(p_1,t) & \text{if } p \equiv (p_1, p_2) \in \bigcup_{l \in E_P} \{P_1^l \times P_2^l\}, t \in T_1 \backslash T_1^{E_T} \\ F_2(p,t) & \text{if } p \in P_2 \backslash P_2^{E_P}, t \in T_2 \backslash T_2^{E_T} \\ F_2(p,t_2) & \text{if } p \in P_2 \backslash P_2^{E_P}, t \equiv (t_1, t_2) \in \bigcup_{l \in E_T} \{T_1^l \times T_2^l\} \\ F_2(p_2,t) & \text{if } p \equiv (p_1, p_2) \in \bigcup_{l \in E_P} \{P_1^l \times P_2^l\}, t \in T_2 \backslash T_2^{E_T} \\ \min\{F_1(p_1,t_1), F_2(p_2,t_2)\} & \text{if } p \equiv (p_1, p_2) \in \bigcup_{l \in E_P} \{P_1^l \times P_2^l\}, \\ & t \equiv (t_1, t_2) \in \bigcup_{l \in E_T} \{T_1^l \times T_2^l\} \end{cases}$$

- Functions $F \in \{\Phi(), \Lambda()\}$ are equal to:

$$F(t) = \begin{cases} F_1(t) & \text{if } t \in T_1 \backslash T_1^{E_T} \\ F_2(t) & \text{if } t \in T_2 \backslash T_2^{E_T} \\ F_1(t_1) & \text{if } t \equiv (t_1, t_2) \in \bigcup_{l \in E_T} \{T_1^l \times T_2^l\} \end{cases}$$

- The initial marking function is equal to:

$$M^0(p) = \begin{cases} M_1^0(p) & \text{if } p \in P_1 \backslash P_1^{E_P} \\ M_2^0(p) & \text{if } p \in P_2 \backslash P_2^{E_P} \\ M_1^0(p_1) + M_2^0(p_2) & \text{if } p \equiv (p_1, p_2) \in \bigcup_{l \in E_P} \{P_1^l \times P_2^l\} \end{cases}$$

- The labeling functions for places and transitions are, respectively, equal to:

$$\psi(x) = \begin{cases} \psi_1(x) & \text{if } x \in P_1 \setminus P_1^{E_P} \\ \psi_2(x) & \text{if } x \in P_2 \setminus P_2^{E_P} \\ \psi_1(p_1) \cup \psi_2(p_2) & \text{if } x \equiv (p_1, p_2) \in \bigcup_{l \in E_P} \{P_1^l \times P_2^l\} \end{cases}$$

$$\lambda(x) = \begin{cases} \lambda_1(x) & \text{if } x \in T_1 \setminus T_1^{E_T} \\ \lambda_2(x) & \text{if } x \in T_2 \setminus T_2^{E_T} \\ \lambda_1(t_1) \cup \lambda_2(t_2) & \text{if } x \equiv (t_1, t_2) \in \bigcup_{l \in E_T} \{T_1^l \times T_2^l\} \end{cases}$$

Definition 8.4. Being the composition associative with respect to place superposition, we use it as an *n*-operand by writing:

$$\mathscr{L}\mathscr{N} = ||_{L_P, \emptyset}^{k=1,...,K} \mathscr{L}\mathscr{N}_k$$

8.1.2   UML State Machines Basic Concepts

UML state machines (UML-SM) can be used to specify behavior of software components (or objects) (UML2 2011). In the following we introduce the basic concepts of UML-SM according to UML2 (2011). This formal definition has been developed in Merseguer and Bernardi (2012), more advanced modeling elements for UML-SM were formalized in Merseguer (2003).

A UML-SM basically consists of *states* and *transitions*. States model situations during which some invariant condition holds, such as the component performing some computational *activity* or waiting for some external *event* to occur. Transitions between states (*external* transitions), labeled as *event/action*, represent how a component in a source state reacts upon receiving an *event*, so performing an *action*, and then entering the target state. The action can also be the sending of a new event to other component. Transitions that do not specify an event are named *completion* transitions, they are implicitly triggered by a *completion event* and fire as soon as the *activity* in the state completes. States can contain *entry/exit* actions and *internal* transitions; entry (exit) actions are executed when the state is entered (exited), internal transitions do not cause a state change and, when triggered, they fire without exiting nor entering the source state.

Definition 8.5. A state machine is a tuple:

$$\mathscr{S}\mathscr{M} = (\Sigma, A_{entry}, A_{exit}, A_{do}, \Theta, E_{trigger}, A_{effect}, source, target)$$

- $\Sigma = \Sigma_{ini} \cup \Sigma_{final} \cup \Sigma_{simple}$ is the set of initial ($|\Sigma_{ini}| = 1$), final (Σ_{final}) and simple (Σ_{simple}) states;
- $A_{entry} : \Sigma \hookrightarrow \mathscr{L}_a$ assigns to a state an optional entry action;
- $A_{exit} : \Sigma \hookrightarrow \mathscr{L}_a$ assigns to a state an optional exit action;
- $A_{do} : \Sigma \hookrightarrow \mathscr{L}_a$ assigns to a state an optional activity;
- $\Theta \subseteq \Sigma \times \Sigma$ is the set of transitions including external, completion and internal transitions, i.e., $\Theta = \Theta_{out} \cup \Theta_\lambda \cup \Theta_{int}$;
- $E_{trigger} : \Theta \to \mathscr{E}$ assigns to each transition a trigger event;
- $A_{effect} : \Theta \hookrightarrow \mathscr{L}_a \bigcup \{\mathscr{SM}_i.ev\}$ assigns to a transition an optional action or the dispatch of an event to other SM $\mathscr{SM}_i$, $ev \in \mathscr{E} \setminus \{\lambda\}$;
- $source : \Theta \to \Sigma$, where $\forall (s, t, s) \in \Theta : source((s, t, s')) = s$; and
- $target : \Theta \to \Sigma$, where $\forall (s, t, s) \in \Theta : target((s, t, s')) = s'$.

where $\mathscr{E}$ is the set of system events that includes the completion event λ and $\mathscr{L}_a$ is the set of system actions.

Transition guards are not explicitly translated in this approach. However, they can be easily ovecome following indication in Merseguer (2003), where a probabilistic interpretation of guards is made.

Unfortunately, UML does not provide sufficient capabilities neither for timing/probabilistic specification, which is a fundamental feature in systems quantitative evaluation nor for dependability modeling. We then provide a formal definition of a SM enriched with those MARTE-DAM annotations which enable the derivation of a dependability LDSPN model.

Definition 8.6. A MARTE-DAM profiled state machine is a tuple:

$$\widehat{\mathscr{SM}} = \langle \mathscr{SM}, pool, demand, prob, ft\_rate, failure, \mathscr{L}_{pred} \rangle$$

where:

- $\mathscr{SM}$ is a state machine, as in Definition 8.5, where the trigger event function is refined to include the (local) fault events, i.e., $\hat{E}_{trigger} : \Theta \to \mathscr{E} \cup \mathscr{E}_{ft}^{\mathscr{SM}}$;
- $pool : \{s_i\} \to \mathbb{N}$ is a function that assigns to a single state, i.e., $\{s_i\} \subseteq \Sigma$, the initial number of components/objects in such a state;
- $demand : A_{do} \hookrightarrow \mathbb{R} \times \{const, mean\}$ is a partial function that assigns to a do-activity the host demand required to execute it, together with the type of statistical qualifier (i.e., a constant value or a mean value);
- $prob : \Theta \hookrightarrow \mathbb{R}$ is a partial function that assigns to a transition the probability of executing it.
- $ft\_rate : \mathscr{E}_{ft}^{\mathscr{SM}} \to \mathbb{R}$ is a function that assigns to each fault event its occurrence rate;
- $failure : \Sigma \to \{true, false\}$ is a function that assigns a boolean value to each state, the $true$ value identifies the failure state;
- $\mathscr{L}_{pred} = \{(type, var)\}$ is a set of pairs, where the first element $type$ is the type of dependability metric (i.e., MTTF, failure distribution or rate) and the second one $var \in \mathbb{R}$ is the corresponding output parameter variable.

8.1.3 *Formal Translation of UML State Machines into DSPN*

The operational semantics of a UML-SM, informally described in UML2 (2011), is herein interpreted by the formal DSPN operational semantics.

Let us assume the system made of n MARTE-DAM annotated SMs that cooperate by exchanging events, $Sys =< \{\widehat{\mathscr{SM}_i}\}_{i=1}^{n}, \mathscr{E}, \mathscr{L}_a >$, where $\mathscr{E}$ is the set of events (including the completion event λ) and $\mathscr{L}_a$ the set of actions.

8.1.3.1 Translation of Simple States

Four different translations for a UML-SM state are given in Fig. 8.1a–d. They depend on whether the state includes activity and/or completion transition. The figure depicts interface transitions, those in pale gray, they are used to compose this model with the models for Θ_{int} (interfaces $t_{end\_int}, t_{int1}, t_{int2}$), Θ_{out} (interfaces t_{out1}, t_{out2}), and Θ_λ (interface t_{ce}). Figure 8.1e, f are variations of the previous ones to show the case when there is no entry action. Although more cases exist, they are just variations of the first four, all of them are formalized below.

These LDSPNs give a formal interpretation of the informal execution semantics UML describes for a state. So, a token in ini_S represents the entrance in the state that is always followed by the execution of the *entry* action. When the do-activity $A_{do}(S)$ exists, then the timed transition t_{do} will be the next to be executed. Note that the exit action $A_{exit}(S)$ is not represented in Fig. 8.1 since it comes after the execution of an external transition.

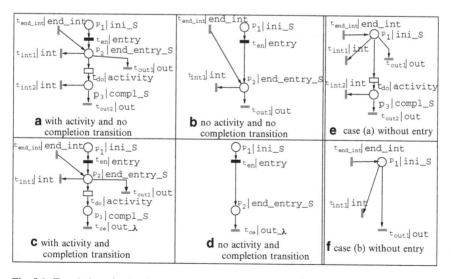

Fig. 8.1 Translation of a simple state

The LDSPN in Fig. 8.1c models a variation of (a) to cope with completion transitions. The only difference is that interface transitions t_{int2} and t_{out2} are omitted, so internal and external transitions cannot take place after the activity. Indeed, transition t_{ce}, whose firing represents the triggering of the completion event, forces the exit of the state. Figure 8.1d has no interfaces for external and internal transitions since they are not allowed for states without activity but with completion transition.

Let $\chi, \overline{\chi}$ be the nonempty-set and empty-set indicator functions, respectively.[1] Then, the sets of places and transitions of the basic LDSPN $\mathscr{BN}_S$, which interprets the state $S \in \Sigma$, are defined as follows:

$$P_{\mathscr{BN}_S} = \{p_1\} \cup \chi(A_{entry}(S)) \cdot \{p_2\} \cup \chi(A_{do}(S)) \cdot \{p_3\};$$

$$T_{\mathscr{BN}_S} = \chi(A_{entry}(S)) \cdot \{t_{en}\} \cup \chi(A_{do}(S)) \cdot \{t_{do}\} \cup \chi(\Theta_{\lambda_S}) \cdot \{t_{ce}\} \cup$$
$$\chi(\Theta_{int_S})\Big[\hat{\chi} \cdot \{t_{int1}, t_{end\_int}\} \cup \Big(\chi(A_{do}(S)) \cdot \overline{\chi}(\Theta_{\lambda_S})\Big) \cdot \{t_{int2}\}\Big] \cup$$
$$\chi(\Theta_{out_S})\Big[\hat{\chi} \cdot \{t_{out1}\} \cup \Big(\chi(A_{do}(S)) \cdot \overline{\chi}(\Theta_{\lambda_S})\Big) \cdot \{t_{out2}\}\Big],$$

where $\Theta_{out_S}, \Theta_{int_S}$, and Θ_{λ_S} are the sets of external, internal, and completion transitions of S, respectively, and $\hat{\chi} = \chi(A_{do}(S)) + \overline{\chi}(A_{do}(S)) \cdot \overline{\chi}(\Theta_{\lambda_S})$. The LDSPN has no inhibitor arcs, i.e., $H_{\mathscr{BN}_S}(p,t) \equiv 0$, while the input and output functions are defined as:

$$I_{\mathscr{BN}_S}(p_1, t) = \begin{cases} 1 & \text{if } t \in \chi(A_{entry}(S)) \cdot \{t_{en}\} \cup \overline{\chi}(A_{entry}(S)) \cdot \Big(\chi(A_{do}(S)) \cdot \{t_{do}\} \cup \\ & \hat{\chi} \cdot \chi(\Theta_{int_S}) \cdot \{t_{int1}\} \cup \hat{\chi} \cdot \chi(\Theta_{out_S}) \cdot \{t_{out1}\} \cup \overline{\chi}(A_{do}(S)) \cdot \chi(\Theta_{\lambda_S}) \cdot \{t_{ce}\}\Big) \\ 0 & \text{otherwise} \end{cases}$$

$$I_{\mathscr{BN}_S}(p_2, t) = \begin{cases} 1 & \text{if } t \in \chi(A_{entry}(S)) \cdot \Big(\chi(A_{do}(S)) \cdot \{t_{do}\} \cup \hat{\chi} \cdot \chi(\Theta_{int_S}) \cdot \{t_{int1}\} \cup \\ & \hat{\chi} \cdot \chi(\Theta_{out_S}) \cdot \{t_{out1}\} \cup \overline{\chi}(A_{do}(S)) \cdot \chi(\Theta_{\lambda_S}) \cdot \{t_{ce}\}\Big) \\ 0 & \text{otherwise} \end{cases}$$

$$I_{\mathscr{BN}_S}(p_3, t) = \begin{cases} 1 & \text{if } t \in \chi(A_{do}(S)) \cdot \Big(\chi(\Theta_{int_S}) \cdot \overline{\chi}(\Theta_{\lambda_S}) \cdot \{t_{int2}\} \cup \\ & \chi(\Theta_{out_S}) \cdot \overline{\chi}(\Theta_{\lambda_S}) \cdot \{t_{out2}\} \cup \chi(\Theta_{\lambda_S}) \cdot \{t_{ce}\}\Big) \\ 0 & \text{otherwise} \end{cases}$$

---

[1]
$$\chi(Q) = \begin{cases} 0 & \text{if } Q = \emptyset \\ 1 & \text{if } Q \neq \emptyset \end{cases} \quad \text{and} \quad \overline{\chi}(Q) = 1 - \chi(Q).$$

$$O_{\mathscr{B}\mathscr{N}_S}(p_1, t) = \begin{cases} 1 & \text{if } t \in \overline{\chi}(A_{entry}(S)) \cdot \chi(\Theta_{ints}) \cdot \hat{\chi} \cdot \{t_{end\_int}\} \\ 0 & \text{otherwise} \end{cases}$$

$$O_{\mathscr{B}\mathscr{N}_S}(p_2, t) = \begin{cases} 1 & \text{if } t \in \chi(A_{entry}(S)) \cdot \left(\{t_{en}\} \cup \chi(\Theta_{ints}) \cdot \hat{\chi} \cdot \{t_{end\_int}\}\right) \\ 0 & \text{otherwise} \end{cases}$$

$$O_{\mathscr{B}\mathscr{N}_S}(p_3, t) = \begin{cases} 1 & \text{if } t \in \chi(A_{do}(S)) \cdot \{t_{do}\} \\ 0 & \text{otherwise} \end{cases}$$

The initial marking $M^0_{\mathscr{B}\mathscr{N}_S}$ and the transition delay $\Lambda_{\mathscr{B}\mathscr{N}_S}$ functions are derived from the formal counterparts *pool* and *demand*, respectively, of the MARTE-DAM annotations (see Definition 8.6). In particular, as shown in Fig. 8.3 (top), the *pool* function corresponds to the *poolSize* tag of the *PARunTInstance* stereotyped state, while the *demand* function corresponds to the *hostDemand* tag of the *GaStep* stereotyped do-activity:

$$p \in P_{\mathscr{B}\mathscr{N}_S} \mapsto M^0_{\mathscr{B}\mathscr{N}_S}(p) = \begin{cases} pool(S) & \text{if } \psi_{\mathscr{B}\mathscr{N}_S}(p) = ini\_S \\ 0 & \text{otherwise} \end{cases}$$

$$t \in T_{\mathscr{B}\mathscr{N}_S} \mapsto \Lambda_{\mathscr{B}\mathscr{N}_S}(t) = \begin{cases} \pi_1(demand(A_{do}(S))) & \text{if } \lambda_{\mathscr{B}\mathscr{N}_S}(t) = A_{do}(S) \\ 1 & \text{otherwise} \end{cases}$$

where π_1 (π_2) is the left (right) projection function. Observe that the timed transition of the LDSPN modeling the do-activity $A_{do}(S)$ will be either deterministic or exponential according to whether $\pi_2(demand(A_{do}(S)))$ is equal to either *const* or *mean*, respectively. A weight equal to one is assigned to the rest of transitions (immediate ones). The priority function $\Phi_{\mathscr{B}\mathscr{N}_S}$ assigns zero priority to the timed transition, representing the do-activity, and one priority to the immediate transitions.

The labeling functions for places and transitions are defined as:

$$\psi_{\mathscr{B}\mathscr{N}_S}(p) = \begin{cases} ini\_\mathscr{S} & \text{if } p = p_1 \\ end\_entry\_\mathscr{S} & \text{if } p = p_2 \\ compl\_\mathscr{S} & \text{if } p = p_3 \end{cases} \quad \lambda_{\mathscr{B}\mathscr{N}_S}(t) = \begin{cases} A_{entry}(S) & \text{if } t = t_{en} \\ A_{do}(S) & \text{if } t = t_{do} \\ end\_int & \text{if } t = t_{end\_int} \\ int & \text{if } t = \{t_{int1}, t_{int2}\} \\ out & \text{if } t = \{t_{out1}, t_{out2}\} \\ \lambda_S & \text{if } t = t_{ce} \end{cases}$$

Finally, we remark that initial and final states match the translation herein presented. Consider that in UML final states have no actions neither external nor internal transitions, while initial ones only own an external transition labeled by the event "create."

8.1.3.2   Translation of Transitions

Figure 8.2 proposes a translation for transitions, it formally interprets the informal execution semantics UML describes for them. In Fig. 8.2a, $t \in \Theta_{out_{s_1}}$ with $source(t) = s_1$, $target(t) = s_2$, $A_{effect}(t) = action$, $E_{trigger}(t) = evx$ and $exit = A_{exit}(s_1)$. The execution semantics of the LDSPN states that when the UML-SM is executing in s_1 and receives event evx, it is accepted and if $action$ and/or $exit$ exist, they are executed, finally s_2 is entered. Note that if evx reaches the UML-SM when it is not executing s_1, the event is lost. So, t_1 has priority over t_3; in the final composed model (8.1), t_1 will have another input place to indeed represent execution of s_1. It is worth noting that the effect of a transition can be a send event to other SM, e.g., $A_{effect}(t) = \mathscr{SM}_i.evy$. The dotted square, in Fig. 8.2, offers the corresponding translation, in this case the label of t_2 will be $\mathscr{SM}_i.evy$. Figure 8.2a is also valid for an external transition t where $source(t) = target(t)$. Then, Fig. 8.2b shows that the only difference between an internal transition and an external with same target and source is that the $exit$ action of the state is not executed by the former. A formalization of these LDSPNs can be obtained similarly as the one developed for the basic state.

As commented in Sect. 8.1.2 transition guards are not explicitly translated. In a well-defined SM, guards should be specified in the case of outgoing transitions leaving the same source state, either external transitions characterized by the same trigger or completion transitions. On the other hand, from the dependability modeling point of view, a probabilistic interpretation of guards can be given by resorting MARTE-DAM annotations. In particular, the SM transitions with guards are stereotyped as *GaStep* and the tagged-value *prob* is used to specify the probability of their execution. The MRS case study of Chap. 5 provides an example of such annotation (see Fig. 5.9—SM of the Redundancy Manager). Such probability value is eventually mapped onto the weight of the LDSPN transition representing the trigger event (labeled e_evx) or the completion event (labeled out_λ).

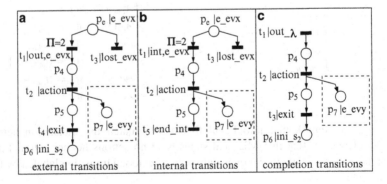

Fig. 8.2 Translation of transitions

8.1.3.3 Composition of Simple States and Transitions

Given a state S with h internal transitions and l external/completion transitions, we get $h+l$ LDSPN models plus the $\mathscr{BN}_S$ that need to be combined to get the LDSPN $\mathscr{LN}_S$. We apply the LDSPN composition operator in definition 8.3.

Let $Lev^P = \{e\_evx, \forall evx \in \mathscr{E} \setminus \{\lambda\}\}$ and $Lstate^P = \{ini\_target, \forall target \in \Sigma\}$. We first compose sub-models of internal and external/completion transitions:

$$INT = \underset{Lev^P,\emptyset}{\overset{i=1,...,h}{||}} INT_i, \quad OUT = \underset{Lstate^P \cup Lev^P,\emptyset}{\overset{j=1,...,l}{||}} OUT_j.$$

Then, the LDSPN $\mathscr{LN}_S$ is obtained by:

$$\mathscr{LN}_S = (INT \underset{Lev^P,\emptyset}{||} OUT) \underset{Lev^P,Ltr^T}{||} \mathscr{BN}_S. \tag{8.1}$$

where $Ltr^T = \{int, end\_int, out, out\_\lambda\}$. This first composition step produces an isolated LDSPN model representing a single SM state plus its outgoing transitions. An exemplification is given in Fig. 8.3 (bottom-left), where the subnet of the *Main* LDSPN model included in the dotted rectangle represents the *Wait4Info* state together with its outgoing transition (Fig. 8.3, top-left).

8.1.3.4 Composition of State Machines

Definition 8.7. The LDSPN that interprets the UML-SM $\mathscr{SM}$ is given by:

$$\mathscr{LN}_{\mathscr{SM}} = \underset{Lev^P \cup Lstate^P,\emptyset}{\overset{s \in \Sigma}{||}} \mathscr{LN}_s.$$

The second composition step produces an LDSPN model representing the whole SM. In the example, the "isolated" LDSPN models *Main* and *Process* of Fig. 8.3 (bottom) are derived from the two homonym SMs of Fig. 8.3 (top). By "isolated," we mean that each LDSPN model owns its event places $e\_create, e\_result, e\_destroy$.

Trigger events of a SM transition can be stereotyped as *DaFaultGenerator*. The function ft_rate of $\widehat{\mathscr{SM}}$, which is the formal counterpart of the MARTE-DAM annotation associated with the stereotyped event, is used to create new LDSPNs. Figure 8.3 (bottom, right) shows the fault generator LDSPN model derived from the MARTE-DAM annotation associated with the *ft* trigger event of the SM Process (Fig. 8.3—top, right). We assume that fault events are local to $\widehat{\mathscr{SM}}$, then, for each fault event $f \in \mathscr{E}_{ft}^{\mathscr{SM}}$ a fault generator LDSPN is defined. The fault generator LDSPNs, which create fault event occurrences, are included in the composition to get the LDSPN of $\widehat{\mathscr{SM}}$.

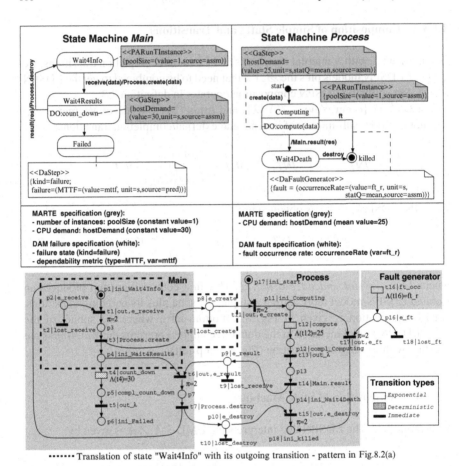

······ Translation of state "Wait4Info" with its outgoing transition - pattern in Fig.8.2(a)

Fig. 8.3 MARTE-DAM annotated SMs (top) and the corresponding LDSPN $\mathscr{LN}_{Sys}$ (bottom)

Definition 8.8. The LDSPN that interprets the UML-SM $\widehat{\mathscr{SM}}$ is given by:

$$\mathscr{LN}_{\widehat{\mathscr{SM}}} = \mathscr{LN}_{\mathscr{SM}} \underset{Lft^P,\emptyset}{||} FT \qquad (8.2)$$

where Lft^P is the set of place labels of fault events, i.e., $Lft^P = \{e\_f, \forall f \in \mathscr{E}_{ft}^{\mathscr{SM}}\}$, $\mathscr{LN}_{\mathscr{SM}}$ is the LDSPN of $\mathscr{SM}$ (Definition 8.7) and FT is the LDSPN including all fault generators associated with $\widehat{\mathscr{SM}}$, i.e.:

$$FT = \underset{\emptyset,\emptyset}{\overset{i=1,...,|\mathscr{E}_{ft}^{\mathscr{SM}}|}{||}} \mathscr{LN}_f^i.$$

The third composition step produces an LDSPN model representing the SM together with the fault assumptions. In the example, the LDSPN models *Process* and *Fault generator* of Fig. 8.3 (bottom, right) are connected by merging the fault event place *e_ft*.

8.1.3.5 Composition of the Final System

Definition 8.9. Given a system *Sys* made of n UML-SMs that cooperate by exchanging events and being $Lev_{Sys}^P = \{e\_evx, \forall evx \in \mathcal{E} \setminus \{\lambda\}\}$, the LDSPN that interprets *Sys* is given by:

$$\mathscr{LN}_{Sys} = \mathop{\|}_{Lev_{Sys}^P, \emptyset}^{i=1..n} \mathscr{LN}_{\widehat{\mathscr{SM}_i}}.$$

The final composition step produces an LDSPN model representing the system consisting of n MARTE-DAM annotated SMs which communicate via mailboxes. In the example of Fig. 8.3 (bottom), as a result of this step, the LDSPN models *Main* and *Process* are connected by merging the common event places *e_create, e_result, e_destroy*.

8.1.3.6 Mapping of Dependability Metrics

Besides the system fault assumptions, failure assumptions and dependability metrics can be specified. Concretely, failure assumptions specify the failure states of the system, those representing an interruption of a system service. Their definition depends on the system requirements and, when several services are specified, different (service) failure modes can be assumed.

The MARTE-DAM annotation, attached to the SM state stereotyped as *DaStep* (Fig. 8.3, top—SM Main), is formalized through the *failure*, $\mathscr{L}_{pred}$ features of $\widehat{\mathscr{SM}}$ (Definition 8.6). In particular, *failure* is used to identify the SM failure state and $\mathscr{L}_{pred}$ to specify the dependability metrics to be computed.

Such annotation enables the formal definition of dependability metrics on the LDSPN model $\mathscr{LN}_{Sys}$ representing the final system (Definition 8.9) in terms of reward functions. A reward function (Chap. 6, Sect. 6.3) partitions the set of reachable markings of $\mathscr{LN}_{Sys}$ into two subsets of markings: the set of system operational states and the set of the system failure states. Then, the problem of translating the failure specification of $\widehat{\mathscr{SM}}$ into LDSPN dependability metrics boils down in:

1. Defining a mapping of an SM failure state onto the subset of markings representing the failure states and,
2. For each pair $(type, var) \in \mathscr{L}_{pred}$, assigning to the output parameter var the corresponding expression (which returns a real value), according to the *type* of dependability metric.

Further details about the mapping of predefined dependability metrics are provided in Merseguer and Bernardi (2012).

8.1.4   Example of Availability Analysis and Assessment

As an example of availability analysis we recall the case study proposed in Sect. 5.3 of Chap. 5. The case study is a MRS, which introduced intrusion-tolerant capabilities for distributed systems. A Use Case Diagram (Fig. 5.7) and a Sequence Diagram (Fig. 5.8) described the main scenario of the system. The UML-SMs (Fig. 5.9) detail the behavior of the system components: payloads, redundancy manager, and message replicator.

MARTE-DAM was used to equip the UML specification with dependability input parameters and measures in MRS. In particular, a measure of service steady-state availability was defined by the modeler as an expression (Use Case Diagram of Fig. 5.7). Such a metric now guides the quantitative analysis and the assessment of the MRS case study. In general, the analysis aims to evaluate numerically the dependability and performance measures, specified in the UML annotated model, and to interpret the results in the application domain. On the other hand, the assessment provides an indication on how to change the design or set the service parameters to guarantee that the system meets its dependability requirements. In MRS, measures of interest are service steady-state availability, response time, and the rate of filtered messages. The latter is used to evaluate the robustness of the MRS under different payloads fault assumptions. The objective of the MRS assessment is to find a (range of) value(s) to be assigned to the time-out duration parameter to ensure a good trade-off between the service availability level (dependability measure) and the service response time (performance measure).

A DSPN model of the MRS is shown in Fig. 8.4. The DSPN sub-models representing the three UML-SMs in Fig. 5.9 (i.e., Message Replicator, Redundancy Manager, and Payload) as well as the fault generator sub-model have been generated applying the translation presented in the previous subsections.

Besides, there is a DSPN sub-model representing the closed workload. All DSPN sub-models are characterized by interface places, labeled as e_ev, that represent mailboxes of events. The DSPN model of the system has been produced by merging the interface places with matching labels of the different DSPN sub-models, as proposed in Definition 8.9.

The DSPN model of the closed workload was manually derived since it relies upon the workload annotation in the SD of Fig. 5.8. Observe that there is not an objective obstacle to a formal transformation since the latter boils in defining a DSPN model similarly to the fault generator one and considering it in the final composition step, defined in Definition 8.9. Some details of interest regarding this manual derivation are discussed in the following.

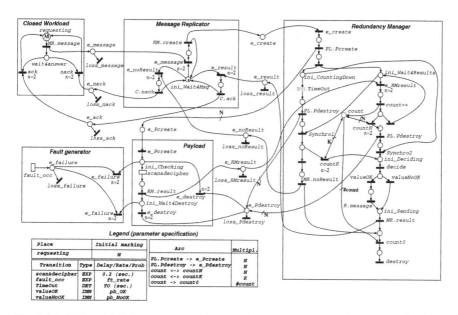

Fig. 8.4 DSPN model of the message redundancy service

The closed workload DSPN sub-model is derived from *GaWorkloadEvent* MARTE-DAM annotation, which appears in the SD in Fig. 5.8. The initial population variable *M* has been used to define the initial marking *M* of place *requesting*. Transition *MR.message* generates tokens (events of the kind message) for the message replicator to start the tasks of the MRS. When the answer (ack or nack) arrives, a new token is placed in *requesting*, which guarantees a constant number of requests in the system as required by the closed workload.

The DSPN model is characterized by several parameters, summarized in legend of Fig. 8.4. In particular, transition firing delays are defined by MARTE *host-Demand* tagged-values attached to UML-SM do-activities GaSteps: mean values are mapped to mean firing delays of exponential transitions (e.g., *scan&decipher* in payload DSPN sub-model) and constant values are mapped to firing delays of deterministic transitions (e.g., *TimeOut* in redundancy manager DSPN sub-model). UML-SM guarded transitions are translated considering a probabilistic interpretation, as proposed in Merseguer (2003). In the MRS, they appear in the redundancy manager UML-SM, transitions with guards [value!=OK] and [value=OK] are then mapped onto a free-choice conflict between DSPN immediate transitions *valueNoOK* and *valueOK* (redundancy manager DSPN sub-model), whose weights (*pb_NoOK* and *pb_OK*, respectively) are defined considering MARTE GaStep tagged-value prob (i.e., the variables pb_NoOK, pb_OK).

According to the objective of the analysis, the measures of interest are the service steady-state availability and response time, and the rate of filtered messages. The *steady-state availability* is a dependability measure and represents the percentage of times the system is able to provide the MRS when requested. The service is correctly performed when either the message is eventually delivered to the receiver or the message is filtered by the redundancy manager (since it is considered corrupted). The service downtime corresponds to each time redundancy manager is not able to decide after a time-out, due to an insufficient number of results (less than three) provided by the payloads. The measure can be computed as the ratio between the throughput of the GaSteps `result(value)/Client.ack()` and `message(receiver,file)/RM.create(receiver,file)` (see the MARTE annotations in Fig. 5.7—UCD—and in Fig. 5.9—Message Replicator SM). In the DSPN model (Fig. 8.4—MR DSPN sub-model), this measure is mapped onto the ratio between the throughputs of transition *e_result*—that represents the reception of the service outcome from the RM, i.e., either delivered or filtered— and transition *e_message*—that models the reception of the service request from the client.

The *response time* is a performance measure and corresponds to the mean time from client request to the reception of a positive ack. It is defined, by applying Little's operational law (Denning and Buzen 1978), as the ratio between the workload M and the throughput of the GaStep `result(value)/Client.ack()` (see MARTE annotations in Fig. 5.8 and in Fig. 5.9—Message Replicator SM). In the DSPN model (Fig. 8.4), the measure is mapped onto the ratio between the initial marking of place *requesting* and the throughput of transition *e_result* (MR DSPN sub-model).

Finally, the *rate of filtered messages* is a performance measure that gives the number of incorrect messages per second detected by the redundancy manager, and then not delivered to the final destination. It provides an indication on the robustness of the MRS and it is specified as the throughput of the GaStep `[value != OK]` of the redundancy manager UML-SM (Fig. 5.9). In the DSPN model (Fig. 8.4— RM DSPN sub-model), the measure is mapped onto the throughput of transition *valueNoOK*.

8.1.4.1 Assessment of the MRS

The MRS case study was deeply assessed by Bernardi et al. (2011c), in the following those results are recalled. The DSPN model is used to compute by simulation the measures of interest. The GreatSPN (2002) tool was used, concretely, its steady-state discrete-event simulator. The measures were computed setting a confidence interval of 99 % and an accuracy of 15 %. The simulated DSPN model assumed an implementation of the MRS with a 4-redundancy level ($N = 4$), a 1-fault tolerance level ($K = 3$), and one client requesting the MRS ($M = 1$).

Considering first, the steady-state availability and response time measures, sensitivity analysis was carried out by varying the values of the fault occurrence rate (*ft_rate* $\in [1ft/s, 1ft/yr]$) and the time-out duration ($TO \in [0.1s, 1s]$). Probability of invalid message detection was set to $pb\_NoOK = 0.5$ ($pb\_OK = 1 - pb\_NoOK$); indeed, this parameter does not affect the measures above. Figure 8.5a shows the steady-state availability of the MRS versus the time-out duration and the payloads fault occurrence rate. Considering that the mean time to scan and decipher the message by a payload is set to 0.2 s, we can observe that the longer the time-out duration is, the greater the system availability; and it becomes closer to 100 % when $TO \geq 0.5$ s. Indeed, the longer the time-out duration is, the lower the probability of false alarms becomes, i.e., a time-out expires but no failure has actually occurred in the payloads. On the other hand, when setting a time-out value and moving along the fault occurrence rate axis in Fig. 8.5a, the curve is basically a constant line. This fact leads to the conclusion that the fault occurrence rate in the payloads does not significantly affect the service availability. Certainly, this suggests to set the time-out TO parameter to a value greater than 0.5 s, in order to guarantee a service availability of at least 91 %.

Figure 8.5b shows the response time of the MRS versus the time-out duration and the payloads fault occurrence rate. At first sight, the result seems to be counter-intuitive: the longer is the time-out duration w.r.t. the time required by the payloads to scan and decipher a message (0.2 s), the smaller should be the response time: indeed, no false alarms should occur and the response time should be influenced only by the time to send a positive ack. Nevertheless, the computed results can be explained considering the possibility of payload failures. Indeed, when several payloads concurrently fail, the system can send a (negative) ack to the client only after the time-out expiration. So, under payload fault assumption, the longer is the time-out duration the longer it takes to send a final response to the client, therefore increasing the overall (positive) response time. On the other hand, the observed metric is influenced by the payloads fault occurrence rate when the time-out duration is greater than 0.6 s. The assessment suggests to set the TO parameter to a value less than 0.6 s to guarantee a reasonable response time (i.e., less than 0.4 s), independently of the assumption on payload fault occurrence rate. Then, considering both the dependability and performance requirements (under the stated

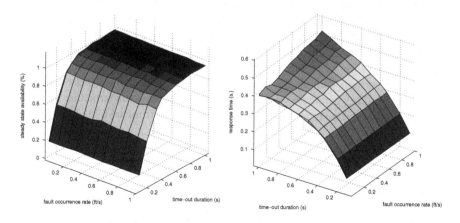

Fig. 8.5 (A) Availability, (R) response time

assumptions for redundancy and fault tolerance levels, and the system workload), the optimal assessed values for the time-out duration should fall in the interval $[0.5s, 0.6s]$.

Unlike the aforementioned measures, the rate of filtered messages is affected by the *pb_NoOK* parameter: so we have conducted sensitivity analysis with *pb_NoOK* ranging between $[0.1, 0.9]$ and under different fault occurrence rate assumptions. As a result of the time-out duration previously assessed, the *TO* parameter has been set to 0.5 s, since this value provides a good trade-off between the service availability and response time. Figure 8.6 shows the measure versus the probability of incorrect message detection and the payloads fault occurrence rate. As expected, the rate of filtered messages is in direct proportion to the *pb_NoOK* parameter, i.e., it increases when the probability of detecting an incorrect message becomes higher. We can observe, also, that the higher the fault occurrence rate is, the lower the rate of filtered messages: the number of filtered messages/second decreases by about 45 % when the fault occurrence rate changes from one fault/year to one fault/second. This result is due to the impossibility of deciding on the message integrity because of payload failures; indeed, since the payloads fail more frequently, Redundancy Manager does not receive enough results from the payloads to formulate a decision. In this case, it is not possible to assess how to set the parameters for optimizing the number of filtered messages, because such parameters (i.e., probability of incorrect message and fault occurrence rate) are not managed by the analysis.

8.2   Reliability Analysis with DFT

Pai and Dugan (2002) propose an approach to derive DFT from UML-based specifications. The latter include UML extensions (i.e., stereotypes and tagged-values) to account for dependability input parameters, system redundancies, and reconfiguration policies. In Chap. 5, we have presented the case study which was used by Pai and Dugan (2002) to exemplify their transformation approach. In particular, we have described the UML specifications of the case study, enriched with DAM annotations which replace the ones originally proposed by the authors. Figure 8.7 shows the transformation process, where the *parser* extracts the logical model of the system with all the information about the system structure and the embedded reliability parameters and produces an encoded system structure. Then, a *synthesis algorithm* generates the DFT from the latter and from the UML behavioral specifications.

8.2.1   The Parser

The parser was customized for the Rational Rose CASE tool (IBM 2012) and was tuned to recognize the UML extensions proposed by Pai and Dugan (2002). It

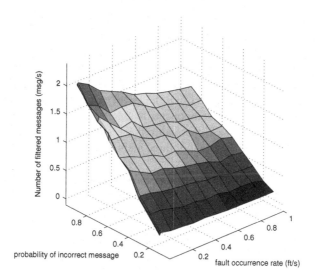

Fig. 8.6 Rate of filtered messages

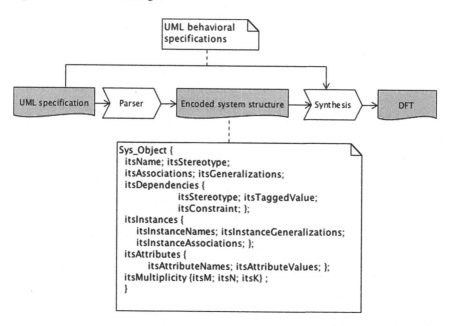

Fig. 8.7 Pai and Dugan (2002) transformation approach

maps the UML structural diagrams to the encoded system structure `Sys_Object`
in Fig. 8.7, shown as a note symbol. Instead, the reconfiguration specifications,
modeled as UML behavioral diagrams (such as state machines), are directly mapped
to DFT constructs by the synthesis algorithm. Herein, we revise the mapping of Pai

and Dugan (2002) by considering UML-DAM system models as input specification. Figure 8.8 (top, left) shows a UML-DAM structural view that will help in describing the transformation approach. The running example is purely syntactical and does not claim to represent a real system: it has been introduced just for illustrative purpose. The system consists of a triplicated bus (*Bus*) connected with three main components (*Main*) and one spare (*Spare*). One working bus is sufficient to enable the communication. The main components belong to a redundant structure with a cold spare (*dormancyFactor=0*) that can replace any of the main components in case of failure of the latter. Two out of three main components are needed at a time (*FTlevel=2*).

The parser generates as many entries in the structure Sys_Object as there are classes which can be subject to failures, that is those stereotyped as *DaComponent*

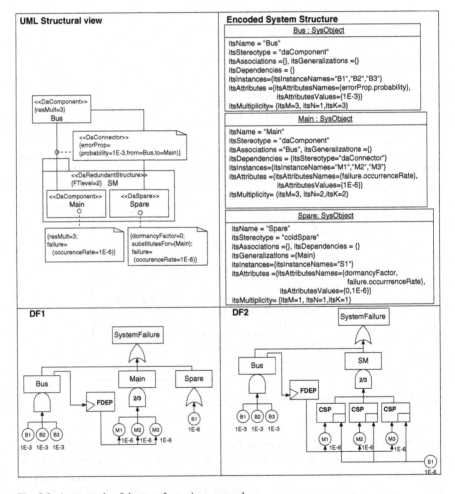

Fig. 8.8 An example of the transformation approach

or *DaVariant* or *DaSpare*. Figure 8.8 (top, right) shows the three entries of such structure that correspond to the clases *Bus*, *Main*, and *Spare*. The *resMult* tagged-values associated with the classes are used to obtain how many components are present in the system.[2] In case of redundant structures, the *DaRedundantStructure* stereotype enables to determine how many components are needed, since the *FTlevel* tagged-value represents the minimum number of components, in the package, that guarantees the service. So, the multiplicities fields `itsM`, `itsN`, and `itsK` of the encoded system structure `Sys_Object` (Fig. 8.7) can be set to the number of system components, the number needed and the number that will cause failure, respectively. Accordingly, the `itsInstanceNames` field is also set.

The field `itsAttributes` collects the probabilistic information needed for reliability analysis, i.e., the failure rate, failure coverage, error propagation probability, restoration, distribution and, in case of spare components, the dormancy factor. The attribute names (values) correspond to the tags (tagged-values) attached to either a component or a connector. In the latter case, the tagged-value attached to a *DaConnector* model element (e.g., an association between two classes) expresses the probability of error propagation from a failed component (e.g., one of the two classes) to the related component (e.g., the other class) and the direction of the error propagation. Then the encoded system structure associated with the failed component will contain the error propagation probability tagged-value.

In the running example, the failure of the buses causes the communication interruption between the main components, so the error propagation probability is encoded in the system structure associated with the bus. On the other hand, the `itsDependencies` field of the system structure associated with the main component is set to the component causing the error.

Table 8.1 summarizes the mapping of the UML-DAM extensions to the encoded system structure `Sys_Object`. In particular, UML model elements stereotyped as *DaSpare* will be characterized by an encoded structure where the `itsStereotype` field is set to either `coldSpare`, `warmSpare` or `hotSpare`, depending on the tagged-value *dormancyFactor* attached to the component in the UML specification. The *substitutesFor* tagged-value is used to update the `itsGeneralizations` field. A *DaVariant* component has a similar mapping. In the example of Fig. 8.8, the `itsGeneralizations` field of the encoded system structure associated with the spare is set to the replaceable main components.

The last row of Table 8.1 describes the mapping of the UML-DAM behavioral specifications to DFT constructs. Actually, the *DaStep* stereotype is the only UML extension applied to specify the reconfiguration policies: the tagged-values are used to determine the trigger event and the dependent components of a functional dependency gate as will be detailed in the next subsection.

---

[2]If the *resMult* tagged-value is not specified, by default, it is assumed that it is equal to one.

Table 8.1 Mapping UML-DAM annotations to the encoded system structure/DFT constructs

Stereotype	Description	Encoded system structure
DaComponent	Number of component instances (*resMult*)	`itsM,itsN,itsK`
	Reliability input parameters (*failure.occurrenceRate, failure.occurrenceDist, failureCoverage, repair.MTTR, repair.rate*)	`itsAttributes`
	Hardware or software component (*origin*)	-
DaVariant	A variant of a software component	`itsStereotype=` `coldSpare`
DaSpare	Hot (*dormancyFactor=1*), warm (*dormancyFactor* ∈ (0, 1)) and cold (*dormancyFactor=0*) spare components	`itsStereotype=` `(hotSpare,` `warmSpare,` `coldSpare)`
	Set of components the spare can substitute for (*substitutesFor*)	`itsGeneralizations`
DaRedundantStructure	Minimum number of components within the redundant structure to still guarantee the service (*FTlevel*)	`itsN, itsK`
DaConnector	Error propagation due to component faults (*errProp*): probability (*errProp.probability*) and direction of the propagation (*errProp.from,errProp.to*). The tagged-value *probability* is mapped to the `itsAttributes` field of the source component (*errProp.from*). The `itsDependencies` field is updated	`itsAttributes,` `itsDependencies,`

Stereotype	Description	DFT construct
DaStep	*kind=failure*: logical expression specifying the failure condition (*failure.condition*) that triggers the step (i.e., element causing the failure and its state)	*FDEP* trigger
	kind=replacement: replaced component (*replace*) within a replacement activity.	*FDEP* dependent component

8.2.2 The Synthesis Algorithm

The algorithm proposed by Pai and Dugan (2002) generates a DFT expressed in the input format of Galileo tool (Sullivan et al. 1999) from the encoded system structure. It consists of three steps (Algorithms 1, 2, and 3, respectively) which are detailed in the following.

Algorithm 1 Generation of *BE, AND, OR, K-of-M* gates

Require: *Sys_Object*
Ensure: DFT_1
 1: Define *TopLevelGate* as *OR*
 2: j = compCount = numberOfComponents(*Sys_Object*)
 3: n = depCount = numberOfDependencies(*Sys_Object.itsName*)
 4: p = instCount = numberOfInstances(*Sys_Object.itsName*)
 5: **for** i=0, <= compCount, i++ **do**
 6:    Create *BE* from *Sys_Object.itsInstances*
 7: **end for**
 8: **while** j ! = 0 **do**
 9:    Assign *Sys_Object.ItsAttributes* to *BE.itsParameters*
10:    Connect *BE* to *TopLevelGate*
11:    **if** (*Sys_Object.itsK* < *Sys_Object.itsM*) && (*Sys_Object.itK* ! = 0, 1) **then**
12:      Define *Gate* as *K-of-M*
13:    **else**
14:      **if** (*Sys_Object.itsK* = *Sys_Object.itsM* = 1) **then**
15:        Define *Gate* as *OR*
16:      **else**
17:        **if** (*Sys_Object.itsK* = *Sys_Object.itsM*) && (*Sys_Object.itsM* > 1) **then**
18:          Define *Gate* as *AND*
19:        **end if**
20:      **end if**
21:    **end if**
22:    Connect *BE* to *Gate* in
23:    Connect *Gate* to *TopLevelGate*
24:    Remove *BE* link to *TopLevelGate*
25:    **for** p>0, p- - **do**
26:      **if** (*Sys_Object.itsDependencies exists*) && FDEP(!*exist*) **then**
27:        Define *Gate* as *FDEP*
28:        Connect *FDEP* normal in to *BE*
29:        **while** n ! = 0 **do**
30:          **if** (*Sys_Object.itsDependencies.itsConstraint* = *OR* || *AND*) **then**
31:            **if** (*OR* || *AND* gate exists) **then**
32:              Connect *OR* || *AND* gate out to *Gate* trigger in
33:            **else**
34:              Define *NewGate* as *Sys_Object.itsDependencies.itsConstraint*
35:              Connect *NewGate* out to *Gate* trigger in
36:              Connect *Sys_Object.itsAssociations* to *NewGate* in
37:            **end if**
38:          **else**
39:            Connect *Sys_Object.itsAssociations* to *Gate* trigger in
40:          **end if**
41:          n- -
42:        **end while**
43:      **else**
44:        **if** (*Sys_Object.itsDependencies exists*) && FDEP exists **then**
45:          Connect *FDEP* normal in to *BE*
46:        **end if**
47:      **end if**
48:    **end for**
49:    j- -
50: **end while**

In the first one (Algorithm 1), a DFT_1 is created that includes the basic events (BEs), the static gates and the functional dependency gates. To this aim, the number of system components, their dependencies and instances are counted (lines 2–4). A BE is created from each instance of a component (lines 5–7). The BE parameters (e.g., failure occurrence rate) are set to the correspondent attributes from the component (line 9)[3] and the BEs are connected to a top level OR gate (line 10).

Thereafter, the component multiplicities itsM and itsK are analyzed in order to define the appropriate gate, either K-of-M, OR or AND, the BEs have to be connected to (lines 11–21). Once the static gate has been defined, the BE-to-gate connections are updated (lines 22–24).

When no dependencies exist between components, then the first step is done. Figure 8.8 (left, bottom) without the functional dependency gate FDEP shows the DFT generated so far by the Algorithm 1. Otherwise, the dependencies of the component instances are determined by itsAssociations field of the encoded system structure. Then, the related BEs are connected to the appropriate functional dependency gates (*FDEP*) normal inputs (lines 25–48). If dependencies have OR/AND constraints, then either an OR or AND gate is created and the trigger BEs are connected to this gate (lines 30–37). Finally, the BEs that are independent, in the dependency relationship, are connected to the appropriate *FDEP* as the trigger (line 39). The DFT of Fig. 8.8 (left, bottom) is characterized by a dependency gate *FDEP* that captures the dependency relations between the buses

---

Algorithm 2 Generation of spare gates

Require: *Sys_Object*, compCount, instCount, DFT_1
Ensure: DFT_2
```
 1:  i=compCount
 2:  while i ! = 0 do
 3:      if (Sys_Object.itsStereotype = "hotSpare" || "warmSpare" || "coldSpare") then
 4:          for p=instCount, p=0, p- - do
 5:              if (HSP || WSP || CSP exists) then
 6:                  Connect BE to SpareGate normal in
 7:              else
 8:                  Define SpareGate as Sys_Object.itsStereotype
 9:                  Connect BE to SpareGate normal in
10:              end if
11:              Connect Sys_Object.itsGeneralizations to SpareGate primary
12:              Connect SpareGate to Gate that BE is connected to
13:              Remove BE link to Gate
14:              InputOrder = Sys_Object.itsTaggedValue
15:          end for
16:      end if
17:      i- -
18:  end while
```

---

[3] All the instances of a component are characterized by the same parameter values.

and the main components according to the error propagation specification annotated with MARTE-DAM.

In the second step (Algorithm 2), spare gates are added to the DFT_1 created from the previous step. The spare components (i.e., hot, warm, and cold) are identified from the logical structure. For each component of the encoded structure, itsStereotype field is used to determine the type of spare (line 3). The appropriate spare gates are then created (line 8) and the BEs, representing the component instances, are connected to either the normal (lines 6 and 9), i.e., spare, or the primary (line 11) connections of the spare gates, depending on the itsGeneralizations field. In particular, if a component is a spare for another component, then the corresponding generalization entry is filled with the name of the BE that it is a spare for. The generalization entry is connected to the primary input of the spare gate and the component itself is connected to the normal input. If the involved BEs were originally connected to other gates (e.g., OR, AND or K-of-M), then the spare gates are then connected to these gates (line 12) and the old connections of the involved BEs are removed (line 13). Observe that, since the primary input of a spare gate should be a basic event, the line 11 of Algorithm 2 subsumes a logical transformation in case a spare can replace several component instances, as it occurs in the running example of Fig. 8.8 (right, bottom).

Algorithm 3 Reconfiguration

Require: Sys_Object, compCount, instCount, DFT_2, UML-DAM behavioral diagram
Ensure: DFT
 1: i=compCount
 2: **while** i ! = 0 **do**
 3:     Locate stereotype "DaStep" with tagged-value "kind=failure"
 4:     Define $ORGate$ as OR
 5:     Define $FDEPGate$ as $FDEP$
 6:     **if** $DaStep$ with $kind = failure$ is found **then**
 7:         **for** p=instCount, p = 0, p- - **do**
 8:             **if** BE connected to $Gate$ **then**
 9:                 Connect $Gate$ out to $ORGate$ in
10:             **else**
11:                 Connect BE to $ORGate$ in
12:             **end if**
13:         **end for**
14:     **end if**
15:     Connect $ORGate$ out to $FDEPGate$ trigger in
16:     Locate stereotype "DaStep" with tagged-value "kind=replacement"
17:     **if** $DaStep$ with $kind = replacement$ is found **then**
18:         **for** p= instCount, p = 0, p- - **do**
19:             Connect $FDEPGate$ normal in to BE
20:         **end for**
21:     **end if**
22:     i- -
23: **end while**

In the third step (Algorithm 3), the DFT_2 created from the previous step is modified to include the reconfiguration policies specified in UML behavioral diagrams (e.g., state machines), if they exist. The *DaStep* stereotyped model elements are used to determine the events that will cause the failure (line 3) and the ones that will trigger the replacement activities (line 16). In particular, from the failure steps the failed components can be determined (*failure=condition=element* tagged-value) and from the replacement steps the replaced components can be identified (*replace* tagged-value). The BEs of the DFT that represent the failed and replaced components are then properly connected to the functional dependency gates and *OR* gates (lines 7–21).

8.2.3   DFT of the Case Study

Figure 8.9 shows the DFT obtained using the Pai and Dugan (2002) approach from the UML-DAM specifications of the MAS. In Chap. 5, the MAS was modeled by both structural (i.e., class and deployment diagrams) and behavioral UML diagrams (i.e., state machine diagram) enriched with DAM annotations. During the first and second steps (Algorithms 1 and 2), the structural diagrams in Figs. 5.11 and 5.12a are considered. In particular, components that do not belong to a redundant structure are mapped to sub-trees, where each one is characterized by as many basic events (BEs) as the component multiplicity connected to an *AND* gate. The top-level gate of each sub-tree is labeled with the name of the component (*BGDataBus, MMBus, VMBus*, and *Memory*).

The sub-trees with top-level gate *4SubSystems* and *VMSS* are generated from the homonym packages of Fig. 5.11 representing redundant structures. Each package in Fig. 5.11 actually contains: (1) a cold spare component and (2) several sub-packages, which in turn are redundant structures consisting of a component and a hot spare. Since the cold spare component has two instances (its multiplicity is equal to two) then two BEs are generated (*SP1,SP2* in the sub-tree *4SubSystems* and *VMSP1,VMSP2* in the sub-tree *VMSS*). Each component or hot spare of a sub-package is mapped to a BE which is connected as a primary connection of a cold spare gate (the gate is labeled with the name of the component or hot spare). The two cold spare BEs are instead connected as normal connections to all the cold spare gates. The *4SubSystems* sub-tree is then characterized by eight cold spare gates connected to a 5-of-8 gate, while the *VMSS* sub-tree is characterized by four cold spare gates connected to a 3-of-4 gate.

The last two sub-trees *FullVersionSoftware* and *MinVersionSoftware* are generated considering the Fig. 5.12a which specifies the software redundancy. In particular, the *FullVersionSoftware* sub-tree is generated considering the dependencies that exist between the model elements in Fig. 5.12a. The *MinVersionSoftware* sub-tree is characterized by two cold spare nodes *PathGenSw* and *SOSw* which are generated from the homonym packages representing software redundant structures. Each package contains a component and its variant, both mapped to a BE. The

BE representing the component is connected to the cold spare gate as primary connection, while the BE representing the variant is connected to the cold spare gate as normal connection.

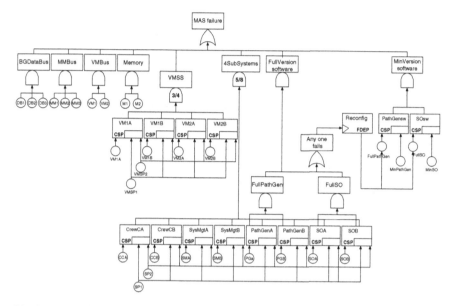

Fig. 8.9 DFT of the MAS case study

Finally, during the last step of the algorithm (Algorithm 3) the functional dependency gate *Reconfig* is created and the trigger event and the dependent BEs are properly connected to the new gate. The trigger event is a sub-tree that represents the failure of the redundant hardware, the *FullSO* software or the *FullPathGen* software. As a consequence, the full version of the software fails (correspondent BEs).

Chapter 9
Conclusions and Advanced Open Issues

Where we are, where we are going...

Abstract Although numerous advances have been made during the last two decades in the area of model-based dependability assessment of software systems, many issues are still open. In this chapter, we present a critical discussion of the state of the art based on the approaches presented in Chap. 7 and identify open issue and present some future work directions in the field.

9.1 Discussion

In this section we discuss, from a critical perspective, the state of the art in the area of model-based dependability assessment of software systems, based on the contributions presented in Chap. 7. More specifically, we surveyed 36 approaches based on 49 papers, which are summarized in Table 7.1 in the order of their presentation. As mentioned before, most of the approaches are using UML as a software modeling language, although a few are using AADL.

9.1.1 Software Engineering and UML Criteria

9.1.1.1 Life Cycle Phase

The support provided by the approaches within the software life cycle spans from the requirements analysis to the deployment phase (Table 9.1); however, the most important contributions are given in the early phases, in particular during the requirements, software architecture, and design specification. This result is not surprising, as it occurred also for performance model-based approaches (Balsamo et al. 2004). It is due to the fact that a major modeling effort is placed early in the life cycle, where the detection of both functional and non-functional (e.g., dependability,

Table 9.1 Contributions by life cycle phase

Approach	Requirements	Architecture	Design	Impl/Deployment
D'Ambrogio		✓		
Yacoub		✓		
Rodrigues		✓		
Singh			✓	
Cortellessa		✓	✓	
Pai			✓	
Grassi			✓	
Bocciarelli		✓	✓	
David			✓	
Bernardi-a			✓	
Genero			✓	
Allenby	✓			
Johannessen	✓			
Hansen		✓		
Iwu	✓	✓	✓	
Liu		✓		
Hawkings	✓		✓	
Pataricza			✓	
Ober			✓	
Zoughbi			✓	
Cancila		✓	✓	
Lu			✓	✓
Goseva		✓		
Hassan		✓		
Bondavalli		✓		
DeMiguel		✓	✓	
Leangsuksun			✓	✓
DalCin	✓		✓	
Addouche	✓		✓	
Bernardi-b	✓		✓	
Mustafiz	✓			
Zarras		✓		
Jürjens			✓	
Bernardi-c	✓	✓	✓	
Bozzano		✓	✓	
Rugina		✓	✓	

performance) problems can be fixed more effectively with less effort and lower costs that late fixes.

We observed that a significant number of works aim at providing solutions for dependability analysis of software systems, while fewer contributions address requirement elicitation or just dependability specification (i.e., how to express dependability characteristics in the software model). Among the surveyed works, only Goseva and Hassan provide methods for risk assessment of safety-critical systems.

The implementation and deployment stages are addressed by only one contribution each (Lu and Leangsuksun, respectively), while none of the considered works focus on testing activities. We think that research efforts should be devoted to combine model-based approaches with experimental ones in the testing phase, e.g., by exploiting use case to drive the testing activities through test cases and to trace back the latter to dependability requirements.

9.1.1.2 UML Diagrams

For the approaches that are based on UML models, class and deployment diagrams are the most frequently used structural diagrams (Table 9.2).

Unlike in performance analysis of UML-based systems, where UML behavioral specifications are necessary to derive a performance model, dependability models can be derived from structural specifications only, although behavioral specifications are also used in many cases.

At the first sight, it seems unusual that deployment diagrams are used in works which address the early phases of the software life cycle. This is justified by the fact that dependability issues often arise not only from software faults but also from hardware faults (e.g., node crashes, broken communication physical links). Therefore, dependability requirements for a software system need to address not only the software but also the platform-dependent architectures of the entire system (usually modeled by deployment diagrams).

Use case, sequence, and state machines are the behavioral diagrams used in many cases. In particular, use case diagrams are used not only in requirement elicitation approaches, but also in the works addressing dependability analysis, mainly to specify the operational profile of interest (e.g., Singh and Cortellessa).

Observe that, apart from Bernardi-c (which provides support for dependability specification for all UML diagrams through a profile), all the other surveyed works consider only a subset of UML diagrams each. Note that Bondavalli is the contribution that enables dependability analysis based on the largest subset of UML diagrams.

The surveyed works rely upon different UML versions (i.e., 1.x and 2.x), mainly according to the year of publication. In general, the most important changes between UML 1.x and 2.x concern behavioral diagrams, more specifically activity and sequence diagrams. However, none of the surveyed approaches that rely upon UML 1.x use activity diagrams. The ones that use sequence diagrams (D'Ambrogio, Yacoub, Singh, Hansen, Goseva, Bondavalli and De Miguel) can, in principle, be applied to UML 2.x, since they consider independent execution scenarios—modeled each one by a simple sequential SD (i.e., without alternative, parallel, optional sub-scenarios). Obviously, the software tools that support such approaches and rely on the UML metamodel (e.g., to produce automatically a formal dependability model) would need to be upgraded to the new UML version. UML2.x supports more types

Table 9.2 UML diagrams

Approach	Class	Object	Use Case	State M.	Activity	Sequence	IOD	Collab.	Comm.	Deploy.
D'Ambrogio						✓				✓
Yacoub						✓				
Rodrigues						✓	✓			
Singh			✓			✓				✓
Cortellessa			✓			✓	✓	✓		✓
Pai	✓	✓		✓						✓
Grassi					✓	✓	✓	✓		✓
David						✓				
Bernardi-a				✓		✓				
Genero	✓									
Allenby				✓						
Johannessen				✓						
Hansen	✓	✓				✓			✓	✓
Iwu	✓			✓		✓				
Liu			✓			✓			✓	
Hawkings	✓			✓		✓				
Pataricza				✓						
Ober	✓			✓						
Zoughbi	✓									
Cancila	✓			✓						
Lu									✓	✓
Goseva			✓	✓		✓			✓	
Hassan			✓			✓				
Bondavalli	✓	✓	✓	✓		✓		✓		✓
DeMiguel	✓			✓		✓		✓		✓
Leangsuksun										✓
DalCin	✓		✓					✓	✓	
Addouche	✓			✓				✓		
Bernardi-b	✓									
Mustafiz			✓		✓					
Zarras		✓				✓				✓
Jürjens				✓	✓	✓				✓
Bernardi-c	✓	✓	✓	✓	✓	✓	✓	✓	✓	✓

of diagrams than UML1.x, in particular the interaction overview diagrams (IOD), which are a combination of activity and sequence diagrams. IOD allow one to model system scenarios using a hierarchical approach. Nevertheless, even though the majority of the surveyed works support UML2.x, very few (i.e., Rodrigues and Bernardi-c) use IOD.

9.1.1.3   Software Development Process

Table 9.3 Contributions by software development process

Approach	General	Use Case	CBSE	SPL
D'Ambrogio			✓	
Yacoub			✓	
Rodrigues			✓	
Singh			✓	
Cortellessa			✓	
Pai	✓			
Grassi			✓	
Bocciarelli			✓	
David	✓			
Bernardi-a	✓			
Genero	✓			
Allenby		✓		
Johannessen		✓		
Hansen	✓			
Iwu	✓			
Liu			✓	✓
Hawkings	✓			
Pataricza	✓			
Ober	✓			
Zoughbi	✓			✓
Cancila	✓			✓
Lu	✓			
Goseva		✓	✓	
Hassan		✓		
Bondavalli	✓			
DeMiguel	✓			
Leangsuksun	✓			
DalCin	✓			
Addouche	✓			
Bernardi-b	✓			
Mustafiz		✓		
Zarras	✓			
Jürjens			✓	
Bernardi-c	✓			
Bozzano			✓	
Rugina	✓			

Most of the approaches follow the traditional software life cycle (Table 9.3). The use case approach is applied in some works to capture dependability requirements, besides the functional requirements. We can observe that there are several contributions using the component-based software development process (CBSE). Only one work, Liu, addresses the software product-line development process (SPL).

9.1.1.4   Software and Application Domains

Most of the works either do not focus on a specific software domain or provide specific support for real-time (embedded) systems. Only Bocciarelli and Zarras' approaches address the service-oriented architecture (SOA) domain.

The majority of the surveyed works support reliability analysis of general software systems, possibly fault-tolerant and distributed systems. We observe that the kind of dependability property to be evaluated is influenced by the software and the application domains considered by a given work. For instance, contributions focusing on real-time (embedded) systems are mainly concerned with safety issues. In particular, considering in detail the application domain (Table 9.4), we notice that most of the works that address aereospace, automotive, railways control software, and healthcare systems are interested in providing support for safety analysis. On the other hand, in the case of transaction applications, it is often desirable to guarantee the continuity and the promptness of service delivery, when requested by the end-user. Therefore, reliability and availability are the main issues addressed by the works dealing with this type of applications.

9.1.1.5   Dependability Specification with UML

The specification of dependability requirements and properties can be done by (a) providing a specific UML profile; (b) providing a set of UML standard extensions (i.e., stereotypes and tagged-values), not structured in a profile[1]; (c) using non-extended UML models; and (d) using the Object Constraint Language (OCL 2006). For the case (c), when non-extended UML models are used, we refer to those approaches that specify the dependability requirements using the very same UML diagrams—like use cases applied in the requirement elicitation approaches—or even ad hoc diagrams—like state-machine variants (Mustafiz, Iwu). Other approaches use UML models to extrapolate dependability information (Genero, Hansen, Goseva). Finally, only two contributions (Hawkings and Lu) use OCL to specify safety related requirements and constraints.

Table 9.5 details the type of specification used by each considered approach. The definition of a UML profile requires more effort to propose a set of extensions, but has the advantage of defining consistent extensions in a structured

---

[1]Observe that the type of specification *(b)* refers to the surveyed works that rely upon UML 1.*.

framework. The majority of the approaches that resort to profiling technique define the profile in the context of existing standard OMG UML profiles, such as the Schedulability, Performance and Time (SPT 2005)—Rodrigues, Grassi, Cortellessa, Bondavalli, Addouche—and the Modeling and Analysis of Real-Time Embedded System (MARTE 2011)—Cancila, Bernardi-c, which has the advantage of exploiting the specification capabilities of the standard profile. Although a lot of efforts have been devoted to propose UML extensions to support dependability

Table 9.4 Application domain

Approach	general	aerospace	automotive	railway	automated	healthcare	transaction
D'Ambrogio	✓						
Yacoub	✓						
Rodrigues	✓						
Singh							✓
Cortellessa	✓						
Pai		✓					
Grassi	✓						
Bocciarelli							✓
David	✓						
Bernardi-a	✓						
Genero	✓						
Allenby		✓					
Johannessen			✓				
Hansen	✓						
Iwu		✓					
Liu						✓	
Hawkings	✓						
Pataricza				✓			
Ober		✓					
Zoughbi		✓					
Cancila				✓			
Lu	✓						
Goseva						✓	
Hassan						✓	
Bondavalli	✓						
DeMiguel	✓						
Leangsuksun	✓						
DalCin	✓						
Addouche					✓		
Bernardi-b					✓		
Mustafiz	✓						
Zarras							✓
Jürjens			✓				
Bernardi-c	✓						
Bozzano		✓	✓				
Rugina		✓	✓				

specification in UML-based systems, less attention has been paid to providing a solution for the unification of the different proposals. Indeed, to the best of our knowledge, only Bernardi-c tackled this issue.

Table 9.5 Dependability specification with UML

Approach	profile	OCL	non-ext. UML	UML extensions
D'Ambrogio			✓	
Yacoub				✓
Rodrigues	✓			
Singh				✓
Cortellessa	✓			
Pai				✓
Grassi	✓			
David			✓	
Bernardi-a	✓			✓
Genero			✓	
Allenby			✓	
Johannessen			✓	
Hansen			✓	
Iwu			✓	
Liu			✓	
Hawkings		✓		
Pataricza				✓
Ober	✓			
Zoughbi	✓			
Cancila	✓			
Lu	✓	✓		
Goseva			✓	
Hassan				✓
Bondavalli	✓			✓
DeMiguel				✓
Leangsuksun				✓
DalCin	✓			
Addouche	✓		✓	
Bernardi-b			✓	
Mustafiz			✓	✓
Zarras				✓
Jürjens				✓
Bernardi-c	✓			

We think that more research should be invested in providing a common UML framework for the modeling and analysis of different NFPs in order to support the consistent specification of different NFPs and their relationships, as well as the trade-off analysis between different NFPs (such as performability, performance and security, security and dependability).

9.1.1.6 Tool Support

The majority of surveyed contributions provide tool support for the approaches they propose. Although most of the tools are research prototypes that do not cover all the aspects, the potential for building more powerful tool support exists. Many approaches could be automated since they propose either rigorous transformation techniques of UML annotated models into formal dependability models or dependability annotations through the UML profiling mechanism. Only a few proposals are difficult to implement or do not provide any indication of an existing implementation. These are mainly approaches that address dependability requirements elicitation via use cases (Allenby and Johannessen) or class diagrams (Bernardi-b), or focus on severity analysis (Hassan).

9.1.2 Dependability Characteristics Criteria

9.1.2.1 Attribute

Concerning the type of dependability attribute, most of the surveyed approaches address either reliability or safety issues, while fewer efforts have been devoted to maintainability and availability. Indeed, the latter are often considered as secondary dependability issues. In particular, the stochastic approaches proposed for reliability analysis can also be used, as claimed by their authors, to compute availability and maintainability measures (e.g., steady-state availability, MTTR) given that the additional quantitative characterization of the repair or recovery activities is provided (e.g., repair rate) as input parameter. A unique exception is Genero, where a set of size and complexity metrics for UML class diagrams are proposed as indicators of the software specification maintainability.

9.1.2.2 Analysis Type

One of the criteria for discussion is the type of dependability analysis proposed, i.e., qualitative or quantitative. Qualitative analysis aims to identify, classify, and rank the hazards or failure modes in the software systems, while quantitative analysis aims to compute dependability measures. We notice that safety-related contributions fall basically in the first category (i.e., qualitative) while the works that focus on reliability, maintainability, and availability belong to the second category (i.e., quantitative). There are some exceptions that support both types of analysis, like the works on safety of Ober, Goseva, Hassan and Cancila, and the works of Bernardi-b, DalCin, Jürjens and Bernardi-c, providing support for dependability specification.

Considering the approaches aimed at quantitative dependability analysis, the majority of them rely on stochastic (or probabilistic) assumptions. Nevertheless, there are also non-stochastic approaches to dependability analysis, like Ober and

Bernardi-b, that support the verification of time-dependent dependability requirements of real-time systems.

9.1.2.3 Analysis Model

Table 9.6 summarizes the techniques adopted by the surveyed works to support dependability analysis of UML-based specifications.

This criterion does not apply to the approaches that provide support only for dependability specification (shown in gray in Table 9.6).

Some of the used techniques are those suggested by dependability standards IEC-60300-3-1 (2003), discussed in Chap. 6. In particular, Fault tree and its variants (e.g., dynamic fault tree) is the mostly used dependability technique, followed by Markov models. Fault trees have been applied in both reliability (D'Ambrogio, Pai, Leangsuksun) and safety contributions (Iwu, Liu , Hawkings, Hassan), and for both qualitative (Iwu, Liu, Hawkings, Hassan) and quantitative (D'Ambrogio, Pai, Leangsuksun) analysis.

Some contributions propose instead techniques which are not traditionally aimed at dependability analysis, e.g., component dependency graphs (Yacoub). Finally, there are a few approaches, like Hassan and Iwu, that suggest the combined use of several complementary techniques.

9.1.2.4 Parameters and Requirements

We observe that the specification of dependability requirements is supported by few approaches. In particular, most of the works that aim at evaluating the system reliability do not provide support for the validation of the estimated reliability measures w.r.t. the requirements.

Concerning the dependability measures, they are often considered as both input parameters and output results in a given approach (D'Ambrogio, Yacoub, Rodrigues, Singh, Pai, Grassi, Cortellessa, DeMiguel, Leangsuksun, Addouche, Bernardi-b, Mustafiz, Bernardi-c). For example, the failure occurrence rate is associated with software component/connectors (i.e., input parameters for the method) and with the system level as well (i.e., output result provided by the method).

None of the surveyed approaches provide any indication on how to assign values to the input parameters. Input parameters are simply assumed values. The value assignment can be trivial for some input parameters, such as MTTF of hardware components that is usually provided by the manufacturer; however, this is not the case for most of the parameters (e.g., how to assign an MTTF value to a software component?).

The most frequent items are reliability measures (**DM.R**) and safety properties (**DM.S**): this is not surprising, since most of the surveyed works address reliability and safety issues.

Table 9.6 Dependability analysis models

Approach	Hazard analysis	FMEA	HAZOP	FFA	Stochastic Petri net	Labeled trans. system	Formal state machine	Dataflow network	Simulation model	Fault Tree	Cost of failure graph	Comp. Dep. Graph	Markov model	Bayesian model	Prob. timed automata	Timed automata	Temporal logics	Block diagram
D'Ambrogio									✓									
Yacoub												✓						
Rodrigues					✓								✓					
Singh													✓					
Cortellessa													✓					
Pai									✓									
Grassi													✓					
Bocciarelli									✓									
David	✓																	
Bernardi-a				✓														
Genero																		
Allenby		✓																
Johannessen			✓															
Hansen		✓																
Iwu		✓					✓		✓									
Liu									✓									
Hawkings									✓									
Pataricza						✓	✓											
Ober																✓	✓	
Zoughbi																		
Cancila																		
Lu																		
Goseva	✓	✓											✓					
Hassan		✓	✓							✓	✓							
Bondavalli					✓													
DeMiguel								✓										
Leangsuksun									✓				✓					
DalCin					✓													
Addouche														✓				
Bernardi-b																	✓	
Mustafiz													✓					
Zarras													✓					✓
Jürjens																	✓	
Bernardi-c					✓													
Bozzano															✓			
Rugina					✓													

Considering other dependability parameters, several are just marginally dealt with, although each item is addressed by at least a contribution. For instance, while special attention has been devoted to the specification of failure modes with respect to the domain (**DT.FMD**) and to the use of hazard guidewords (**DT.HGW**), fewer works consider other classifications of failure modes, such as failure detectability (**DT.FMDet**) and consistency (**DT.FMC**). Another example: few efforts have been devoted to maintenance issues, i.e., modifications (**M.M**—Genero) and repair (**M.R**—Bernardi-c), and to supporting a comprehensive specification of redundancy in fault-tolerant systems. For instance, only one contribution (Zarras) provides UML extensions to specify the maximum number of replica failures that can be tolerated (**R.F**).

9.1.3 Quality Criteria

9.1.3.1 Validation and Compliance with Standards

The validation of the proposed methods is not a primary issue in the surveyed approaches; indeed about a third of them does not consider validation at all. However, when validation is considered, it is carried out mainly to show the applicability and/or the scalability of the method to realistic examples, i.e., through case studies. The approaches that present a case study are: Singh, Pai, David, Bernardi-a, Allenbi, Johannessen, Hansen, Iwu, Liu, Patarizca, Ober, Goseva, Hassan, Zoughbi, Bondavalli, Bernardi-b, Zarras, Jürjens, and Bernardi-c. Only a few works (Genero and Mustafiz) conduct empirical analysis in an academic environment, to assess not only the applicability of the proposed approaches but also their effectiveness.

We observed that all approaches providing support for quantitative dependability analysis are in fact missing the validation of the correctness of the proposed methods. This could be achieved, e.g., by comparing the analysis results with results obtained from testing activities by injecting faults during the system execution.

Concerning the compliance of the method with respect to dependability engineering standards, only a third of the approaches adheres to some standard. Most of the compliant approaches focus on safety issues in the development of real-time and embedded systems (Allenbi, Johannessen, Iwu, Goseva, Hassan, Cancila, Zoughbi, Lu) for which a certification from third parties is required.

9.1.3.2 Presentation of Results

The majority of the approaches addressing dependability analysis provide a basic support to present the results of the analysis. The most common way is textual, followed by graphical and tabular presentation. We observed that sensitivity analysis is supported by several works that address reliability and availability analysis. The most promising approaches are those that feed back the results to the original UML specification (Rodriguez, Liu, Pataricza, Hassan and Jürjens); this makes the analysis process transparent to the software analyst.

However, more research is needed to address this issue. In particular, the problem of how to identify the critical elements of the system specification which are the cause of unsatisfactory dependability properties is still open. Good solutions would provide useful information to the software engineers for changing the design accordingly.

9.1.3.3 Limitations

Almost all the surveyed approaches present limitations, as summarized in detail in Table 9.7.

In particular, several proposals aimed at reliability analysis assume failure independence for the system components (Yacoub, Rodrigues, Singh, Grassi, Zarras, Leangsuksun). However, this assumption, which facilitates the analysis of the derived reliability model, may not hold for systems characterized by tightly coupled components. An example of such systems are the very demanding complex, large-scale ICT infrastructures that control distributed embedded systems (e.g., distributed SCADA systems controlling power production and distribution plants located in a given geographical area). Another limitation that is common to some approaches is low scalability (Bernardi-a, Hansen, Hawkings) that can make the validation and verification activities time consuming and risky—or, even worse, unfeasible—from the software process management point of view.

9.2 Discussion Summary

This section summarizes the conclusion of the discussion from the previous section and identifies open issues that emerged from the study. Firstly, most of the works focus on reliability and safety, and fewer efforts have been devoted to availability and maintainability modeling and analysis. Moreover, we have not found any work addressing specifically how to extend UML with integrity NFP, which is also a dependability concern.

Secondly, the surveyed works provide support mainly in the early phases of the software life cycle (i.e., from requirements to design), while there is a lack of support for later phases, as, for example, for testing dependability NFPs guided by selected use cases.

Thirdly, the contributions using model transformations mainly focus on obtaining formal models which can be used for dependability analysis. Only a few go one step further to provide feedback from the analysis results to the original UML model specification, in order to pinpoint the causes for requirement inconsistencies or design flaws. It is also worth noticing that tool support and method validation are

Table 9.7 Limitations

Approach ID	Limitations
D'Ambrogio	Lack of UML extensions. Informal treatment of spatial redundancy.
Yacoub	Execution scenario independent assumption. Parallel execution of components is not supported. Component failure independence assumption
Rodrigues	Component failure independence assumption.
Singh	Component/connector failure independence assumption. Time-independent failure probability.
Cortellessa	No annotations for hw failure supported.
Pai	Use of class diagrams to represent hardware components and explicit error propagation associations between hardware components.
Grassi	Failure independence assumption.
Bocciarelli	The NFP extensions are introduced in the BPMN metamodel with the drawback that one needs to extend the tool support, as existing tools do not understand the new metaclasses.
David	A Dysfunctional Behavior dababase needs to be constructed.
Bernardi-a	Limited scalability that may lead to the generation of intractable dependability models from the analysis point of view.
Genero	Lack of guidelines about how to use the proposed metrics to evaluate the maintainability of the UML specifications.
Allenby	Operations in emergency/degraded states and multiple failure identification are not supported.
Johannessen	
Hansen	Limited scalability that may lead to a time consuming activity.
Iwu	Lack of relationships between UML specification and PFS requirements.
Liu	The state-based modeling technique is not suitable for testing border (exact) time values.
Hawkings	Limited scalability in the hazard detection approach that may lead to an uncontrolled generation of mutant transitions.
Pataricza	
Ober	
Zoughbi	Use of dynamic concepts (defined with the profile) to extend static concepts. This leads to mixed static/dynamic views in the same diagram (CD).
Cancila	
Lu	Timing specification issues are vaguely dealt.
Goseva	Use case/scenario independent assumption.
Hassan	Low traceability of the results derived from each applied severity technique.
Bondavalli	Introduction on unnecessary redundant information in the UML models, since some input parameters require the joint use of more than one stereotype.
DeMiguel	
Leangsuksun	Node failure independence assumption, single-failure assumption.
DalCin	Lack of support to the modeling of the interaction among dependability mechanisms and the system components.
Addouche	Poor separation of concerns (new classes need to be defined and introduced in the system model, beside the classes representing the system components).
Bernardi-b	Expertise of the modeler required to specify the predicates/axioms in TRIO language.
Mustafiz	Failure assumptions limited to failures coming from the system environment (hw sensor failure). Use of no standard state-charts (DA-Chart).
Zarras	Object failure independence assumption.
Jürjens	
Bernardi-c	Lack of support for the specification of path properties. Limited support for the specification of FT mechanism (only redundancy aspects are dealt with).
Bozzano	
Rugina	

crucial factors to make an approach effective. Although the majority of the surveyed approaches are characterized by a high automation degree, most of them are not fully supported by software tools. Moreover, in many cases method validation consists only in applying the proposed method to a case study. Considering the approaches that provide support for quantitative dependability analysis, the validation of the correctness of the proposed methods is in fact missing. More efforts should be devoted to the validation of the methods themselves.

Last but not least, more research work should be invested in providing a standard common UML framework for the modeling and analysis of several NFPs, in order to support the consistent specification of different NFPs and their relationships, as well as the trade-off analysis between different NFPs (such as performability, performance and security, security and dependability).

Finally, an important issue to consider for future work is to investigate the current request for proposals (RFPs) for UML-related standards that are now being considered and their potential impact to the area of dependability modeling with UML.

9.3 Advanced Open Issues

Experience in conducting model-driven NFP analysis in the context of model-driven development shows that the domain is still facing a number of challenges.

Human qualifications. Software developers are not trained in all the formal models used for the analysis of different non-functional properties (NFPs), which leads to the idea that we need to hide some of the analysis details from developers. However, the software models have to be annotated with extra information for each NFP and the analysis results have to be interpreted in order to improve the designs. A better balance needs to be made between what needs to be hidden and what to be exposed to the software developer.

Round-trip NFP analysis. The concept of round-trip software engineering means consistently refining a high-level model of a software system into a lower-level model (forward engineering) and abstracting a low-level model into a higher-level one (reverse engineering). The round-trip concept can be applied also to the model-driven NFP analysis, as shown in Fig. 1.2, where the forward trip transforms a software model into a formal model, and the reverse trip produces feedback from the analysis results to the original software model. This raises the need for automated diagnosis tools specific to different formal models. It also raises the need for better traceability links between corresponding software and analysis model elements. It also brings us to the next step: the need allow the designer to ask specific dependability questions in UML terms (for instance, what is the total down time for a given component due to a certain use case) which should be translated automatically into a specific query in terms of the formal model used for analysis. Assuming that the formal model is Petri Nets, the query translation needs to map the dependability values related to the given UML model elements to Petri Nets measures related to the corresponding places and transitions. Such queries should be supported by special model transformations.

Abstraction level. The analysis of different NFPs may require different views of the UML software models at different levels of abstraction/detail. The challenge is to keep all these views consistent not only at the beginning, but also throughout the development process, when changes are applied to the model in order to add new features or to improve different properties.

Software process. Integrating the analysis of multiple NFPs raises software process issues. For each NFP, it is necessary to explore the state space for different design alternatives, configurations, and workload parameters in order to diagnose problems and decide on improvement solutions. The challenge is how to compare and rank different solution alternatives that may improve some NFPs and deteriorate others, and how to decide on the trade-offs.

Analysis of multiple NFPs. Another advanced open issue is the fact that by integrating the analysis of multiple NFPs, we need to handle (i.e., generate, analyze, and diagnose) different formal analysis models. How do we iterate between different analysis models? Are the analysis models obtained from exactly the same software model, or from different views and/or abstractions of the software model? If this is the case, how do we keep these software views consistent? When we change one to improve one NFP, how do the other change?

Design space exploration. Another issue is using optimization techniques over multiple NFPs to obtain the best system design and configuration. How do we explore the state space? Some kind of parameterizations would be necessary, that would allow an automatic experiment manager to modify "in synch" all the analysis models included in the optimization procedure.

Incremental propagation of changes through the model chain. Currently, every time the software design is changed to improve some properties, a new analysis model is derived from scratch in order to redo the analysis. The challenge is to develop incremental transformation methods for propagating a certain change from the software model to the analysis model, thus keeping different model consistent, instead of starting from scratch after every model improvement.

Multi-paradigm modeling. A research direction that gets attention these days in the field of model-driven development, called *multi-paradigm modeling*, is looking at how to use multiple modeling languages and formalisms to solve a larger problem. The questions are as follows: how to interface and bridge different modeling languages that are used in a large problem, how to query not only one model but different related models, how to trace-link related model element in different models (e.g., a software and a corresponding analysis model), how to carry results from one model to another, how to control complex experiments, how to integrate the tool support, etc. The idea is to accept that we have to handle different related models expressed in different modeling languages that cannot be joined together in a single super modeling language. Instead, we need to learn how to navigate between different models and to do overall reasoning. In other words, we could approach the idea of analyzing multiple NFPs as a multi-paradigm modeling problem.

Tool interoperability. There are many kinds of tools that need to work together: editors for the software model, model transformations, solver for the analysis models, optimization, experiment controllers, etc. Some of the extended abilities we propose (e.g., incremental propagation of change, translation of queries from a domain to another, synchronization of different software model versions) require new tools. Software engineering will need more engineering methods and better tool support to take advantage of the verification of NFPs as proposed in the book. Experience shows that it is difficult to interface and integrate seamlessly different tools, which may have been created at different times with different purposes and maybe running on different platforms.

In conclusion, our vision is of a model-driven software development process that integrates the verification of multiple NFPs by generating and analyzing formal models. The NFPs considered in the book are dependability related, with focus on RAMS (reliability, availability, maintainability, and safety) properties.

Appendix A
The MARTE Profile

Abstract The appendix introduces the basic concepts of the MARTE profile, standardized by OMG, which is extended by the DAM profile described in Chap. 4. The focus is on MARTE concepts used by DAM.

A.1 MARTE Overview

The architecture of the MARTE profile, which contains three main parts: *Marte Foundations*, *Marte Design Model*, and *Marte Analysis Model*, is shown in Fig. A.1. The MARTE profile was built with two main goals in mind: to model real-time and embedded systems (supported by the *MARTE Design Model*) and to add annotations to UML models in order to enable the analysis of system properties (supported by the *MARTE Analysis Model*). These two main parts share common concepts described in the shared package *MARTE foundations*.

The packages contained in *MARTE Foundations* have the following roles: *CoreElements* defines the basic behavior concepts for the real-time embedded domain, such as a causality model; *NFP* defines a common framework for annotating models with quantitative and qualitative non-functional information; *Time* defines the time modeling as used within MARTE; *GRM* (Generic Resource Modeling) specifies how to describe at system level resource models; *Alloc* (Allocation modeling) defines concepts required to describe allocation concerns.

The *Marte Analysis Model* contains the following packages: *GCM* (General Component Model) introduces a general component model suitable for real-time embedded systems; *HLAM* (High-Level Application Modeling) defines high-level concepts for designing qualitative and quantitative concerns (e.g., concurrency and synchronization); Detailed Resource Modeling is split into two parts dedicated to detailed modeling of software *SRM* (Software Resource Modeling) and hardware *HRM* (Hardware Resource Modeling), respectively.

The *Marte Analysis Model* part defines so far profiles for two different types of analysis: schedulability (supported by *SAM*) and performance analysis (supported by *PAM*). The concepts common to these two quantitative analyses are contained in the *GQAM* profile (described in Sect. A.3.1), which is in turn specialized by *SAM* and *PAM*. It is important to note that the *DAM* profile for dependability modeling and analysis defined in Chap. 5 of the book also specializes the GQAM profile.

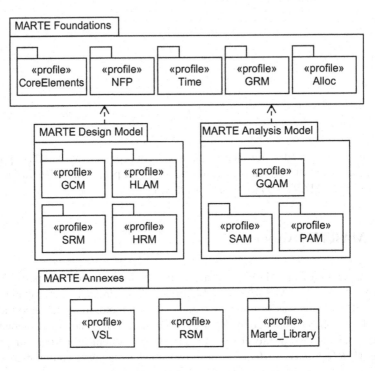

Fig. A.1 The architecture of the MARTE profile

MARTE contains also some annexes, as shown in Fig. A.1. The *VSL* profile defines an expression language for specifying the values of constraints, properties, and stereotype attributes, particularly related to non-functional aspects. VSL was originally designed as an integral part of MARTE, but later was extracted as an independent annex that can be used by other UML-based specifications interested in extending the base expression infrastructure provided by UML. An example of such specification is SySML. Another annex, *RSM* (Repetitive Structure Modeling) is intended for the design of intensive computation embedded systems with repetitive structures. *Marte_Library* is another important annex that defines MARTE primitive data types, a set of predefined NFP types and units of measures.

In the following sections we will give more details about the parts that are important for the definition of the DAM profile.

It is important to note that the MARTE specification defines for every package first the domain model (i.e., the concepts and their relationship) and then the corresponding profile, obtained by mapping the domain concepts to UML extensions, i.e., to stereotypes, tagged-values, and constraints that can be attached to UML model elements in order to extend them.

A.2 Non-functional Properties

UML lacks modeling features needed to express and support the specification and analysis of non-functional characteristics. As a general purpose language, UML leaves out domain-specific details but provides instead standard extension mechanisms that allow for future refinements. The NFP modeling framework deals with the following requirements: how to specify NFPs, how to attach NFPs to UML model elements, how to define relationships between different NFPs, and how to express constraints on or between NFPs.

MARTE includes a so-called *Value Specification Language (VSL)* as an annex, which defines a set of language constructs and a textual grammar supporting extended values, expressions, and data types used particularly for specifying non-functional properties. The NFP package from the MARTE Foundations imports VSL. The NFP package realizes the following requirements for non-functional properties:

- *NFP Qualitative or Quantitative nature.* A quantitative property may be characterized by a set of measures expressed in terms of *magnitude* and *unit*. A qualitative property may be denoted by a label (e.g., *periodic, sporadic*, and *bursty* for an event arrival patterns) representing an abstract characterization with a certain meaning for designers or tools.
- *Qualifiers* can characterize the precision, accuracy, statistical measure (e.g., *mean, maximum, minimum, variance*) or source (showing how a given value was obtained, e.g., *required, measured, estimated, simulated, or calculated.*)
- *Variables and Expressions*, beside concrete values, raise the level of abstractions of the specified properties, allowing to derive ones from the others.
- *Trade-off between usability and flexibility.* Usability suggests the merit of declaring a set of standard property types and their available operations for a certain domain, while flexibility allows for user-defined properties.

As mentioned before, VSL extends directly the concepts of UML value specification and data type metamodel. It defines the following data types: Bounded Subtype, IntervalType, CollectionType, TupleType, and ChoiceType). VSL also defines also four kinds of composite value specifications: collection, interval, tuple, and choice. A few typical examples are:

```
{1, 2, 5, 88} // simple numerical collection
[5..4] // simple integer interval
(value=5.2, unit=mW, source=calc) // tuple value for power
```

The value specifications defined in VSL can be attached to stereotype attributes or used in constraints, as shown in the example of annotated model from Sect. A.3.3.

A.3   MARTE Analysis Model

A.3.1   *Generic Quantitative Analysis Model*

In MARTE, the fundamental concepts shared by different quantitative analysis domains are joined in a single package called Generic Quantitative Analysis Model (GQAM), which is further specialized by the domain models for schedulability (SAM) and performance (PAM). Figure A.2 shows the relationships between the *GQAM* package of the MARTE domain model, which imports the MARTE Foundations packages NFP, Time and GRM and the *MARTE_Library* containing NFP type definitions and units of measures. The domain models for performance analysis (*PAM*) and schedulability analysis (*SAM*) import and specialize *QGAM*. Other domain models for quantitative analysis may be defined by specializing *QGAM*; an example is the *Dependability Analysis Model (DAM)* described in Chap. 5. The core GQAM concepts describe how the system behavior uses resources

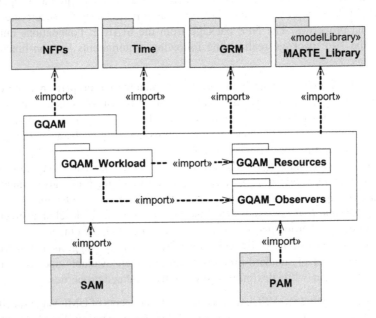

Fig. A.2 The GQAM domain model package

over time, and contains three main categories of concepts: resources, behavior, and workloads.

A.3.1.1 GQAM Resource Concepts

The GQAM domain model package describing the resource-related concepts is represented in Fig. A.3. A resource is based on the abstract *Resource* class defined

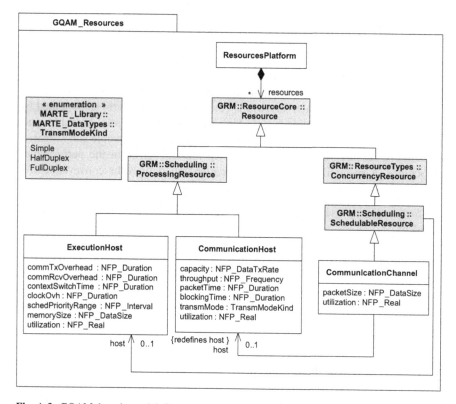

Fig. A.3 GQAM domain model: Resources

in the *General Resource Model* and contains common features such as scheduling discipline, multiplicity, services. The following types of resources are important in GQAM:

- *ExecutionHost*: a processor or other computing device on which are running processes;
- *CommunicationsHost*: a communication network or a bus connecting processing nodes and/or devices;
- *SchedulableResource*: a software resource managed by the operating system, like a process or thread pool;
- *CommunicationChannel*: logical channel that conveys messages.

In order to be executed, a *SchedulableResource* must be allocated to an *ExecutionHost* and a *CommunicationChannel* to a *CommunicationHost*.

Services are provided by resources and by sub-systems. A sub-system service associated with an interface operation provided by a component may be identified as a *RequestedService*, which in turn is a subtype of *Step*, and may be refined by a *BehaviorScenario*.

A.3.1.2   GQAM Behavior/Scenario Concepts

The class *BehaviorScenario* describes a behavior triggered by an event, composed of *Steps* related by predecessor–successor relationships. Scenarios define execution paths with externally visible end points, to which Quality of Service (QoS) requirements may be attached. Each scenario is composed from scenario steps joined by predecessor–successor relationships, which may include fork/join, branch/merge, and loops. A step may represent an elementary operation or a whole sub-scenario. Quantitative resource demands for each step must be given in the performance annotations. A specialized step, *CommunicationStep*, defines the conveyance of a message. Resource usage is attached to behavior in different ways:

- a *Step* implicitly uses a *SchedulableResource* (representing a process, thread, or task);
- each primitive *Step* executes on a host processor;
- specialized steps, AcquireStep or ReleaseStep, explicitly acquire or release a Resource; and
- *BehaviorScenarios* and *Steps* may use other kind of resources, so *BehaviorScenario* inherits from *ResourceUsage* which links resources with concrete usage demands.

A.3.1.3   GQAM Workload Concepts

Each scenario is executed by a workload, which may be open (i.e., requests arriving in some predetermined pattern) or closed (a given number of users or jobs). Different workloads correspond to different operating modes, such as takeoff, in-flight and landing of an aircraft or peak-load and average-load of an enterprise application. A workload is represented by a stream of triggering events, *WorkloadEvent*, generated in one of the following ways:

- by a timed event (e.g., a periodic stream with jitter);
- by a given arrival pattern (periodic, aperiodic, sporadic, burst, irregular, open, closed);
- by a generating mechanism named *WorkloadGenerator*;
- from a trace of events stored in a file.

A.3.1.4   GQAM Profile

The GQAM profile stereotypes and their attribute expressed as tagged-values are obtained by mapping the domain model concepts to UML extensions. More specifically, Fig. A.4 shows the GQAM profile package containing the stereotypes for resources.

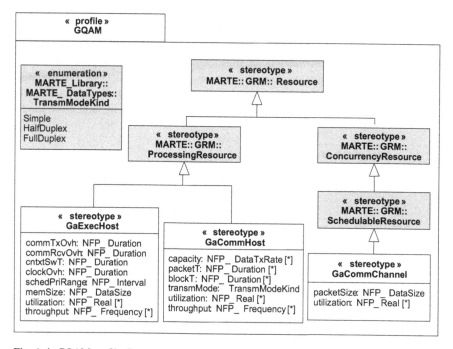

Fig. A.4   GQAM profile: Resources

A.3.2   Performance Analysis Model

Performance is determined by how the system behavior uses system resources. The resources used by the software can be active or passive, logical or physical, software or hardware. Some of these resources belong to the software itself (e.g., critical section, software server, lock, buffer), others to the underlying platforms (e.g., process, thread, processor, disk, communication network). Scenarios define execution paths with externally visible end points. Quality of Service (QoS) requirements (such as response time, throughput, probability of meeting deadlines, etc.) can be placed on scenarios. Each scenario is executed by a workload, which may be open (i.e., requests arriving in some predetermined pattern) or closed (a given number of users or jobs).

As mentioned above, the Performance Analysis Model (PAM) specializes the GQAM domain model. It is important to mention that only a few new concepts were defined in PAM, while most of the concepts are reused from GQAM (reused concepts are shaded in diagrams). The same is true for the Schedulability Analysis Model (SAM).

In terms of resources, PAM reuses *ExecutionHost* for processor, *Schedulable Resources* for processes (or threads) and adds a *LogicalResource* defined by the software (such as semaphore, lock, buffer pool, critical section). A runtime object instance *PaRunTInstance* is an alias for a process or thread pool associated in behavior specifications to the role responsible for the actions on lifelines or swimlanes. The PAM domain model package describing the resource-related concepts is represented in Fig. A.5 PAM specializes a *Step* to include more kinds

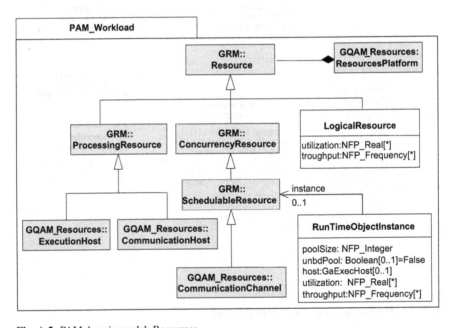

Fig. A.5 PAM domain model: Resources

of operation demands during a step. For instance, it allows for a non-synchronizing parallel operation, which is forked but never joins (*noSync* property). A new step subtype, *PassResource*, indicates the passing of a shared resource from one process to another. The PAM profile is obtained by mapping the PAM domain model to UML. Figure A.6 shows the GQAM profile package containing the stereotypes for resources. Only two new stereotypes are defined in this package, and the rest (shaded) are reused from the GQAM profile.

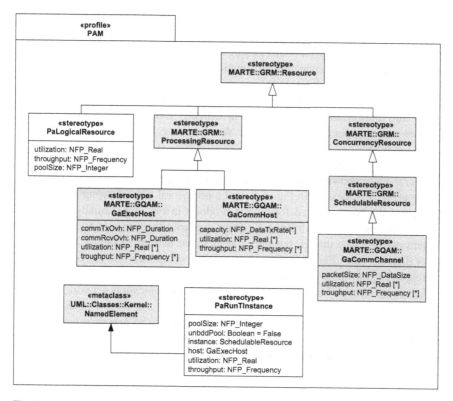

Fig. A.6 PAM profile: Resources

A.3.3   Example of UML Model with MARTE Annotations

A UML model intended for performance analysis should contain a structural view representing the software architecture at the granularity level of concurrent runtime components and their allocation to hardware resources, as well as a behavioral view showing representative scenarios with their respective resource usage and workloads. In this section is given an example of UML model with performance annotations for an electronic commerce system (the static view in Fig. A.7 and the dynamic view for a selected scenario in Fig. A.8).

The components of the case study system TPC-W, a transactional web e-Commerce benchmark (TPC-W 2000), are logically divided into three tiers: (a) a set of emulated web browsers (*EB*), (b) a web tier including web servers and image servers, and (c) a persistent storage tier. TPC-W emulates customers browsing and buying products from a web site, with 14 different web pages that correspond to typical customer operations. The user starts at the Home page that includes the company logo, promotional items and navigation options to best selling books, new books, search pages, the shopping cart, and order status pages. At every page, the user is offered a selection of pages that can be visited next. The user may browse pages containing product information, perform searches with different keys, and put items in the cart. A new customer has to fill out a customer registration page; for returning customers, the personal information is retrieved from the database. Before ordering, the user may update the shopping cart content. When deciding to buy, the user enters the credit card information and submits the order. The system obtains credit card authorization from a *Payment Gateway Emulator (PGE)* and presents the user with an order confirmation page. At a later date, the user can view the status of the last order.

The UML model with MARTE performance annotations is composed of a structural view showing the concurrent runtime component instances and their deployment to processors in Fig. A.7, and a behavioral view showing the scenario for one of the pages needed for buying products in Fig. A.8. Usually the source model contains several performance-critical scenarios that are used to generate the system performance model, but only one is given here as example. The deployment diagram from Fig. A.7 shows the runtime components at the bottom, their corresponding artifacts and the deployment on processing nodes. The processing nodes are stereotyped as *GaExecHost* and the communication network nodes as *GaCommHost*. The stereotype attributes *commRcvOvh* and *commTxOvh* are host-specific costs of receiving and sending messages, *resMult=5* describes a symmetric multiprocessor with five processors, while *blockT* and *capacity* describe a pure latency and bandwidth for the link.

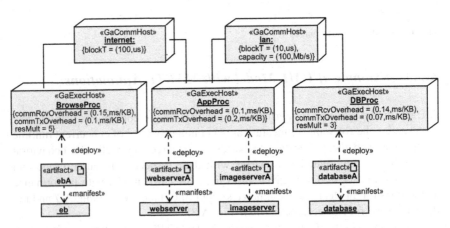

Fig. A.7 Example of deployment diagram with MARTE performance annotations

The scenario *GetBuyConfirm* is represented by a sequence diagram in Fig. A.8. The scenario transfers the shopping cart content into a newly created order for the registered customer, executes a payment authorization, and returns a page with the details of the order to the EB. The following operations are performed:

- *EB* issues a request to *WebServer* for buy confirm page;
- *WebServer* gets the corresponding shopping cart object;

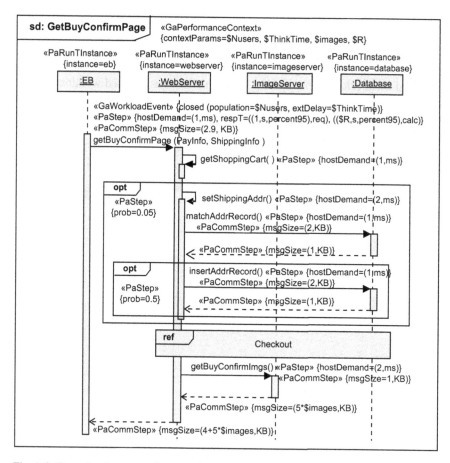

Fig. A.8 Example of sequence diagram with MARTE performance annotations

- With 5% probability (modeled as an *opt* fragment), a shipping address is obtained and *WebServer* tries to match it with information from the database;
- If no address record is found, insert a new address record (modeled as a nested *opt* fragment)
- Invoking the Checkout sub-scenario (modeled as a *ref* fragment invocation, whose details are not shown here);
- *WebServer* gets necessary images from *ImageServer*;
- *WebServer* constructs the html code for the buy/confirm page and returns it to *EB*.

Some examples of MARTE performance annotations used in the scenario model indicate the scenario steps, the workload and the concurrent runtime instances corresponding to the lifeline roles. Two kinds of step stereotypes are applied to messages: *PaStep* representing the execution of the operations invoked by the message and *PaCommStep* for the communication costs involved with passing the message. Examples of execution step attributes are *hostDemand* giving the value and unit for the required execution time and *prob* giving the probability for the optional steps. The communication steps have an attribute *msgSize* giving the value and unit of the message size. The first step of the scenario has the scenario workload *GaWorkloadEvent* attached to it, which defines a closed workload with a population given by the variable *$Nusers* and a think time for each user given by the variable *$ThinkTime*. Each lifeline role is related to a runtime concurrent component instance, as indicated by *PaRunTInstance*.

Appendix B
Classes in the Dependability Domain Model

Abstract This appendix details the classes, and its attributes, in the dependability domain model described in Chap. 2.

B.1 Classes in the Core Model

Table B.1 Core model description

Class/Attribute	Description
Component	Hardware/software components that may be affected by threats. A component provides and requests basic services and interacts with the other components through connectors. It must either provide or request at least one basic service. A component may consist of a set of other components.
Attribute	
stateful	(true) Faulty component can be characterized by an error latency, so it can be restored before failure. (false) Faulty component is considered as failed (Bondavalli et al (2001b); Majzik et al (2003)).
origin	Hardware or software component (Bondavalli et al (2001b); Majzik et al (2003)).
failureCoverage	Percentage of failure coverage (Pai and Dugan (2002)).
/percPermFault	Percentage of permanent faults (Bondavalli et al (2001b); Majzik et al (2003)). Derived from *fault* association-end and *persistency* attribute of Threats::Fault class.
/ssAvail	Steady state availability percentage (Sahner et al (1996); Bernardi et al (2004a)). Derived from *MTTF* (Threats::Failure) and *MTTR* (Maintenance::Repair) attributes.
unreliability	Probability that the time to failure random variable is less than (or equal to) the time t - time dependent (Sahner et al (1996)).
	Continued on next page

S. Bernardi et al., *Model-Driven Dependability Assessment of Software Systems*, DOI 10.1007/978-3-642-39512-3, © Springer-Verlag Berlin Heidelberg 2013

Table B.1 (continued)

/reliability	Survival function (Evans et al (2000)): probability that the component is functioning correctly during the time interval $(0, t]$ - time dependent (Sahner et al (1996)).
missionTime	The maximum period of time for which a component can be used. After this time, it must be replaced. Mission time should be declared by the manufacturer of the component. Equivalent to *lifetime* (IEC-62061 (2005)).
availLevel	Availability level associated to the nines of availability. E.g., very high corresponds to 99,9% of ssAvail, etc. (application specific).
reliabLevel	Reliability level (application specific).
safetyLevel	Safety level (application specific).
complexity	Complexity metric quantifies the component failure proneness (Bernardi et al (2004a); Jürjens (2003); Jürjens and Wagner (2005); Goseva-Popstojanova et al (2003)).
Association-end	
subComponents	A component may consist of a set of sub-components.
interacts-via	A component interacts with other components through one or more connectors.
provides/requests	A component may provide (request) services to other components. The OCL constraint states that a component cannot be isolated, i.e., it provides (or requests) at least a service to another component.
Connector	Logical connectors represent either potential or actual communications between components. Such connectors carry the error propagation between components.
Attribute	
coupling	Coupling metric in Goseva-Popstojanova et al (2003). It is related to error propagation proneness.
Dependability Analysis Context	This concept corresponds to the one used in the GQAM of MARTE to declare the model parameters.
Attribute	
contextParams	Set of global variables for the given context.
Association-end	
components	The set of components the system under analysis consists of.
services	The set of services the system under analysis consists of.
	Continued on next page

Table B.1 (continued)

Service	Service provided by the system to the users.
Attributes	
execProb	Service execution probability in Goseva-Popstojanova et al (2003); Hassan et al (2005); Cortellessa and Pompei (2004).
/ssAvail	Steady state availability percentage in Bernardi et al (2002, 2004a); Bondavalli et al (2001b); Majzik et al (2003). The steady state availability can be defined as in Sahner et al (1996): MTTF/MTBF or MTTF/(MTTF+MTTR) or MTTF/(MTTF+recoveryDuration). It can be derived then from associations connecting Service with Failure or Recovery classes, and from the homonym attributes defined in the latter.
instAvail	Probability that the provided service at time t is correct (time dependent) as in Sahner et al (1996). Used in Bondavalli et al (2001b); Majzik et al (2003).
unreliability	Unreliability, that is the probability that the time to failure random variable is less than (or equal to) the time t (time dependent), Sahner et al (1996).
/reliability	Reliability, used in Bondavalli et al (2001b); Majzik et al (2003), is the probability that the time to failure random variable is greater than time t (time dependent) or, in other words, that the service provided to the user is correct during the time interval $(0,t]$ as in Sahner et al (1996). It is defined as 1-unreliability. It is a *survival function* in Evans et al (2000).
missionTime	The maximum period of time for which a service can be used.
availLevel	Availability level associated to the nines of availability. E.g., high corresponds to 99% of ssAvail, etc.
reliabLevel	Reliability level.
	Continued on next page

Table B.1 (continued)

safetyLevel	Safety level.
complexity	Complexity metric, appears in Bernardi et al (2002, 2004a); Jürjens (2003); Jürjens and Wagner (2005); Goseva-Popstojanova et al (2003). There are many complexity metrics in the literature (e.g., Halstead's Software Metric, McCabe's Cyclomatic Complexity). This attribute provides a quantitative characterization of the service complexity which is related to the service failure proneness.
Association-end	
basicServices	The set of basic services, provided/required by the system components, that constitute the service.
steps	The set of ordered steps that need to be executed to fulfill the service.
ServiceRequest *Attributes*	The user that requests one or more services to the system.
accessProb	Probability that the user accesses to the system, Cortellessa and Pompei (2004).
serviceProb	Probability that the user, once accessed to the system, requires a certain service, Cortellessa and Pompei (2004). It is a vector of real values ordered according to the list *requests*.
Attributes	
requests	Ordered list of services requested by the user.
Step	Action/state of a system component during execution of a service.

B.2   Classes in the Redundancy Model

Table B.2 Redundancy model description

Class/Attribute	Description
Adjudicator, Controller, Variant *(Adjudicator) Attribute*	The three terms come from the software FT concept of "recovery block" Lyu (1995).
errorDetecCoverage	It is the error detection coverage associated to the adjudicators (e.g., a tester that checks the results produced by the variants). Used in Majzik et al (2003); Bondavalli et al (2001b).
(Variant) Attribute	
multiplicity	Number of variant copies (required or assumed).
Component *Association-end*	Concept defined in System::Core.
substitutedBy	The set of spares that may replace the component in case of failure of the latter.
FT Component	Abstract concept that indicates a kind of component that plays a specific role within a redundant structure.
Spare *Attribute*	This term is mainly referred to hardware components, however it can be also used for software components.
dormancyFactor	Ratio between failure rate in standby mode and failure rate in operational mode. Its value is also used to discriminate the type of spare (i.e., hot, cold, warm). Used in Pai and Dugan (2002).
Association-end	
substitutesFor	The set of components the spare can substitute for. The OCL constraints states that the spare cannot substitute itself.
Redundant Structure *Attribute*	It is a container of components. This concept has been introduced to specify impairments that may affect (simultaneously) a set of components belonging to the redundant structure.
FTlevel	The minimum number of components required to still guarantee a service.
Association-end	
comp	The set of components (at least two) included in the redundant structure. The OCL constraint states that the number of components within a redundant structure should be as many as those indicated by the attribute *FTlevel*.

B.3   Classes in the Threats Model

Table B.3 Threats model description

Class/Attribute	Description
Component *Association-end*	Concept defined in System::Core.
fault	The faults associated to the component.
error	The errors associated to the component.
impairment	The impairments (failures or hazards) associated to the component.
Connector *Association-end*	Concept defined in System::Core.
errProp	The error propagations carried by the connector.
impairment	The impairments (failures or hazards) associated to the connector.
Error *Attributes*	Description of a system error.
latency	Time elapsed between the error occurrence and the error detection, used in Bernardi et al (2002, 2004a).
probability	Probability of an error occurrence, used in Bernardi et al (2002, 2004a).
Association-end	
cause	The set of faults that cause the error.
effect	The set of failures that are provoked by the error (the set can be empty).
Error Propagation *Attribute*	Error propagation relation between interacting components (represents the concept of external error propagation). It is characterized by a direction.
probability	Error propagation probability, used by Majzik et al (2003); Bondavalli et al (2001b); Bernardi et al (2002, 2004a).
Association-end	
from	The (failed) component that originates the error.
to	The component that becomes erroneous due to the error propagation.
effect	The error caused in the target component (to).
cause	The failure in the source component (from) that causes the error propagation.
Error Propagation Relation	The relation is defined over the set of error propagation relations to express non trivial relationships among the latter, including sequence dependencies ("order" constraint attached to the relation).
	Continued on next page

Table B.3 (continued)

Attribute	
propagationExpr	It is a logical expression that models non trivial error propagation relationships. It is introduced to support the approach in Pai and Dugan (2002) based on the derivation of dynamic fault trees.
Association-end	
errProp	The ordered set of basic terms (at least two) of the logical expression. Each basic term expresses an error propagation between two components.
Error Step	An erroneous state/action.
Failure	Description of a failure.
Attributes	
occurrenceRate	Failure occurrence rate, i.e., number of failures per unit time. Used as either input parameter D'Ambrogio et al (2002); Pai and Dugan (2002); Grassi et al (2005, 2007) or requirement Bernardi et al (2002, 2004a).
MTTF	Mean Time To Failure. It can be either a requirement, or metric or input parameter (see comments for "occurrenceDist"). Used by Bernardi et al (2002, 2004a); Majzik et al (2003); Bondavalli et al (2001b).
MTBF	Mean Time Between Failures. It can be either a requirement, or metric or input parameter (see comments for "occurrenceDist"). Used by Bernardi et al (2002, 2004a).
occurrenceDist	Failure occurrence distribution (time dependent). Depending on the affected system level, it can be either a requirement, or metric (e.g., top-level service unreliability in Majzik et al (2003); Bondavalli et al (2001b)) or an input parameter (e.g., component failure assumption in D'Ambrogio et al (2002); Pai and Dugan (2002); Grassi et al (2005, 2007)).
domain	Failure domain (Avizienis et al, 2004), i.e., content, early timing, late timing, halt or erratic. Used by Pataricza (2000); Bernardi et al (2002, 2004a); Bernardi and Merseguer (2006); Jürjens and Wagner (2005); Jürjens (2003).
detectability	Failure detectability (Avizienis et al, 2004), i.e., signaled or unsignaled.
consistency	Failure consistency (Avizienis et al, 2004), i.e., consistent or inconsistent.

Continued on next page

Table B.3 (continued)

consequence	Failure consequence (Avizienis et al, 2004), i.e., minor, marginal, major, or catastrophic. Used by Bernardi et al (2002, 2004a); Goseva-Popstojanova et al (2003); Hassan et al (2005).
condition	Logical condition that leads to the failure. Used to express relationships among component failure states in Addouche et al (2004, 2006); Bobbio et al (2003).
Failure Step	It has various meanings. State/activity affected by failure in Grassi et al (2005, 2007); state reached after failure occurrence in Bernardi and Merseguer (2006); Bondavalli et al (2001b); Majzik et al (2003) and failure event/transition/call that leads to a failure state in Bondavalli et al (2001b); Majzik et al (2003); Pai and Dugan (2002); D'Ambrogio et al (2002).
Fault	Description of a fault.
Attributes	
occurrenceRate	Fault occurrence rate, e.g. number of faults per year. Used by Majzik et al (2003); Bondavalli et al (2001b); Bernardi and Merseguer (2006).
latency	Fault latency is the time elapsing between a fault occurrence and the instant in which it is perceived by the component(s). Used by Bernardi and Merseguer (2006).
occurrenceProb	Probability of a fault occurrence (time independent). Used by Cortellessa and Pompei (2004).
occurrenceDist	Probability of a fault occurrence within time t (time dependent). E.g., it can be specified as negative exponential distribution with input parameter the occurrenceRate attribute.
persistency	Indicates the type of fault w.r.t. persistency (Avizienis et al, 2004), that is either transient or permanent. Used by Pataricza (2000); Bernardi and Merseguer (2006).
duration	Fault duration (from its occurrence). This attribute can be used to discriminate the fault persistency Bernardi et al (2002, 2004a).
Association-end	
effect (Error)	The set of errors caused by the fault (it can be empty).
effect (Impairment)	The set of impairments, i.e., failures, hazards, caused by the fault (it can be empty).

Continued on next page

Table B.3 (continued)

Fault Generator	Fault injector. This concept can be modeled, for example, by a UML state machine that represents the behavior of the injected fault(s). Used by Pataricza (2000); Bernardi and Merseguer (2006).
Attribute	
numberOfFaults	Number of faults that affect simultaneously the system (for analysis purposes).
Association-end	
fault	The fault characterization generated by the fault injector.
Fault Step	A faulty state.
Hazard	Description of a hazard (Leveson, 1995).
Attribute	
origin	Depending on the factors that provoked it, it can be classified as endogenous (due to factors inherent in the system) or exogenous (due to external phenomena).
severity	Worst possible accident that could result from the hazard given the environment in its most unfavorable state.
likelihood	Likelihood of hazard occurring (qualitative).
/level	Derived attribute: it is a combination of severity and likelihood.
latency	Duration from its occurrence to an accident.
accidentLikelihood	Likelihood of hazard leading to an accident.
guideword	Guideword that describes the hazard. Used by Hassan et al (2005), e.g., applied in FFA.
accident	Accident on the system environment that may be provoked by the hazard.
Hazard Step	Similar meaning of failure step but referred to hazard.
Impairment	Abstract concept that may correspond to either failure or hazard.
Attribute	
occurrenceProb	Occurrence probability of the impairment (time independent). It has been used in Bernardi et al (2002, 2004a); Hassan et al (2005).
/risk	Risk factor used in Goseva-Popstojanova et al (2003). It is a derived attribute, when applied to failure is a combination of (failure) occurrence probability and of failure consequence. When applied to hazards, is a combination of (hazard) latency and accidentLikelihood.

Continued on next page

Table B.3 (continued)

cost	Cost of the impairment (accepted measure of conse-quences). Used by Hassan et al (2005).
Association-end	
cause (Fault)	The set of faults that originate the impairment.
cause (Error)	The set of errors that originate the impairment.
RedundantStructure	Concept defined in System::Redundancy.
Association-end	
commonMode	The common impairments (failures or hazards) affecting all the components within the redundant structure.
Service	Concept defined in System::Core.
Association-end	
impairment	The impairments (failures or hazards) affecting the ser-vice.
Step	Concept defined in System::Core.
Association-end	
error	The errors affecting the step.
impairment	The impairments (failures or hazards) affecting the step.
fault	The fault affecting the step.

B.4   Classes in the Maintenance Model

Table B.4 Maintenance model description

Class/Attribute	Description
Activation Step *Attribute*	Activates the system behavior as a consequence of failure steps.
priority	Priority associated to the activation step.
preemption	(true) The activation step can be preempted by another activation step with a higher priority. (false) The activation step cannot be pre-empted.
Association-end	
agents	The agent groups that carry out this step.
cause	The failure steps that cause this step.
Agent Group *Attribute*	A group of external agents.
skill	Technicians of hardware or software.
correctness	Probability to have a successful maintenance.
/agentsNumber	Number of external agents that compose the group. The OCL con-straints states that this number a derived attribute (equal to the size of the set *agents* given by the association-end.
Association-end	
agents	The external agents belonging to the group.
Component *Association-end*	Concept defined in System::Core
repair	The actions carried out to repair the component.
External Agent	This class represents an external actor that undertakes repair actions on system component affected by threats, e.g., repairman, test equip-ment, remote reloading software, etc.
Maintenance Action *Attribute*	Abstract concept that includes both repair and recovery actions.
rate	Rate of the maintenance action.
distribution	Probability distribution associated to the maintenance action, that is time to repair/recover (time dependent). Used in Bernardi and Merseguer (2006).
Maintenance Step *Association-end*	Abstract concept that includes both reconfiguration and activation steps.
maintenance	The maintenance actions performed in this step.

Continued on next page

Table B.4 (continued)

Reallocation Step	Reconfiguration step in which an ordered set of sw components are reallocated onto an ordered collection of hw spare components. Used by Pai and Dugan (2002). The OCL constraint states that the number of sw components must be equal to the cardinality of the collection of the hw components.
Association-end	
map	The ordered set of software components to be reallocated.
to	The ordered collection of hardware spare components that host the software component.
Reconfiguration Step	Abstract concept that represents a step in which a reconfiguration technique is carried out. The latter consists of either switching in (spare or variant) components or reallocating sw components among non failed hw components (Avizienis et al, 2004).
Recovery	Recovery descriptor. A recovery activity/action is usually carried out by the system itself as a part of an implemented fault tolerance strategy (Avizienis et al, 2004).
Attribute	
duration	Recovery duration.
coverageFactor	Probability of recovery given that a fault is occurred in the system.
Repair	Repair descriptor. A repair activity/action is carried out on system components by external agents.
Attribute	
MTTR	Mean Time To Repair. Used by Bernardi et al (2002, 2004a); Bernardi and Merseguer (2006); Bondavalli et al (2001b); Majzik et al (2003).
Replacement Step	Reconfiguration step in which an ordered set of failed components are replaced with an ordered set of components (spares or variants). Used by Pai and Dugan (2002).
Association-end	
replace	The ordered set of failed components.
with	The ordered set of component that replace the failed ones.
Service	Concept defined in System::Core
Association-end	
recovery	The recovery actions undertaken to restore the service.

References

AADL (2006) The Architecture Analysis & Design Language (AADL): An Introduction. Technical Note CMU/SEI-2006-TN-011

AADL (2009) Architecture Analysis & Design Language. SAE International

AADL-EM (2006) SAE-AS5506/1 Architecture Analysis and Design Language Annex (AADL): Vol 1, annex E:Error Model. International Society of Automotive Engineers

Addouche N, Antoine C, Montmain J (2004) UML models for dependability analysis of real-time systems. In: Proceedings of the international conference on systems, man and cybernetics, vol 6. IEEE Computer Society, Silver Spring, pp 5209–5214

Addouche N, Antoine C, Montmain J (2006) Methodology for UML modeling and formal verification of real-time systems. In: International Conference on Computational Intelligence for Modelling Control and Automation (CIMCA 2006), International Conference on Intelligent Agents, Web Technologies and Internet Commerce (IAWTIC 2006). IEEE Computer Society, Silver Spring, p 17

Ajmone MM, Chiola G (1987) On Petri nets with deterministic and exponentially distributed firing times. In: Advances in Petri nets 1987, covers the 7th European workshop on applications and theory of Petri nets. Springer, London, pp 132–145

Ajmone-Marsan M, Balbo G, Conte G, Donatelli S, Franceschinis G (1994) Modeling with generalized stochastic Petri nets. Wiley series in parallel computing. Wiley, West Sussex

Allenby K, Kelly T (2001) Deriving safety requirements using scenarios. In: 5th IEEE international symposium on requirements engineering. IEEE Computer Society, Washington, pp 228–235

ANSI/IEEE (1991) Standard Glossary of Software Engineering Terminology. Technical Report STD-729-1991, ANSI/IEEE

ANSI/IEEE-STD-352 (1987) IEEE guide for general principles of reliability analysis of nuclear power generating station safety systems

Arnold T (1973) The concept of coverage and its effect on the reliability model of a repairable system. IEEE Trans Comp 22:251–254. doi: http://doi.ieeecomputersociety.org/10.1109/T-C.1973.223703

ARP-4754 (1994) Certification considerations for highly-integrated or complex aircraft systems. Society of Automotive Engineers (SAE), Warrendale

ARP-4761 (1995) Guidelines and methods for conducting the safety assessment of civil airbone systems and equipment. Society of Automotive Engineers (SAE), Warrendale

AUTOSAR (2011) AUTomotive Open System ARchitecture. Version 3.0. www.autosar.org. Accessed 30 Sept 2010

Avižienis A (1967) Design of fault-tolerant computers. In: Proceedings of the fall joint computer conference, AFIPS '67 (Fall). ACM, New York, pp 733–743

Avizienis A (1985) The N-version approach to fault-tolerant software. IEEE Trans Software Eng 11(12):1491–1501

Avizienis A, Laprie JC, Randell B, Landwehr C (2004) Basic concepts and taxonomy of dependable and secure computing. IEEE Trans Dependable Secur Comput 1(1):11–33

Baarir S, Beccuti M, Cerotti D, DePierro M, Donatelli S, Franceschinis G (2009) The GreatSPN tool: recent enhancements. SIGMETRICS Perform Eval Rev 36(4):4–9

Balsamo S, Di Marco A, Inverardi P, Simeoni M (2004) Model-based performance prediction in software development: A survey. IEEE Trans Software Eng 30(5):295–310

Béounes C, Kanoun K, Aguera M, Laprie JC, Arlat J, Metge S, Bachmann S, de Souza JM, Bourdeau C, Powell D, Doucet JE, Spiesser P (1993) SURF-2: a program for dependability evaluation of complex hardware and software systems. In: The 23rd annual international symposium on Fault-Tolerant Computing (FTCS-23). IEEE Computer Society, Toulouse, pp 668–673

Bernardi S, Merseguer J (2006) QoS assessment via stochastic analysis. IEEE Internet Comput 10(3): 32–42

Bernardi S, Donatelli S, Horváth A (2001) Special section on the pratical use of high-level Petri Nets: implementing compositionality for stochastic Petri nets. Int J Software Tool Tech Tran (STTT) 3(4):417–430

Bernardi S, Donatelli S, Dondossola G (2002) Methodology for the generation of the modeling scenarios starting from the requisite specifications and its application to the collected requirements, IST Project 25434 DepAuDE - Deliverable D1.3b, 2002

Bernardi S, Donatelli S, Dondossola G (2004a) A class diagram framework for collecting dependability requirements in automation systems. In: Proceedings of the 1st international symposium on leveraging applications of formal methods (ISOLA'04), Department of Computer Science, University of Cyprus, Paphos (Cyprus)

Bernardi S, Donatelli S, Dondossola G (2004b) Towards a methodological approach to specification and analysis of dependable automation systems. In: Proceedings of the 1st international joint conference on formal modelling and analysis of timed systems (FORMATS) and on formal techniques in real-time and fault tolerant system (FTRTFT). Springer, Grenoble (France), pp 36–51

Bernardi S, Campos J, Merseguer J (2011a) Timing-failure risk assessment of UML design using Time Petri Net bound techniques. IEEE Trans Ind Informat 7(1):90–104

Bernardi S, Flammini F, Marrone S, Merseguer J, Papa C, Vittorini V (2011b) Model-driven availability evaluation of railway control systems. In: 30th international conference, SAFECOMP11, Naples. LNCS, vol 6894. Springer, pp 15–28

Bernardi S, Merseguer J, Petriu D (2011c) A dependability profile within MARTE. Software Syst Model 10(3):313–336

Bernardi S, Merseguer J, Petriu D (2012) Dependability modeling and analysis of software systems specified with UML. ACM Comput Surv 45(1):2

Bernardi S, Flammini F, Marrone S, Mazzocca N, Merseguer J, Nardone R, Vittorini V (2013) Enabling the usage of UML in the verification of railway systems: the DAM-rail approach. Reliab Eng Syst Safety. http://dx.doi.org/10.1016/j.ress.2013.06.032

Berthomieu B, Diaz M (1991) Modeling and verification of time dependent systems using time Petri nets. IEEE Trans Software Eng 12(3):259–273

Biba KJ (1977) Integrity considerations for secure computer systems. Tech Rep MTR-3153, Mitre Corporation, Bedford MA

Billinton R, Allan RN (1992) Reliability evaluation of engineering systems: concepts and techniques. Plenum, New York

Bobbio A, Ciancamerla E, Franceschinis G, Gaeta R, Minichino M, Portinale L (2003) Sequential application of heterogeneous models for the safety analysis of a control system: a case study. Reliab Eng Syst Saf 81:269–280

Bocciarelli P, D'Ambrogio A (2011a) A BPMN extension for modeling non functional properties of business processes. In: Wainer GA, Traoré MK, Heckel R, Himmelspach J (eds) Proceedings of the 2011 symposium on theory of modeling & simulation: DEVS integrative M&S symposium (TMS-DEVS) held within the spring simulation multi-conference, SpringSim '11, vol 4. SCS/ACM, Boston, pp 160–168

Bocciarelli P, D'Ambrogio A (2011b) A model-driven method for describing and predicting the reliability of composite services. Software Syst Model 10(2):265–280

Boehm B (1984) Verifying and validating software requirements and design specifications. IEEE Software 1:75–88, doi: http://doi.ieeecomputersociety.org/10.1109/MS.1984.233702

Bondavalli A, Dal Cin M, Latella D, Majzik I, Pataricza A, Savoia G (2001a) Dependability analysis in the early phases of UML-based system design. Int J Comput Syst Sci Eng 16(5):265–275

Bondavalli A, Chiaradonna S, Di Giandomenico F, Mura I (2004) Dependability modeling and evaluation of multiple-phased systems using DEEM. IEEE Trans Reliab 53(4):509–522

Bondavalli A, et al. (2001b) Dependability analysis in the early phases of UML-based system design. Int J Comput Syst Sci Eng 16(5):265–275

Bozzano M, Cimatti A, Katoen JP, Nguyen VY, Noll T, Roveri M (2011) Safety, dependability and performance analysis of extended AADL models. Comput J 54(5):754–775

BPEL (2007) Web Services Business Process Execution Language. Version 2.0

BPMN (2011) Business Process Modeling Notation. Version 2.0 - OMG Standard document formal/2011-01-03

BS-5760-5 (1991) Reliability of systems, equipment and components. Guide to failure modes, effects and criticality analysis (FMEA and FMECA)

Campos J, Silva M (1992) Structural techniques and performance bounds of stochastic Petri net models. Lecture notes in computer science, vol 609. Springer, Heidelberg, pp 352–391

Cancila D, Terrier F, Belmonte F, Dubois H, Espinoza H, Gérard S, Cuccuru A (2009) Sophia: a modeling language for model-based safety engineering. In: Van Baelen S, Weigert T, Ober I, Espinoza H (eds) 2nd international workshop on model based architecting and construction of embedded systems, CEUR. Denver, Colorado, pp 11–26

Cao H, Yan T, Pereira LR, Das SR, Lewis B (2006) Use AADL to analyze and design embedded systems. www.embedded.com. Accessed 19 Aug 2007

Chillarege R, Bhandari IS, Chaar JK, Halliday MJ, Moebus DS, Ray BK, Wong MY (1992) Orthogonal defect classification-a concept for in-process measurements. IEEE Trans Software Eng 18:943–956

Chiola G, Dutheillet C, Franceschinis G, Haddad S (1993) Stochastic well-formed colored nets and symmetric modeling applications. IEEE Trans Comput 42(11):1343–1360

Choi H, Kulkarni VG, Trivedi KS (1994) Markov regenerative stochastic Petri nets. Perform Eval 20:337–357

Clark DD, Wilson DR (1987) A comparison of commercial and military computer security policies. In: Proceedings of the IEEE symposium on security and privacy. IEEE CS, Oakland, California, pp 184–195

Clark G, Courtney T, Daly D, Deavours D, Derisavi S, Doyle JM, Sanders WH, Webster P (2001) The Möbius modeling tool. In: Proceedings of the 9th international workshop on Petri nets and performance models, pp 241 –250

Contini S, Scheer S, Wilikens M, DeCola G, Cojazzi G (1999) ASTRA, an integrated tool set for complex systems dependability studies. Tech. rep., European Commission Joint Research Centre (JRC) – JRC n. 18415, jRC n. 18415

Cortellessa V, Grassi V (2007) A modeling approach to analyze the impact of error propagation on reliability of component-based systems. In: Proceedings of the 10th international conference on component-based software engineering, CBSE'07. Springer, Berlin, pp 140–156

Cortellessa V, Mirandola R (2000) Deriving a queueing network based performance model from UML diagrams. In: Proceedings of the second international workshop on software and performance (WOSP2000). ACM, Ottawa, pp 58–70

Cortellessa V, Pompei A (2004) Towards a UML Profile for QoS: a contribution in the reliability domain. In: Proceedings of the fourth international workshop on software and performance (WOSP'04). Redwood Shores, California, pp 197–206

Cox D, Miller H (1965) The theory of stochastic processes. Chapman and Hall, London

Csertan G, Huszerl G, Majzik I, Pap Z, Pataricza A, Varro D (2002) VIATRA – VIsual Automated TRAnsformations for formal verification and validation of UML models. In: Proceedings of the

17th IEEE international conference on automated software engineering (ASE). IEEE Computer Society, Washington, DC, pp 267–270

Dal Cin M (2003) Extending UML towards a useful OO-language for modeling dependability features. In: Proceedings of 9th IEEE international workshop on object-oriented real-time dependable systems (WORDS 2003 Fall). IEEE Computer Society, Anacapri (Capri Island), Italy, pp 325–330

D'Ambrogio A, Iazeolla G, Mirandola R (2002) A method for the prediction of software reliability. In: Proceedings of the 6-th IASTED software engineering and applications conference (SEA2002), Cambridge, MA

David P, Idasiak V, Kratz F (2009) Improving reliability studies with SysML. In: RAMS09: Proceedings of the reliability and maintainability symposium. IEEE Computer Society, Fort Worth, Texas

DeMiguel M, Lambolais T, Piekarec S, Betgé-Brezetz S, Péquery J (2001) Automatic generation of simulation models for the evaluation of performance and reliability of architectures specified in UML. In: EDO'00: revised papers from the second international workshop on engineering distributed objects. Springer, London, pp 83–101

Denning P, Buzen J (1978) The operational analysis of queueing network models. ACM Comput Surv 10(3):225–261

Devanbu PT, Stubblebine S (2000) Software engineering for security: a roadmap. In: Proceedings of the conference on the future of software engineering, ICSE'00. ACM, New York, pp 227–239

Donatelli S, Franceschinis G (1996) The PSR methodology: integrating hardware and software models. In: Billington J, Reisig W (eds) Application and theory of Petri nets. LNCS, vol 1091. Springer, Berlin, pp 133–152

Dugan JB, Trivedi KS, Geist R, Nicola VF (1985) Extended stochastic petri nets: applications and analysis. In: Proceedings of the 10th international symposium on computer performance modelling, measurement and evaluation, Performance '84. North-Holland Publishing Co., Amsterdam, The Netherlands, pp 507–519

Dugan JB, Bavuso SJ, Boyd MA (1992) Dynamic fault-tree models for fault tolerant computer systems. IEEE Trans Reliab 41(3):363–373

Dugan JB, Venkataraman B, Gulati R (1997) DIFtree: a software package for the analysis of dynamic fault tree models. In: Proceedings of the 1997 reliability and maintainability symposium (RAMS). IEEE Computer Society, Washington, DC, pp 64–70

EAST-ADL2 (2010) EAST-ADL Profile Specification. The ATESST2 Consortium: deliverable D4.1.1

Evans M, Hastings N, Peacock B (2000) Statistical distributions. Wiley, New York

Genero M, Piattini M, Manso E, Cantone G (2003) Building UML class diagram maintainability prediction models based on early metrics. In: METRICS '03: Proceedings of the 9th international symposium on software metrics. IEEE Computer Society, Washington, DC, p 263

Genero M, Manso E, Visaggio A, Canofra G, Piattini M (2007) Building measure-based prediction models for UML class diagram maintainability. Empir Software Eng 12:517–549

Gharbi N, Dutheillet C (2011) An algorithmic approach for analysis of finite-source retrial systems with unreliable servers. Comput Math Appl 62(6):2535–2546

Ghezzi C, Mandrioli D, Morzenti A (1990) Trio: a logic language for executable specifications of real-time systems. J Syst Software 12(2):107–123

Goseva-Popstojanova K, Trivedi KS (2000) Stochastic modeling formalisms for dependability, performance and performability. In: Haring G, Lindemann C, Reiser M (eds) Performance evaluation: origins and directions, Lecture notes in computer science, vol 1769. Springer, Berlin, pp 403–422

Goseva-Popstojanova K, Hassan AE, Guedem A, Abdelmoez W, Nassar DEM, Ammar HH, Mili A (2003) Architectural-level risk analysis using UML. IEEE Trans Software Eng 29(10):946–960

Graaf B, van Deursen A (2007) Visualisation of domain-specific modelling languages using UML. In: 14th annual IEEE international conference and workshop on engineering of computer based systems (ECBS 2007), 26–29 March 2007, IEEE Computer Society, Tucson, Arizona, pp 586–595

Grassi V, Mirandola R, Sabetta A (2005) From design to analysis models: a kernel language for performance and reliability analysis of component-based systems. In: Proceedings of the fifth international workshop on software and performance (WOSP'05). Palma de Mallorca, Illes Balears, pp 25–36

Grassi V, Mirandola R, Sabetta A (2007) Filling the gap between design and performance/reliability models of component-based systems: A model-driven approach. J Syst Software 80(4):528–558

GreatSPN (2002) University of Torino. http://www.di.unito.it/_greatspn. Accessed 6 Sept 2013

Hansen K, Wells L, Maier T (2004) HAZOP analysis of UML-based software architecture description of safety-critical systems. In: Koskimies K, Kuzniarz L, Lilius J, Porres I (eds) Second Nordic workshop on UML, modeling, methods and tools, TUCS. Turku, Finland

Harel D (1987) Statecharts: a visual formalism for complex systems. Sci Comput Program 8(3):231–274

Hassan A, Goseva-Popstojanova K, Ammar H (2005) UML based severity analysis methodology. In: Proceedings of annual reliability and maintainability symposium (RAMS 2005), Alexandria, VA

Haverkort BR, Marie R, Rubino G, Trivedi K (2001) Performability modelling. Wiley, Chichester

Hawkings R, Toyn I, Bate I (2003) An approach to designing safety critical systems using the unified modelling language. In: Workshop on critical systems development with UML, San Francisco, pp 3–18

HAZOP (2000) HAZOP studies on systems containing programmable electronics. UK Ministry of Defence, Glasgow (UK)

Hosford J (1960) Measures of dependability. Oper Res 8(1):204–206

Huang Y, Kindala C (1996) Software fault tolerance in the application layer. In: Lyu MR (ed) Software fault tolerance. Wiley, New York, Chap 10, pp 231–248

IAEA-478 (1988) Component reliability data for use in probabilistic safety assessement. Technical document issued by the International Atomic Energy Agency, Vienna (Austria)

IBM (2012) Rational rose modeler. http://www-01.ibm.com/software/rational/. Accessed 6 Sept 2013

IEC-60300-3-1 (2003) Dependability Management. Part 3: Application Guide, Section 1: Analysis Techniques for dependability: Guide on methodology

IEC-60300-3-15 (2009) Dependability Management. Part 3–15: Guidance to engineering of system dependability

IEC-60812 (1985) Analysis techniques for system reliability - Procedure for failure mode and effects analysis (FMEA)

IEC-61025 (2006) Fault tree analysis (FTA)

IEC-61078 (2006) Analysis techniques for dependability – Reliability block diagram and boolean methods

IEC-61131-1 (1992) Programmable controllers, part 3: Programming languages. International Electro-technical Commission

IEC-61165 (2006) Application of Markov techniques

IEC-61508 (1998) Functional safety of electrical/electronic/programmable electronic safety-related systems. International Electro-technical Commission

IEC-61882 (2001) Hazard and operability studies (HAZOP studies) – Application guide

IEC-62061 (2005) Safety of machinery – Functional safety of safety-related electrical, electronic and programmable electronic control systems

IEC-62502 (2010) Analysis techniques for dependability – Event tree analysis (ETA). Ed1.0

Isograph (2012) FaultTree+ software package. URL http://www.isograph-software.com. Accessed 6 Sept 2013

ISO/IEC 14764 (2006) Standard for software engineering – software life cycle processes - maintenance. International organization for standardization/International electro-technical commission

ISO/IEC-15909-1 (2004) Systems and software engineering – High-level Petri nets. Part 1: Concepts, definitions and graphical notation

ISO/IEC-9126-1 (2001) Software engineering – Product quality. Part 1: Quality Model

ISO/IEC9126-1.2 (2001) Information technology – software product quality. Part 1: quality model. International Electro-technical Commission

ITU-TS (1995) ITU-TS Recommendation Z.120: Message Sequence Charts (MSC). International Telecommunication Union, Geneva

Iwu F, Galloway A, McDermid J, Toyn I (2007) Integrating safety and formal analyses using UML and PFS. Reliab Eng Syst Saf 92(2):156–170

Jürjens J, Wagner S (2005) Component-based development of dependable systems with UML. In: Atkinson C, Bunse C, Gross HG, Peper C (eds) Component-based software development for embedded systems. LNCS, vol 3778. Springer, Berlin, pp 320–344

Johannessen P, Grante C, Alminger A, Eklund U, Torin J (2001) Hazard analysis in object-oriented design of dependable systems. In: Proceedings of the international conference on dependable systems and networks (DSN01). IEEE Computer Society, Washington, DC, pp 507–512

Johnson BW (1989) Design and analysis of fault-tolerant digital systems. Addison-Wesley, Reading, MA

Jouault F, Kurtev I (2006) Transforming models with ATL. In: Proceedings of the 2005 international conference on satellite events at the MoDELS, MoDELS'05. Springer, Berlin, pp 128–138

Jürjens J (2003) Developing safety-critical systems with UML. In: Proceedings of UML 2003. LNCS, vol 2863. Springer, San Francisco, pp 360–372

Kelling C (1996) Conventional and fast simulation techniques for stochastic Petri nets. Bericht (Technische Universität Berlin. Fachbereich 20, Informatik), Technische Universität Berlin, Fachbereich 13, Informatik

Kulkarni VG (1995) Modeling and analysis of stochastic systems. Chapman & Hall, London

Lagarde F, Espinoza H, Terrier F, Gérard S (2007) Improving UML profile design practices by leveraging conceptual domain models. In: Stirewalt REK, Egyed A, Fischer B (eds) 22nd IEEE/ACM international conference on automated software engineering (ASE 2007). ACM, Atlanta (USA), pp 445–448

Lamport L, Shostak R, Pease M (1982) The byzantine generals problem. ACM Trans Program Lang Syst 4:382–401

Leangsuksun C, Shen L, Liu T, Song H, Scott SL (2003) Availability prediction and modeling of high availability OSCAR cluster. In: IEEE international conference on cluster computing. IEEE Computer Society, Washington, DC, p 380

Leveson N, Stolzy J (1987) Safety analysis using Petri nets. IEEE Trans Software Eng 13(3): 386–397

Leveson NG (1995) Safeware: system safety and computers. Addison-Wesley, Reading

Lindemann C (1998) Performance modelling with deterministic and stochastic Petri nets. Wiley, New York

Littlewood B, Strigini L (1993) Validation of ultrahigh dependability for software-based systems. Commun ACM 36:69–80, doi: http://doi.acm.org/10.1145/163359.163373

Liu J, Dehlinger J, Lutz RR (2007) Safety analysis of software product lines using state-based modeling. J Syst Software 80(11):1879–1892

Lu S, Halang WA (2007) A UML profile to model safety-critical embedded real-time control systems. In: Krämer BJ, Halang WA (eds) Contributions to ubiquitous computing, studies in computational intelligence, vol 42. Springer, Berlin, pp 197–218

Lyu M (1995) Software fault tolerance. Wiley, New York

Lyu MR (ed) (1996) Handbook of software reliability engineering. IEEE Computer Society, New York

Majzik I, Pataricza A, Bondavalli A (2003) Stochastic dependability analysis of system architecture based on UML models. In: Architecting dependable systems. LNCS, vol 2677. Springer, Berlin, pp 219–244

MARTE (2011) UML Profile for MARTE: Modeling and analysis of real-time and embedded systems. Version 1.1, OMG document: formal/2011-06-02

Martin J, Odell J (1997) Object-oriented methods: a foundation, 2nd edn. Prentice Hall, Englewood Cliffs

Mauri G (2000) Integrating safety analysis techniques, supporting identification of common cause failures. PhD thesis, Department of Computer Science, University of York

Merseguer J (2003) Software performance engineering based on UML and Petri nets. PhD thesis, University of Zaragoza, Spain

Merseguer J, Bernardi S (2012) Dependability analysis of DES based on MARTE and UML state machines models. Discrete Event Dyn Syst 22(2):163–178

Meyer J (1980) On evaluating the performability of degradable computing systems. IEEE Trans Comput 29:720–731

MIL-STD-1629a (1980) Military standard: procedures for performing a failure mode, effect and criticality analysis

MIL-STD-882c (1993) Military standard: system safety program requirements

MIL-STD-882d (2000) Military standard: standard practice for system safety

MOF (2006) Meta Object Facility (MOF) Specification. OMG document: formal/2006-01-01

Muppala J, Ciardo G, Trivedi K (1993) Modeling using stochastic reward nets. In: Schwetman HD, Walrand JC, Bagchi KK, DeGroot D (eds) MASCOTS '93, Proceedings of the international workshop on modeling, analysis, and simulation on computer and telecommunication systems, 17–20 January 1993. The Society for Computer Simulation, La Jolla, San Diego, pp 367–372

Mustafiz S, Kienzle J (2009) DREP: a requirements engineering process for dependable reactive systems. In: Butler MJ, Jones CB, Romanovsky A, Troubitsyna E (eds) Methods, models and tools for fault tolerance. Lecture Notes in Computer Science, vol 5454. Springer, Berlin/Heidelberg, pp 220–250

Mustafiz S, Sun X, Kienzle J, Vangheluwe H (2008) Model-driven assessment of system dependability. Software Syst Model 7(4):487–502

Nicol D, Sanders W, Trivedi K (2004) Model-based evaluation: from dependability to security. IEEE Trans Sependable secur Comput 1(1):48–65

de Niz D (2007) Diagrams and languages for model-based software engineering of embedded systems:UML and AADL. White Paper, www.sei.cmu.edu/library

NPRD11 (2011) Nonelectronic parts reliability data. Reliability Information Analysis Center, Department of Defence (USA)

Ober I, Graf S, Ober I (2006) Validating timed UML models by simulation and verification. STTT 8(2):128–145

OCL (2006) Object constraint language. OMG document: formal/2006-05-01, v2.0

OpNet (1999) OpNet modeler. Http://www.opnet.com/solutions/network_rd/modeler.html. Accessed 6 Sept 2013

OSATE (2012) Open Source AADL Tool Environment. International Society of Automotive Engineers. http://www.aadl.info. Accessed 6 Sept 2013

Pai GJ, Dugan J (2002) Automatic synthesis of dynamic fault trees from UML system models. In: Proceedings of 13th international symposium on software reliability engineering (ISSRE-02). IEEE Computer Society, Annapolis, pp 243–256

Papoulis A (1965) Probability, random variables and stochastic processes. McGraw Hill, New York

Pataricza A (2000) From the general resource model to a general fault modelling paradigm? In: Workshop on critical systems, held within UML'2000. CiteSeer Computer and Information Science Publications, Digital Library

Pataricza A, Majzik I, Huszerl G, Várnay G (2003) UML-based design and formal analysis of a safety-critical railway control software module. In: Tarnai G, Schnieder E (eds) Proceedings of symposium formal methods for railway operation and control systems (FORMS03), Budapest (Hungary), pp 125–132

Powell D (1992) Failure mode assumptions and assumption coverage. In: Fault-tolerant computing, 1992. FTCS-22. Twenty-second international symposium on Digest of Papers. IEEE computer society, Boston, pp 386–395

QoS&FT (2008) UML Profile for Modeling Quality of Service and Fault Tolerant Characteristics and Mechanisms. V1.1, formal/08-04-05

QVT (2011) Query/View/Transformation Specification. OMG document: formal/2011-01-01

Rai S, Veeraraghavan M, Trivedi K (1995) A survey on efficient computation of reliability using disjoint products approach. Networks 25(3):147–163

Rauzy A (1993) New algorithms for fault trees analysis. Reliab Eng Syst Saf 5(59):203–211

Rodrigues GN, Rosenblum DS, Uchitel S (2005) Reliability prediction in model-driven development. In: Briand LC, Williams C (eds) Model driven engineering languages and systems, 8th international conference (MoDELS 2005). Lecture Notes in Computer Science, vol 3713. Springer, Montego Bay, Jamaica, pp 339–354

RTCA (1992) Software considerations in airbone systems and equipment certification. Radio Technical Commission for Aeronautics (RTCA), European Organization for Civil Aviation Electronics (EUROCAE), no.DO-178B/ED-12B

Rugina AE, Kanoun K, Kaâniche M (2007) A system dependability modeling framework using AADL and GSPNs. In: de Lemos R et al. (eds) Architecting dependable systems IV. Lecture Notes in Computer Science, vol 4615. Springer, Berlin/Heidelberg, pp 14–38

Rugina AE, Kanoun K, Kaâniche M (2008) The ADAPT tool: From AADL architectural models to stochastic Petri nets through model transformation. In: Seventh European dependable computing conference, EDCC-7. IEEE Computer Society, Kaunas, Lithuania, pp 85–90

Rugina AE, Kanoun K, Kaâniche M (2011) Software dependability modeling using AADL. Int J Performability Eng 7(4):313–325

Rumbaugh JE, Blaha MR, Premerlani WJ, Eddy F, Lorensen WE (1991) Object-oriented modeling and design. Prentice-Hall, Englewood Cliffs

SAE-ARP-4761 (1996) Guidelines and Methods for Conducting the Safety Assessment Process on Civil Airborne Systems and Equipment

Sahner R, Trivedi K, Puliafito A (1996) Performance and reliability analysis of computer systems: an example-based approach using the SHARPE Software Package. Kluwer, Boston

Sahner RA, Trivedi KS (1987) Reliability modeling using SHARPE. IEEE Trans Reliab 36(2):186–193

Sailer R, Zhang X, Jaeger T, van Doorn L (2004) Design and implementation of a tcg-based integrity measurement architecture. In: Proceedings of the 13th conference on USENIX security symposium, vol 13, SSYM'04. USENIX Association, Berkeley, pp 223–238

Sanders W, Meyer J (2001) Stochastic activity networks: formal definitions and concepts. In: Brinksma E, Hermanns H, Katoen JP (eds) Lectures on formal methods and performance analysis, First EEF/Euro summer school on trends in computer science, Berg en Dal, The Netherlands, 3–7 July 2000, Revised Lectures, Springer, Lecture Notes in Computer Science, vol 2090, pp 315–343

Schmidt DC (2006) Guest editor's introduction: model-driven engineering. Computer 39(2):25–31

Selic B (2003) The pragmatics of model-driven development. IEEE Software 20(5):19–25

Selic B (2007) A systematic approach to domain-specific language design using UML. In: Tenth IEEE international symposium on object-oriented real-time distributed computing (ISORC 2007), 7–9 May 2007. IEEE Computer Society, Santorini Island, Greece, pp 2–9

de Souza e Silva E, Gail HR (1989) Calculating availability and performability measures of repairable computer systems using randomization. J ACM 36:171–193, doi: http://doi.acm.org/10.1145/58562.59307

Singh H, Cortellessa V, Cukic B, Gunel E, Bharadwaj V (2001) A bayesian approach to reliability prediction and assessment of component based systems. In: 12th international symposium on software reliability engineering (ISSRE 2001), Hong Kong, China, 27–30 November 2001. IEEE Computer Society, Washington, pp 12–21

Smith C, Lloyd G (2003) Software performance engineering. In: Lavagno L, Martin G, Selic B (eds) UML for real: design of embedded real-time systems. Kluwer, New York, pp 343–365

SoaML (2012) Service oriented architecture modeling language. Version 1.0.1 - OMG Standard document formal/2012-05-10

SPT (2005) UML Profile for schedulabibity, performance and time specification. Version 1.1, formal/05-01-02

Stapelberg RF (2008) Handbook of reliability, availability, maintainability and safety engineering design. Springer, London

Sterbenz JPG, Hutchison D, Çetinkaya EK, Jabbar A, Rohrer JP, Schöller M, Smith P (2010) Resilience and survivability in communication networks: strategies, principles, and survey of disciplines. Comput Network 54(8):1245–1265

Sullivan KJ, Dugan JB, Coppit D (1999) The Galileo fault tree analysis tool. In: Proceedings of the 29th annual international symposium on fault-tolerant computing. IEEE Computer Society, Madison, pp 232–235

SysML (2012) System Modeling Language. Version 1.3, OMG document formal/2012-06-01

TCG (2011) Http://www.trustedcomputinggroup.org. Accessed 6 Sept 2013

TPC-W (2000) Tpc-w. Http://www.tpc.org/tpcw/. Accessed 6 Sept 2013

Trivedi K (2001) Probability and statistics with reliability, queuing, and computer science applications. Wiley, New York

Trivedi KS (2002) SHARPE 2002: Symbolic hierarchical automated reliability and performance evaluator. In: Proceedings of the 2002 international conference on dependable systems and networks (DSN 2002). IEEE Computer Society, Bethesda, p 544

UML-EDOC (2001) UML profile for enterprise distributed object computing. Version 1.0

UML2 (2011) Unified modeling language: superstructure. Version 2.4.1, OMG document: formal/2011-08-05

Vita L, Scarpa M, Puliafito A (1995) Concurrent generalized petri nets. In: Proceedings of the second international workshop on the numerical solution of Markov chain. Kluwer, Railey, North Carolina, pp 359–382

Weyuker EJ (1982) On testing non-testable programs. Comput J 25(4):465–470

Yacoub SM, Cukic B, Ammar HH (2004) A scenario-based reliability analysis approach for component-based software. IEEE Trans Reliab 53(4):465–480

Zang X, Sun H, Trivedi KS (1999) A BDD-based algorithm for reliability evaluation of phased mission system. IEEE Trans Reliab 48(1):50–60

Zarras A, Vassiliadis P, Issarny V (2004) Model-driven dependability analysis of web services. In: Meersman R, Tari Z (eds) On the move to meaningful internet systems 2004: CoopIS, DOA, and ODBASE, OTM confederated international conferences, Agia Napa, Cyprus, 25–29 October 2004, Proceedings, Part II. Lecture notes in computer science, vol 3291. Springer, Berlin/Heidelberg, pp 1608–1625

Zimmermann A (2012) Modeling and evaluation of stochastic Petri nets with TimeNET 4.1. In: 6th international ICST conference on performance evaluation methodologies and tools, Cargese, Corsica, France, 9–12 October 2012. IEEE, New York, pp 54–63

Zoughbi G, Briand L, Labiche Y (2006) A UML profile for developing airworthiness-compliant (RTCA DO-178B) safety-critical software. Tech. rep., Carleton University, Canada, tech.rep.SCE-05-19

Zoughbi G, Briand L, Labiche Y (2007) A UML profile for developing airworthiness-compliant (RTCA DO-178B), safety-critical software. In: Engels G (ed) Proceedings of models 2007. LNCS, vol 4735. Springer, Berlin, pp 574–588

Index

AADL, 5, 35
    example, 37
    vs. UML, 39
Activity diagram, 31
Analysis techniques, 73
    ETA, 75, 84
    FFA, 85
    FMEA, 85
    FMECA, 85
    FTA, 75–77
    HAZOP, 85
    markov analysis, 86
    PHA, 86
    PN, 80
    RBD, 87
    truth table, 87
AUTOSAR, 5
Availability, 10, 18

BPEL, 5
BPMN, 5

CBSE, 137
Class diagram, 22
Common mode impairments, 60
Communication diagram, 24
Component diagram, 31

D-DSML, 5, 6
DAM, 6, 51
    application, 59
    basic dependability types, 58
    case study, 62, 67

complex dependability types, 57
    extensions, 53
    library, 57
Dependability, 1, 10
    availability, 1
    domain model, 41
    errors, 11
    failures, 12
    faults, 11
    formulae, 16
    hazards, 13
    integrity, 1
    maintainability, 1
    means, 13
    measures, 16
    properties, 16
    reliability, 1, 10
    requirements, 16
    safety, 1
    threats, 10
Dependability tools, 88
    DEEM, 89
    FaultTree+, 90
    Galileo, 89
    GreatSPN, 89
    Möbius, 89
    SHARPE, 88
    StarsStudio-Astra, 90
    SURF-2, 88
    TimeNET, 89
Deployment diagram, 32
Domain model, 41
DSML, 5, 41, 51
DSPN, 106
    composition, 107
    translation, 111
Dynamic fault trees, 122

S. Bernardi et al., *Model-Driven Dependability Assessment of Software Systems*,
DOI 10.1007/978-3-642-39512-3, © Springer-Verlag Berlin Heidelberg 2013

EAST-ADL2, 5
Error, 11

Failure, 12
Fault, 11
    prevention, 15
    tolerance, 15

Integrity, 10
Interaction diagrams, 24
Interaction overview diagram, 24

Maintainability, 10, 17
Maintenance, 15
MARTE, 5, 45, 151
    example, 159
    GQAM, 154
    PAM, 157
MDD, 3
    assessment, 4
Metamodel, 20, 23
Model, 15
    dependability model, 15
MOF, 51

NFP, 1, 3, 51, 153

OCL, 33, 56
OMT, 19
OOA&D, 19
OOSE, 19

Package, 43
    core, 43
    diagram, 33
    maintenance, 43, 48
    redundancy, 46
    system, 43
    threats, 43, 47
Performability, 2
Performance, 2
Proposals
    availability, 96
        Addouche, 101
        Bernardi-a, 96
        Bernardi-b, 102
        Bernardi-c, 103

Bondavalli, 100
Bozzano, 104
DalCin, 101
DeMiguel, 101
Leangsuksun, 101
criteria, 93
maintainability, 97
    Addouche, 101
    Bernardi-b, 102
    Bernardi-c, 103
    Bozzano, 104
    Genero, 97
reliability, 94
    Addouche, 101
    Bernardi-b, 102
    Bernardi-c, 103
    Bocciarelli, 96
    Bondavalli, 100
    Bozzano, 104
    Cortellessa, 95
    D'Ambrogio, 95
    DalCin, 101
    David, 96
    DeMiguel, 101
    Grassi, 95
    Jürjens, 103
    Leangsuksun, 101
    Mustafiz, 102
    Pai, 95, 122
    Rodrigues, 95
    Singh, 95
    Yacoub, 95
    Zarras, 103
risk assessment
    Goseva, 99
    Hassan, 99
safety, 97
    Allenby, 97
    Bernardi-c, 103
    Bozzano, 104
    Cancila, 99
    Hansen, 98
    Hawking, 98
    Iwu, 98
    Jürjens, 103
    Johannessen, 97
    Liu, 98
    Lu, 99
    Mustafiz, 102
    Ober, 99
    Pataricza, 98
    Zarras, 103
    Zoughbi, 99

Reliability, 17

Safety, 10, 18
Security, 2
Sequence diagram, 24
SoaML, 5
Software life-cycle, 3
Software product line, 138
SPN, 80, 106
    DSPN, 106
State machine diagram, 27
SysML, 5, 41

Timing diagram, 24

UML, 5, 19

activity diagram, 31
class diagram, 22, 135
communication diagram, 24, 135
component diagram, 31
deployment diagram, 32, 135
interaction diagrams, 24
interaction overview diagram, 24, 135
object diagram, 135
package diagrams, 33
run-time semantics, 21
run-to-completion, 27
sequence diagram, 24, 135
state machine diagram, 27, 109, 135
    translation, 111
timing diagram, 24
use case, 30
use case diagram, 135
Use case, 30

Printed in the United States
By Bookmasters